About The Author

Ian Wishart is an award-winning journalist and author, with a 30 year career in radio, television and magazines, a #1 talk radio show and five #1 bestselling books to his credit. Together with his wife Heidi, they edit and publish the news magazine *Investigate* and the news website www.investigatedaily.com.

For Levi

The Great Divide

Ian Wishart

HOWLING AT THE MOON PUBLISHING LTD

First edition published 2012
Howling At The Moon Publishing Ltd
PO Box 188, Kaukapakapa
Auckland 0843, NEW ZEALAND

www.howlingatthemoon.com
email: editorial@investigatemagazine.com

ISBN 978-0-9876573-6-7

Typeset in Adobe Garamond Pro and Baskerville Cyrillic
Cover concept: Ian Wishart, Heidi Wishart, Bozidar Jokanovic
Book Design: Bozidar Jokanovic

To get another copy of this book airmailed to you anywhere in the world, or to
purchase a fully text-searchable digital edition, visit our website:
WWW.HOWLINGATTHEMOON.COM

LEGAL NOTICE: Criticisms of individuals in this book reflect the author's honest
opinion, for reasons outlined in the text or generally known at the time of writing

Contents

Our Story

"Had Captain Hobson been able to conceive what was entailed in the piece-meal purchase of a country held under tribal ownership, it is difficult to think that he would have signed the Treaty without hesitation.

"He could not, of course, imagine that he was giving legal force to a system under which the buying of a block of land would involve years of bargaining, even when a majority of its owners wished to sell; that the ascertainment of a title would mean tedious and costly examination by courts of experts of a labyrinth of strange and conflicting barbaric customs; that land might be paid for again and again, and yet be declared unsold; that an almost empty wilderness might be bought first from its handful of occupants, then from the conquerors who had laid it waste, and yet after all be reclaimed by returned slaves or fugitives who had quitted it years before, and who had been paid for the land on which they had been living during their absence.

"Governor Hobson could not foresee that cases would occur in which the whole purchase money of broad lands would be swallowed up in the costs of sale, or that a greedy tribe of expert middlemen would in days to come bleed Maori and settler alike."

As an opening shot in the war that has become the Treaty of Waitangi, those words just quoted are hard to beat. They encapsulate all the cynicism, doubt and eye-rolling frustration that have surrounded the Treaty in recent years.

So which perceptive commentator made that statement? Hone Harawira? Don Brash? Rodney Hide?

None of the above is the correct answer. The passage was written way back in 1898, while the ink was still 'wet' on the 1840 Treaty in a legal

6

sense, and the massive treaty settlement upheavals of the 1990s and today were but a distant dream. The man who wrote it was William Pember-Reeves, a former New Zealand journalist turned cabinet minister, historian and lifelong socialist, in his book *The Long White Cloud*, a brief history of New Zealand.

There's been a lot of revisionist history written in New Zealand in more recent years in my view, politically-correct stuff or agenda-laden texts from social and political change merchants posing as historians or researchers. What I wanted to capture in this book was something different, what I consider to be the "authentic" voices from New Zealand's past without being filtered through the pen and prejudices of academia. Naturally, and I can hear the screams already, some will say this book is filtered through the prejudices of a journalist. Perhaps. You can be the judge of that. But I think you will find this book plays the issue with a straight bat. I report it the way I found it, and provide references all the way through if you want to read the source documents for yourself.

I have no particular dog in the ring, except for my support of a written constitution to provide certainty moving forward. I am married to a woman of Maori-Italian extraction, and my children proudly share a slice of Ngati Whatua heritage – a couple have enough of the "tar brush", as their Maori grandfather so quaintly puts it, that Maori mums at school or daycare have wondered which local hapu they came from. Under the terms of the Treaty of Waitangi Act, my children are "Maori". They are also Scot and Irish, direct descendants of John McGechean who arrived in Wellington on the *Bengal Merchant* on 20 February 1840, literally 14 days after the Treaty of Waitangi was signed, and also of the Allison and Laurie families on board Auckland's "First Fleet" of migrants in September 1842 - the ships *Duchess of Argylle* and the *Jane Gifford*. In that extent, my family is typical of many in New Zealand today – blended ethnicities, authentic Kiwi 'mongrel'. As Captain Hobson predicted at Waitangi all those years ago, 'He iwi tahi tatou' – we have indeed become one people.

One hundred and fourteen years ago, in 1898, William Pember-Reeves already had a pretty good handle on why the Treaty had turned into a legal minefield, and it seems little has changed. There have been a number of "full and final" treaty settlements since then involving the same portions of land and tribes, and somehow what was once deemed "settled" suddenly turns out not to be quite so.

Behind it all lies a labyrinth of cultural differences – fundamentally the Maori concept of land ownership was collective, whilst Europeans were used to individual title. The assumption that was often made – that those Maori currently occupying the land in question were its owners – was not always the case.

So who were these two "Treaty Partners" that modern legislation and court rulings talk of? What did each bring to the table, and what did they expect to gain or lose? Does a document essentially drafted on the equivalent of a café napkin in 1840 have legal relevance, and if so how should we look at it as we move towards a new Constitution?

To answer these questions, we need to set the scene; to go back in time and re-live some of those early moments of New Zealand history through the eyes of those who were there. It is only after hearing their voices that we can arguably put in context the arguments of modern Treaty commentators and advocates.

History comes alive when it lifts off the pages in front of you, and what I've tried to do in this book is give you the major waypoints on New Zealand's journey to nationhood, in living colour. Some of what you read will challenge what you've read in other popular history books.

My preference has been to use original texts wherever possible – eye-witness reports – and commentaries as close to the events in question as possible, in order to give readers a feel for how people more intimately connected to those events interpreted them. I've quoted liberally from old texts and books long out of print, deliberately, so that readers can get the full context of what's being said, rather than mere snippets dropped in to reinforce a point.

The downside to that is you can see some examples of what we would now call racist attitudes, but we're all smart enough to make allowances for writers speaking to us from 100 to 300 years ago as creatures of their times. You will also notice archaic spelling, which I have not changed either given the context.

There is a difference between items of factual reportage, and items of opinion. All of us, including the voices from the past, are entitled to our opinions however outrageous. The facts however can speak for themselves. You can judge for yourself the merits of this approach, setting New Zealand's past free from the biases of its cultural and political gatekeepers.

It is the experiences of real people, on all sides of an event, that define how the event is seen in history. The story of New Zealand is not some dry, dusty compendium of old parchments written by a collection of fusty academics; it is a story of life and death, of triumph and tragedy, of two peoples meeting for the first time in history – with wildly different backgrounds – struggling to find balance, honour and a new way forward.

It is the story of change, of how things never stay the same no matter how much we wish them to, and how 'adapt or die' is the overarching driving force that has filled humanity's sails since the beginning of time. It was the wind of change that drove the first humans from the warmth of the tropical Pacific down to temperate New Zealand, and the same wind that blew European explorers onto our shores either hundreds of – or as little as 300 depending on who you believe – years later.

History was not forged by the politically correct. It was forged by people with strong beliefs, strong prejudices and all the passion you'd expect from people at the earth's last civilisational frontier.

Maori or Pakeha, the making of New Zealand is a story we can all be proud of, something we can and should celebrate.

It's our story.

CHAPTER ONE

The First New Zealanders

If you listen to the usual tales, Maori arrived in this country in the "Great Migration" of canoes somewhere around 1200 to 1300 AD. Although modern ethnographers no longer believe in the one-off great fleet theory – preferring instead evidence of a number of isolated canoe arrivals at different times – they do think Maori only arrived in this country some time after 1200 AD, based on radio-carbon dating of known human settlement sites in the Bay of Plenty against a known volcanic eruption.[1]

Those of you who have read the late Michael King's *Penguin History of New Zealand* will find this chapter on somewhat of a collision course with King, although he says he has left the door open in his book to being corrected:

"A thirteenth century date for the initial settlement of New Zealand...is more soundly based on the range of evidence currently verifiable. *It is still an informed guess, however* [emphasis added], and there is always a possibility that new evidence will provoke a further twist of the kaleidoscope that will move the settlement pattern towards different configurations."[2]

Some of New Zealand's earliest explorers, however, would be shaking their heads in disbelief at that statement if they were still alive, because there's actually considerable evidence of ancient pre-European settlement of New Zealand.

---

1 From Hogg et al. 2002: *"Various authors have shown that there are no human archaeological contexts in New Zealand which pre-date the 12th century AD"* (Anderson 1991; McFadgen 1994; McFadgen et al. 1994; Higham & Hogg 1997; Higham et al. 1999). *"Recent archaeological and radiocarbon evidence now suggests strongly that the earliest settlers in the New Zealand archipelago arrived around c. 1250–1300 AD"* (McFadgen et al. 1994; Higham & Hogg 1997; Higham et al. 1999). See their paper "A wiggle-match...", http://researchcommons.waikato.ac.nz/bitstream/handle/10289/5248/A%20wiggle-match.pdf?sequence=1
2 *The Penguin History of New Zealand*, Michael King, Penguin 2003, p51

At Bruce Bay on the South Island's West Coast, rainforest comes almost down to the waterline. It's said to be the place where mythical Polynesian voyager Maui first set foot in New Zealand.[3] It's also the location of a puzzling archaeological mystery.

Explorer Julius von Haast arrived in 1868 to inspect an archaeological discovery by gold miners. The miners had dug down 14 feet, nine inches (nearly five metres) below the surface of the ground, at a spot some 565 feet (172 metres) inland from the beach. The area they were prospecting had once been the seashore, long, long ago, but the sea had long since retreated. What they were looking for were gold deposits in an ancient gravel bed buried under layers of sediment laid down over time, upon which a massive forest had grown on top of. What they found was something vastly more valuable than gold:

"In one of the claims in this last described forest-belt, on the bottom of the wash-dirt, reposing directly upon the argillaceous gravel, a party of miners, consisting of S. Fiddean, J. Sawyer, and T. Harrison, found a stone chisel and a sharpening-stone lying close to each other; the former was broken, having been accidentally struck by the pick when the miners were loosening the wash-dirt," writes Haast.[4]

"The stone chisel is made of a dark greenish chert, and is partly polished; the sharpening-stone is formed of a coarse greyish sandstone, which I found *in situ* about ten miles south of this locality, near the mouth of the river Paringa. The two stone implements now in the Canterbury Museum, were found a few days before my arrival."

These stone tools were found five metres underground, and one of them had evidently been crafted from a sandstone sourced ten miles away, but that's not the most staggering revelation. Here's what the goldminers first had to remove from the surface before they could even begin digging in their gold claim:

"After having removed the large trees growing here, sometimes 4 feet in diameter, and standing closely together…"

How long does it take for tree trunks on the West Coast to reach 1.2 metres in diameter? How long does it take for time to bury a human settlement to a depth of five metres? According to Haast, the forest was ancient even by 1868 standards.

---

3   http://www.makaawhio.maori.nz/marachistory.html
4   *Geology of the Provinces of Canterbury and Westland, New Zealand : a report comprising the results of official explorations*, by Julius von Haast, 1879, see http://www.nzetc.org/tm/scholarly/tei-HaaGeol-t1-body1-d3-d16-d1.html

Sir Julius Von Haast, K.C.M.G., Ph.D., F.R.S., F.G.S.,

"In the same forest, many and larger trees are lying prostrate on the ground, and in all stages of decay; sometimes their former existence being indicated only by long mossy ridges, so that we may safely conclude that the present forest vegetation is not the first one, but that it was preceded by trees of the same species, and often of large dimensions, formerly growing there."

The forests at Bruce Bay are predominantly rimu, a native conifer that reaches heights of 60 metres and two metres across, in the course of a thousand year life-span. The biggest trees had already lived and died, what Haast was looking at was second generation trees, themselves already monsters. Remember, the first generation of those trees had to grow on that gold-mining site *after* the human tools had already been covered by sediment to a depth of five metres. It's possible that site could have been 1,500 or even 2,000 years old.

The tools may not be capable of being carbon dated, but the circumstances of their discovery five metres underground are fully documented. If King is right about the earliest NZ settlement happening after 1200AD, how does he explain tools at such a depth, beneath a thousand year old forest in the 1860s? It's not the first problem King will face in this chapter.

Haast speculated the tools belonged to a people he called "the Moa hunters" – a race he believed pre-dated traditional Maori settlement of New Zealand. In fact, the discovery of tools so deep underground suggested to Haast, "it is not impossible, man [may] already have lived in New Zealand during the latter part of the Great Glacier period." In other words, at the end of the last Ice Age, 10,000 years ago. That's certainly far earlier than current scientific belief, but then again Haast was on the actual spot, looking at tools found five metres under the earth. The impact of looking at polished stone tools on the ground at your feet, then up to the daylight at the entrance of a five metre deep hole you are standing in, is lost somewhat when modern researchers examine those same tools in a museum case.

The possibility of New Zealand being populated almost as far back as Australia was raised with the tantalising discovery in Auckland of a chopped-down tree stump. No big deal, you might say, but the report to the New Zealand Institute in 1874 (now the Royal Society of NZ) lays out just why this stump was special:

"I have to record this evening a discovery giving a trace of human life on this island, and in this locality, reaching back beyond history, and supporting the Maori tradition that this island was inhabited before their arrival here," reported John Goodall, a civil engineer for the city of Auckland.[5]

"Heavy excavations have been carried on at and about the Albert Barracks by the Auckland Improvement Commissioners for the purpose of making new streets for the benefit of the city. During last March, while works were being carried on in Coburg Street, near the junction of Wellesley Street East, the workmen came upon the tree stump, now before you (see Pl. VI.), lying in the centre of a narrow channel below the road level, this channel having been cut for the purpose of laying sewer pipes. Through the intelligence of Mr. James Williamson, the contractors overseer, who at once recognised its value, it was saved. Shortly after I was on the spot, and my attention was drawn to it.

"It being important that the discovery should be verified by undoubted authority, I immediately went for, and returned accompanied by Theophilus Heale, Esq., Inspector of Surveys, who satisfied himself as to the genuineness of the discovery, and the undisturbed stratification of the volcanic débris of about 25 feet lying above. The place where the stump was found is shown on plan and section (Pl. VI.).

"In the section I have shown the stump as when found resting on the clay. It was in its natural position, upright, with its roots penetrating the clay, of which fact I satisfied myself by digging deeply below to a depth of over two feet, and found the traces of roots going down. The surface of the clay has loam in it.

"The top of the stump was embedded in volcanic mud, and above it

5   "On the discovery of a cut stump of a tree", by John Goodall C.E. *Transactions & Proceedings of the NZ Institute*, Vol 7, 1874 See http://rsnz.natlib.govt.nz/volume/rsnz_07/rsnz_07_00_001820.html

there were 25 feet of débris in perfect stratification, as shown in section. These stratified beds of ooze and débris can be traced till they reach the beds of cinders, and thence to the conglomerated mass of scoria and basaltic lava, which occurs adjacent to the volcanic centre. The clay in which the stump once grew occurs immediately above the tertiary rocks, and and is from 10 to 15 feet thick.

"This stump is asserted by those who have a knowledge of New Zealand woods to be of tea-tree (manuka) the wood that has been chiefly used by Maoris for making paddles. It has an undoubted appearance of having been cut by some tool, and being so must have been by the hand of man. I leave it to any one to satisfy themselves by a personal examination whether it be so or not.[6] The cut seems to be too fresh to refer back to so remote a period as the volcanic era, but with the evidence we have of the finest markings of ferns, shells, etc., being preserved from ages vastly more remote, surely we may expect it from this, which in comparison is but recent.

"Undoubted as these facts may appear it may yet be well to consider by what other means they may have been produced. The stump may have been lodged where found by a landslip, it may have been burnt off, or it may have belonged to a rotten tree and been broken down by the wind, or by the flow of the volcanic ooze in which it is embedded.

"That the stump was not lodged there by a landslip may be seen by the section which shows the overlying strata perfectly undisturbed, and it is further evident that it must have grown on the spot where found as its roots were penetrating the lower clay; everywhere above the clay abundant remains of trees occur and roots in the clay, showing that the place was wooded at the time prior to its being covered by the volcanic débris.

"That it was not burnt off is certain, from the sharpness of the edges of the surface, the absence of charcoal, or even of a charred appearance, and the presence of a projecting piece of wood in the centre of the stump, which must have held the tree upright to the last, and which would not have existed had it been fired.

"That it did not result from a rotten tree is equally evident, for it could not now be in so good preservation, the bark would not have remained on it, the sharpness of the edges would not have existed, and the wood would not now be fibrous; decayed wood would have lost its fibrous structure.

"It is therefore beyond any doubt that we have evidence of the existence

---

6 A report in New Zealand's *Southern Cross* newspaper at the time, suggesting a stone adze was found beside the stump, appears to be wrong. Goodall was the first senior official at the scene and does not record the discovery of a tool.

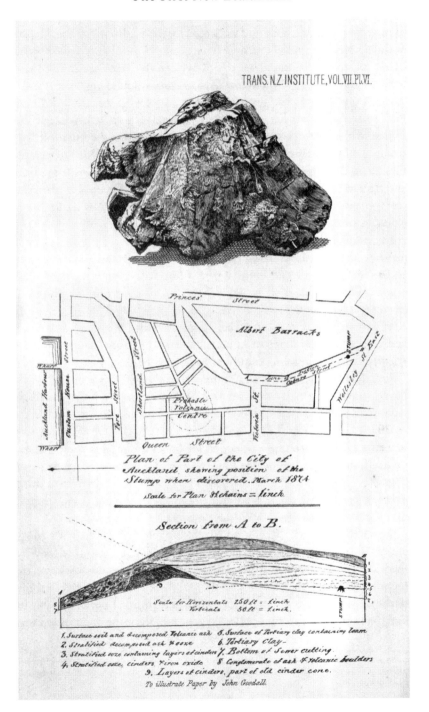

TRANS. N.Z. INSTITUTE, VOL.VII. Pl.VI.

Plan of Part of the City of
Auckland, shewing position of the
Stump when discovered. March 1874.
Scale for Plan 8 chains = 1 inch.

Section from A to B.

Scale for Horizontals 250 ft = 1 inch.
" Verticals 50 ft = 1 inch.

1. Surface soil and decomposed Volcanic ash
2. Stratified decomposed ash & ooze
3. Stratified ooze containing layers of cinders
4. Stratified ooze, cinders, & iron oxide
5. Surface of Tertiary clay containing loam
6. Tertiary clay
7. Bottom of Sewer cutting
8. Conglomerate of ash & Volcanic boulders
9. Layers of cinders, part of old cinder cone.
To illustrate Paper by John Goodall.

of man long before the period indicated by the traditions of the Maoris of their advent to this island, and at a period before what is probably the oldest volcano in Auckland became extinct. In the Maori traditions there is no mention of any of the volcanos near Auckland having been active."

Given that the tree had grown on the inside of what was the old Albert Park crater, it's a fair bet the 250,000 year old Albert Park was not the source of the ash and scoria in the clay 25 feet above the sawn-off tree stump. A more likely culprit for that layer of debris was the Mt Eden crater further up the ridgeline, which last exploded somewhere between 14,000 and 24,000 years ago.[7] The Taupo eruption of 286 AD could explain the surface debris, as it laid an ash layer 60cm thick across Auckland, but it would not explain the volcanic mud flows above the tree stump.

The point being, more than seven metres below a layer of volcanic deposits, in perfectly stratified clay, workmen overseen by a civil engineer and a chief surveyor had found a tree stump with clear evidence it had been chopped down, and no sign of the rest of the tree – which you'd expect if it had been a natural felling.

At two ends of the country, then, Auckland and Westland, scientists had prima facie evidence of human habitation at times when modern scientists assume humans could not have been here.

Researching caves on Banks Peninsula on the other side of the South Island (then known as "Middle Island"), Julius Haast found a lot more archaeological evidence of these "moa hunter" people, and that evidence again led him to believe they came before the Maori. One of his reasons for stating this was the appearance of dog bones in the Moa cooking pits. Of itself, this might be nothing unusual, but Haast found no evidence of dogs ever being fed at these sites. The dogs that lived in the time of these people were being caught wild and eaten, they were not domesticated pets sharing the fire space with their owners.

"From the manner the dog bones are broken and mixed with Moa-bones, "it is evident that the dog was also considered a favourite food by the Moa-hunters, but it is difficult to believe that it was domesticated by them[8]. Although I have examined thousands of bones collected in these refuse heaps, many of them very minute and delicate, I never was able to find the least trace that they had been gnawed. The same observation was

---

7 "Age of the Auckland Volcanic Field," Jan Lindsay and Graham Leonard, IESE Report 1-2009.02 | June 2009, see http://www.iese.co.nz/LinkClick.aspx?fileticket=gI9F5esXBzQ%3D &tabid=344
8 Dr. James Hector in Vol. IX. of the *Transactions of the New Zealand Institute* page 248

made by me at the Moa-hunter encampment, at the mouth of the Shag river, Otago. Thus, we are compelled to believe that the Moa-hunters only chased the dog then living in a wild state in New Zealand, without having as yet domesticated it.

Moa-hunter oven pits

"Admitting the Maori traditions, which state distinctly that they brought the domestic dog (Kuri) with them from Hawaiki, it is evident that these kitchen middens of the Moa-hunters must date back to a period much anterior [before] to their arrival in New Zealand. No human bones were found in connection with these kitchen middens, so that there is strong presumptive evidence for believing that the Moahunters were not addicted to anthropophagy [cannibalism]."

What Haast did find is that spearheads and other stone tools found in these ancient sites were being made in precisely the same manner as stone age tools from European cave-dwellers and North American Indian tribes.

"The figure of this "teshoa" a [American Indian] name which I wish to adapt for similar stone implements in New Zealand, is so like one of the latter that it would be impossible to distinguish them if placed side by side. At the same time I wish to observe that the description and figures of the flint-flakes, roughly chipped, found in Indian graves, etc., are so much like those obtained in the Moa-hunter encampment that there is no doubt that the former aborigines of New Zealand employed the same mode of manufacture and used the same form of rude stone implements as the primitive races of Europe and North America."[9]

At the same time, however, there was evidence the Moa hunters also had the ability to polish and sharpen stone in the more modern Maori fashion, based on the discovery of polished tools on both the west and east coasts. Clearly the Moa hunters shared something in common with Maori.

At Warrington, near Dunedin, carbon dating of one Moa-hunter site suggests it may have been in use as early as 900 to 1000AD.[10] Clearly the

9   http://www.nzetc.org/tm/scholarly/tei-HaaGeol-t1-body1-d3-d16-d1.html#n445
10 "Marine Shell, Charcoal and Moa Egg Shell Conventional Radiocarbon Dates from New Zealand Moa-hunting Archaeological Sites", Matthew Schmidt. http://nzarchaeology.org/

1350AD migration story couldn't account for that, which lends weight to the idea that Polynesian seafarers settled in New Zealand in random fashion over a number of centuries, rather than one mighty voyage. Initial settlement would have been small, with the population growing as food allowed. It took several hundred years before human population grew significant enough to finally extinguish the moa from our landscape.

Whoever the Moa-hunters were, they were big eaters – scientists estimate up to 8,000 moa were cooked in 1,200 ovens at the Waitaki River mouth alone.[11] Nor were moas the only diet. Seals, sea leopards, the aforementioned dogs and even bellbirds were on the menu.

One odd discovery in the 1870s was made in the Earnscleugh caves in Otago. Researchers with the Otago Museum found a lizard jaw and a vertebral rib from the same creature.

"It may be the last cervical of a reptile," wrote Captain F W Hutton, a fellow of the Royal Society, "although it seems to be too robust and too flattened for the rib of a lizard. It more nearly resembles the first thoracic rib of a mammal, but…it is, indeed, unlike anything known to me."

Hutton examined the jaw and believed its teeth were even stronger that those of an iguana. Its tooth structure was "pleuordont", meaning it could not have been from a tuatara, but could have been anything from a very large skink or gecko through to a monitor lizard or even a komodo dragon type of creature.

Hutton, with the assistance of the Otago and Canterbury museums who'd also been involved in the research, presented his findings in 1898 to the Royal Society of New Zealand and speculated the law and bone may "provisionally, be supposed to belong to the extinct kumi, or ngarara, of the Maoris."

Just what was this strange creature the museums had found?

Sir Julius von Haast gave a keynote address to the Royal Society that year that threatened to shed more light on the discovery. In Haast's case, it was a series of ancient cave paintings in the Canterbury and north Otago regions depicting "crocodiles…gigantic lizards…snakes".

In New Zealand?

"In [figure] No. 4, we have the representation of a large snake possessing a swollen head and a long protruding tongue. This figure is nearly three

elecpublications/schmidtmoa.htm
11 "The Archaeology of Canterbury in Maori Times", Aidan J. Challis, 1995, see http://conservation.govt.nz/upload/documents/science-and-technical/sr89.pdf. Michael King asserts up to 90,000 moa were cooked at the Waitaki River mouth but provides no cited source (see *Penguin History of New Zealand*, p63)

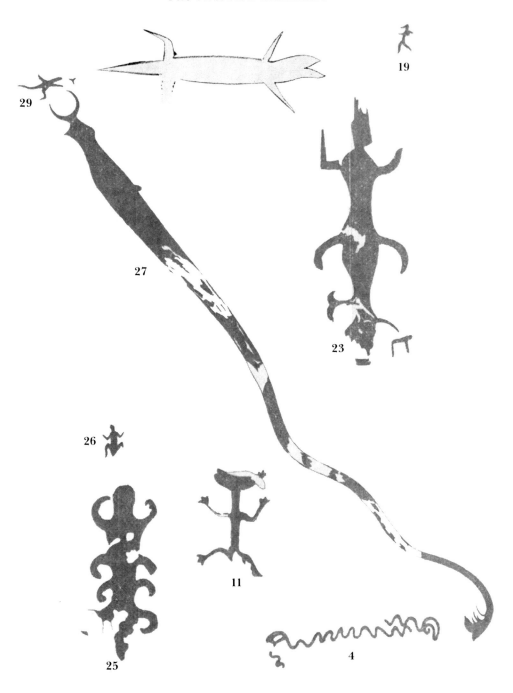

The Great Divide

feet long [on the cave wall], and shows numerous windings."

In figure number 11 Haast described "a gigantic fabulous lizard which is said to have watched the moa."

The cave painter, at Weka Pass about 70km north of Christchurch, was also perhaps also familiar with catastrophic volcanic eruptions.

"In No. 19 we have doubtless the picture of a human being, who is running away from No. 17, the object from the top of which issues fire and smoke." Haast also identifies "a similar figure running away from the monster No. 27...a huge snake-like animal fifteen feet long", possibly "a boa constrictor". The creature in image 27 was "in the act of swallowing a man".

Nearby were images 23 and 25 which appeared to be "large lizards or crocodiles", and the question Haast found himself asking was why Canterbury cave painters, "in a country without snakes, could not only have traditions about them but actually be able to picture them, [unless] that had received amongst them immigrants from tropical countries who had landed on the coasts of New Zealand from some cause or another."

Today, modern Maori mythology still runs deep on the 'taniwha', and modern construction projects have been delayed or abandoned on the basis of failure to give the mythological creature his due. As Haast reminded his audience 114 years ago, however, the cave evidence of crocodiles, giant lizards and snakes is not the end of the story.

"You are well aware that on the second visit of Captain Cook, Tawai-hura, a native chief[12] of Queen Charlotte Sound, gave an account of enormous snakes and lizards to him, and drew a representation of both animals so distinctly that they could not be mistaken, [yet] hitherto the researches of naturalists for so many years have failed to reveal their existence in these islands."

In the 1770s, was it possible that New Zealand was still home to some kind of giant reptiles?[13] With no television, no books and no reliable

12 You will come across references to "chiefs" frequently in the historic writings quoted in this book. It is a generic term referring to citizen-members of tribes. As Samuel Marsden found, "there is no middle class of people in New Zealand: they are all either chiefs or (in a certain degree) slaves." Within the higher levels of a tribe there were different ranks of 'chief' – rangatira to denote leaders within hapu and senior officials, and ariki – the highest ranking by virtue of their genealogy back to the tribal ancestors. There are constant references in most history books and school books to Pakeha settlers insulting the mana of a 'chief'. In nearly every case, the insult was to an ordinary Joe Public tribal member just like you or I.
13 By way of example, although no other European had ever reported seeing one, a respected European naturalist, Charles Douglas, may have shot and killed the last breeding pair of either Haast's Eagle or a giant New Zealand hawk, the Eyle's Harrier, in 1870, for food. He wrote: "The expanse of wing of this bird will scarcely be believed. I shot two on the Haast, one was

20

communication with the outside world, how on earth were Marlborough Sounds Maori able to draw pictures of such beasts? Cook's journals touch on the dilemma of his discussions with Tawaihura.

"We had another piece of intelligence from him, more correctly given, though not confirmed by our own observations, that there are snakes and lizards there of an enormous size. He described the latter as being eight feet in length, and as big round as a man's body. He said, they sometimes seize and devour men; that they burrow in the ground; and that they are killed by making fires at the mouths of the holes. We could not be mistaken as to the animal; for, with his own hand, he drew a very good representation of a lizard on a piece of paper; as also of a snake, in order to shew what he meant."[14]

Forty years later, when European whalers and sealers had by this time become well established on the New Zealand coast, another Maori chief from north Auckland made a similar claim, recorded by a British seafarer who found the idea dubious.

"Duaterra, however, informed us, that a most destructive animal was found in the interior of the country, which made great havoc among the children, carrying them off and devouring them, whenever they came in its way. The description he gave of it corresponded exactly with that of the alligator; but I should still doubt that either this or any other predaceous animal of so formidable a description exists in New Zealand. The chief had never seen the animal himself, but received his accounts from others; and hence it appears to me very probable that his credulity might have been imposed upon."[15]

For the record, in a country with a resident population of 4.5 million, no one has found an "alligator" roaming wild in New Zealand in the modern era. But interestingly enough we used to have one. Scientists have found remains of a fossil crocodile from 16 million years ago, believed to be a Mekosuchine crocodile. These primitive crocs –ranging between two and five metres in length – were common in Australia, New Guinea and evidently New Zealand at some point in the distant past. In Australia they

---

8 feet 4 inches (2.54 m) from tip to tip, the other was 6 feet 9 inches (2.06 m), but with all their expanse of wing they have very little lifting power, as a large hawk can only lift a duck for a few feet, so no one need get up any of those legends about birds carrying babies out of cradles, as the eagle is accused of doing." See *Mr Explorer Douglas* by John Pascoe, 1957, republished by Canterbury University Press, 2000.

14 Cook – *A Voyage to the Pacific Ocean*, vol. 1, pp. 142-3, Dublin, 1786.

15 http://www.nzetc.org/tm/scholarly/tei-Bes02Reli-t1-body-d4-d6-d2.html, "Maori Religion & Mythology Part 2", Elsdon Best, quoting Nicholas in his *Narrative of a Voyage to New Zealand* 1817, vol. 2, p. 126.

greeted the first aborigines 40,000 years ago and died out soon after, either hunted to extinction or killed by the much larger saltwater crocodiles that appeared on the scene. Surprisingly, however, the Mekosuchines island-hopped across the Pacific, spreading out to Vanuatu, Fiji and even New Caledonia – New Zealand's largest and nearest tropical neighbour just to the north. The last of these crocodiles was hunted to extinction in New Caledonia possibly around the same time the first settlers arrived in New Zealand – remains of one dating back to 400 AD have been found and it was unlikely to have been New Caledonia's last one.[16]

We know this crocodile lived in New Zealand. We don't know when it became extinct or why. It's a big creature and would have needed sizeable prey. Were they still around when the first humans arrived? Did they die out because humans killed them, as hinted at in Captain Cook's journals[17], or from starvation as humans competed with them for food?

Or do the cave paintings represent the first writings of our first settlers as they tried to tell the story of the lands they'd left behind? Were the cave paintings intended to be a history lesson of the homeland for the children and descendants of those first New Zealanders?

But here's the twist. The only known habitats for the Mekosuchine crocs were New Zealand, Australia, and the Melanesian islands of Fiji, Vanuatu and New Caledonia. Maori are Polynesian. What are they doing with cultural memories of Melanesian crocodiles and pythons? When Maori interacted with Cook and those who followed in the nineteenth century, they had already lost their cultural memory of the extinct moa and giant eagle. How could they forget more recent creatures yet be able to recall and draw beasts presumably from offshore and a time long, long ago? If the Melanesian crocs had in fact died out hundreds of years earlier, this lingering memory becomes even more difficult to explain.

Historian Michael King throws down a gauntlet at the opening of chapter two of his book:

"Despite a plethora of amateur theories about Melanesian, South Ameri-can, Egyptian, Phoenician and Celtic colonisation of New Zealand, there is not a shred of evidence that the first human settlers were anything other than Polynesian."[18]

---

16 "The small, recently extinct, island-dwelling crocodilians of the South Pacific" Darren Naish, http://scienceblogs.com/tetrapodzoology/2009/05/mekosuchines_2009.php
17 If they were present in NZ within the time of human settlement, why weren't Maori swanning around with crocodile skin shoes and handbags? After all, they used moa, kiwi and dog skins. Not one ancient Maori has been found buried with a pair of Crocs.
18 *Penguin History of New Zealand*, p29

ABOVE: A Mekosuchine croc of the type that once roamed New Zealand and New Caledonia. RIGHT: Cave drawings from the South Island, possibly of a croc-like creature with a serated tail, swallowing a person; and a more stylistic – possibly skeletal – representation of a beast, possibly with spears stuck in it. Either way, apart from the taniwha legends there is no cultural memory of an animal capable of attacking humans in New Zealand or Polynesia, only in Melanesia and Australia The lower cave drawing stands 7 feet tall on the cave wall

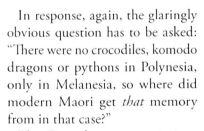

In response, again, the glaringly obvious question has to be asked: "There were no crocodiles, komodo dragons or pythons in Polynesia, only in Melanesia, so where did modern Maori get *that* memory from in that case?"

The Canterbury cave paintings certainly prompted Sir Julius von Haast to wonder, out loud, whether New Zealand's first "Maori" might in fact have been Melanesian, not Polynesian.[19]

"However, the strongest proof of their being foreign to native handicraft, is the character of these paintings, consisting as they do of primitive representations of serpents, lizards, whales, quadrupeds, many of them in monstrous forms, together with drawings of other objects, representing

---

[19] Modern anthropologists believe the first settlers were simply "archaic" Maori who were superseded by a more advanced Maori culture in subsequent waves of immigration. They could well be right, but that doesn't answer the question of how they were able to draw komodo dragon-type lizards, crocodiles and pythons, in caves bordering the Canterbury plains.

probably weapons, implements or clothing, all of which the Maoris do not possess, nor do they know their use," testified Haast.[20]

One of the controversies over New Zealand's first residents has been when they arrived. As the textbooks all note, New Zealand was the last major landmass in the world to be colonised by humans. Yet we have a long coastline, and in truth any number of voyagers blown off course could have ended up here. Most of course would be men-only crews, meaning they could eke out a Robinson Crusoe existence but with no hope of descendants. Once they died, the forests and the weather would have taken care of any evidence of their existence. So the first settlement of New Zealand cannot have been based upon random shipwrecks, but on a deliberate and active attempt to migrate, in vessels carrying women as well as men, probably after 'scouts' had successfully returned to the islands and confirmed New Zealand's whereabouts.[21]

We've already seen that the first settlers had memories of things not seen in East Polynesia, where we know through DNA that the modern Maori hailed from. If the crocodiles were not still living in New Zealand when the first people arrived, then their memory can only have come from New Caledonia where the crocs still roamed up to around 800 AD. Was such a voyage from Melanesia to New Zealand feasible?

"Computer simulations show that it was just as easy for voyaging canoes to sail to New Zealand from New Caledonia, Fiji, or West Polynesia, as it was from East Polynesia. An early canoe landing in New Zealand from this region remains a possibility," states the *Encyclopedia of New Zealand*.[22]

One of the markers used to determine the time when New Zealand was colonised is the Polynesian rat, *Rattus exulans*. Based on the fact that no undisputable evidence of rats in New Zealand can be found before about 1200 AD, and because the Polynesian rat can only swim three metres before drowning (and therefore clearly did not arrive here under its own steam naturally), the assumption has been made that humans cannot have been in New Zealand before that time otherwise we would have seen the rats earlier as well.

The only problem with that theory is that absence of evidence is not

---

20 http://www.nzetc.org/tm/scholarly/tei-HaaGeol-t1-body1-d3-d16-d1.html#n450

21 Demographers have estimated that a base population of 200, including at least 50 women, would have been needed in 1300 AD to explain a 100,000 population by the 1800s. Of course, if settlement occurred hundreds of years earlier, the initial numbers could have been much lower (which explains why their settlement sites have been hard to find) and multiplied more slowly over time.

22 "When Was New Zealand First Settled?" – http://www.teara.govt.nz/en/when-was-new-zealand-first-settled/6

Polynesian rat. Wikipedia Commons Licence/User cliff1066

evidence of absence. Just because you can't find a trace of something, doesn't mean it wasn't there. The Polynesian rat hated water and was not a natural boat stowaway. It was deliberately chucked into the canoe with a few more of its furry little rat mates to be food for the voyage. If it was a swift and speedy voyage, little rat might be rewarded with freedom at the end. On the other hand if the canoe got blown around by storms, bad currents or simply drifted on languid summer days with no wind, there's every possibility the onboard supply of rats might have been exhausted by the hungry crew long before they actually hit the beach at New Zealand. Human settlers could have arrived here, in other words, without any rats to share the love.

It is therefore entirely feasible that human colonisers arrived much earlier on these islands than scientists have so far been able to ascertain. The lack of early rat evidence[23] does not disprove this, it just means that any rats deliberately taken on board (as they had to be; they were as fond of water and boats as cats were) had been eaten in transit – an early Polynesian version of drive-through takeaways. At some point, during

---

23   For the record, there's a scientific 'debate' about the first rats. Richard Holdaway has dated the first rat remains to as far back as 10AD, but his critics reckon the carbon dating is wrong, and cite the fact that they can't find any rat-gnawed seeds or snail shells prior to 1200AD as proof that rats were not active until then, meaning humans were not here either. As shown in the main argument above, it's possible that Option C, hungry humans arriving early without any live rats left in the boat, is the best explanation of all.

a later migration wave after 1200AD, once the trade route was well and truly established, someone let the rats out and the clock officially began ticking on human colonisation as far as archaeologists are concerned.[24]

Michael King concedes that Polynesian rat DNA proves at least some of New Zealand's rats came from colonies in Fiji (Melanesian) and West Polynesia (closer to New Guinea)[25], but he explains this "variance" away as "this contact may have been fleeting and not part of the organised settlement of the country". King's *History of New Zealand* – in this particular regard – appears to be clutching desperately to a theory increasingly going against the evidence. We have proof of Melanesian cultural memories in the cave paintings and stories told to Captain Cook. We have evidence of Melanesian rats. "Nothing to see here, move on", appears to be the catch-cry of modern academics to this inconvenient evidence, however.

Since Michael King published his book back in 2003, new genetic studies have further clarified the ancestry of the Maori. Modern Maori predominantly trace back through Polynesia, Micronesia and East Asia to an aboriginal tribe living in modern Taiwan. That's the ultimate turangawaewae for the first Polynesians. But as they moved through Melanesia they did intermarry – to a limited extent – with some coastal Melanesian tribes.[26] It's always possible that on their journey of migration into Polynesia one of these half-caste family groupings were either blown off course or chose a different navigational path to end up in New Zealand much earlier than the Maori who eventually followed them.

If you accept the word of the *Encyclopedia of New Zealand*, the "oldest" archaeological site in the country is the Wairau Bar at the top of the South Island, dated to around 1280 AD. But what are we to make of Haast's polished stone tools found five metres underground beneath a forest of 1000 year old rimu? How long does it take for five metres of perfectly layered soil to accumulate? There's no explaining that one away in a hurry. New Zealand archaeologists who say they can't find evidence

24 For a fascinating bring-together of the rat debate, see I. A. E. Atkinson & D. R. Towns (2001): "Advances in New Zealand mammalogy 1990–2000: Pacific rat", *Journal of the Royal Society of New Zealand*, 31:1, 99-109, available online here http://www.tandfonline.com/doi/abs/10.1080/0 3014223.2001.9517641

25 "Prehistoric Mobility in Polynesia: MtDNA Variation in *Rattus exulans* from the Chatham and Kermadec Islands", Matisoo-Smith et al, *Asian Perspectives*, Vol. 38, No.2, 1999, see http://scholarspace.manoa.hawaii.edu/bitstream/handle/10125/17126/AP-v38n2-186-199. pdf?sequence=1

26 "The genetic structure of Pacific Islanders", Friedlaender et al, PLoS, 2008, see http:// www.plosgenetics.org/article/info:doi/10.1371/journal.pgen.0040019

of human habitation earlier than 1280 need to also explain a second discovery reported by Sir Julius von Haast.

"Since then [the Bruce Bay discovery] I have received another adze made of sandstone, possessing a well-polished cutting edge, found at Hunt's Beach, West Coast, eighteen feet below the ground, amongst the roots and stumps of an ancient forest, which last June, during the progress of gold mining operations, was laid bare."[27]

Hunt's Beach is about 12 kilometres north of the earlier find at Bruce Bay. In this case the tool was buried nearly six metres beneath an ancient forest. Somebody lived there, long before the trees began growing in 800AD and therefore much earlier again than our "official" oldest site from 1280AD. You could argue that a prankster finding ancient Maori artefacts was re-burying them in forests in the hope that somebody would stumble across them if they happened to be passing – six metres underground! A more logical explanation is that evidence of the first New Zealanders is buried much deeper than we normally look.

Haast wasn't alone in such discoveries. Explorer Joshua Rutland reports on the Nelson area:[28]

"Large, very old slow-growing trees are found in and beside many of the [kitchen] pits. Every part of the Sounds furnishes the same unmistakeable evidence, that the forest has taken possession of land once occupied by man.

"From the remains brought to light by the destruction of the forest along the shores of Pelorus Sound, we learn that the district was formerly inhabited by a people differing widely in their habits from the Maoris of Cook's or the early missionary times, and that these ancient people occupied the land at a period sufficiently remote to allow our slow-growing forest trees to come up and attain their full dimensions where their habitations once stood or where their fires were lighted.[29]

"Shortly after settling in the Pelorus valley my attention was directed to a black horizontal seam in a perpendicular clay bank, formed by the

27 "Moa and Moa Hunters" by Julius von Haast, *Transactions & Proceedings of The New Zealand Institute*, Vol. IV 1871

28 "Traces of Ancient Human Occupation in the Pelorus District, Middle Island, New Zealand", Joshua Rutland, *Journal of the Polynesian Society*, Volume VI, 1897, see http://www.jps.auckland.ac.nz/document/Volume_3_1894/Volume_3,_No.4,_December_1894/Traces_of_ancient_human_occupation_in_the_Pelorus_district,_Middle_Island,_New_Zealand,_by_Joshua_Rutland,_p_220-232/p1

29 In other words, the earliest settlers lived and died, then a forest grew up over where they'd had their village, and then centuries later people have repopulated the area. There was a huge gap between the deaths of the original inhabitants, and the decision by Maori to later settle the area.

encroachment of the Pelorus river on a small island at the head of the tide-way.

"The seam consisted of charcoal mixed with burnt stones and large mussel-shells, the whole evidently the remains of a cooking place. From one of the shells I examined the lime portion had almost disappeared, but the more durable horny cuticle was intact. Above this ancient cooking place there was about three feet of solid clay, over which again stood a large Matai tree more than three feet in diameter.[30]

"Between the time when the fire was lighted and the discovery of the remains...the clay must have accumulated and the Matai sprung into existence, but more than that, the narrow channel separating the island from the mainland must have been still narrower, or probably it was not the bed of the Pelorus when the old inhabitants tarried beside it to cook their food. It could be plainly seen when the seam of charcoal attracted attention, that the island had been a point of land severed from the mainland by the river working its way into a stream that drained a small gully a little to the westward. The wide shallow channel on the south side of the island, now only carrying water in flood-time is plainly the old Pelorus bed.

"This was the first indication that the district had been inhabited longer than was commonly supposed. Subsequently the washing away of the clay bank continuing, exposed the burnt earth and stones of a Maori *kapa* (or oven) ten feet below the surface of the island, showing that at some period a filling up or raising of the land had taken place; and that men had occupied the spot occasionally or regularly during the time."

This was a four hundred to 1,000 year old tree that had sprouted –at the latest – around 1400AD, on top of a metre of accumulated clay, beneath which someone had once cooked a feed of mussels. Two metres further underground another oven was located. Who lived there and when, and have modern archaeologists failed to find evidence of old human habitation simply because they are not digging deep enough?[31]

30 Matai trees of this size can be as old as 1,300 years, see http://www.conservation.co.nz/upload/documents/science-and-technical/Sfc113.pdf , section 5.3
31 The scale of the problem – trying to find evidence of human habitation up to two thousand years ago – can be seen from the immense difficulty archaeologists are having in finding evidence of *European* habitation in NZ from only 200 years ago: "To date, remains of this kind from the earliest phases of European settlement have been difficult to recover. Little survives from the first ephemeral settlements in the last decade of the 18th century, or from those of commercial sealers in the first two decades of the 19th century. A handful of sites including Codfish Island (Smith & Anderson 2007, 2009), Te Puna (Middleton 2008), Oashore (Smith & Prickett 2006) and Te Hoe (Smith & Prickett 2008) at which occupation commenced in the two decades from 1825, thus far provide the earliest secure evidence of household and community life in 19th century New Zealand." If New Zealand's best archaeologists can find only the barest

Arguably, modern researchers are at a bit of a disadvantage. Many of the discoveries took place 150 years ago as the land was first cleared or mining first got underway. It's too difficult now, perhaps, to try and find ancient needles in a modern haystack of changed land use.

In the Marlborough Sounds, however, these ancient people were Waitaha or even older, the Turehu or Patupaiarehe – the same possibly Melanesian or Melanesian-influenced tribes named as the Moa hunters and cave painters who were wiped out by Ngai Tahu in the 1700s. Joshua Rutland in the late 1800s interviewed local iwi still living in the Pelorus valley to find out what they knew.[32]

"I shall therefore close this article by giving briefly the substance of what I have been able to collect from my Maori neighbours regarding the ancient inhabitants whose remains have been described. Premising that my information has not been obtained from one individual, or at one time, but little by little, only one item resting on a single statement. The district now called the County of Sounds [the Marlborough Sounds], including Rangitoto and Arapaoa Islands was originally inhabited by a small dark-complexioned Maori-speaking people, who were very numerous, peaceable, and industrious.

"Being agriculturists they kept large areas of land in cultivation, but as seamen they displayed little ability, constructing only small canoes. These canoes when not in use were dragged by means of ropes up the hills, where the population generally resided; the numerous pits scattered along the shores of the Sounds and on the islands, being the remains of their habitations. The aborigines were acquainted with the Moa, which according to the accounts they have handed down was sixteen feet in height. Whether they only knew the great bird in the open country and hunted it for food, or whether they had them like the tame cassowaries kept by the New Guinea Natives, there is no tradition.

---

trace of European settlements from two centuries ago, in areas where we know for a fact they existed right down to the patch of land they lived on, how much credence should we really give their claims about the certainty of New Zealand only being settled by Maori after 1280AD? What real hope have they got of finding a beachside village from 400AD when they don't even know where to look, or where rising sea levels or ancient tsunami have buried the evidence? See Department of Conservation report, http://www.doc.govt.nz/conservation/historic/by-region/northland/bay-of-islands/marsden-cross-historic-reserve/archaeological-investigation/about-the-project/

32 *Journal of the Polynesian Society*, Volume 3 1894 > Volume 3, No.4, December 1894 > Traces of ancient human occupation in the Pelorus district, Middle Island, New Zealand, by Joshua Rutland, p 220-232, see http://www.jps.auckland.ac.nz/document/Volume_3_1894/Volume_3,_No.4,_December_1894/Traces_of_ancient_human_occupation_in_the_Pelorus_district,_Middle_Island,_New_Zealand,_by_Joshua_Rutland,_p_220-232/p1

"Upon this peaceful population the ancestors of the modern Maoris descended from the north in their large canoes; having only to encounter an unwarlike people, they destroyed all before them. A few of the inhabitants were enslaved, their descendants being still pointed out amongst the Pelorus Natives. One family in particular, the Pokiki, is said to be a remnant of the old race. The only individuals bearing the name with whom I am acquainted, certainly correspond with the traditional descriptions of the Natives, being shorter of stature and darker-complexioned than the Maoris, generally differing from them also in features. From the ancient inhabitants the Maoris obtained a knowledge of the greenstone, and how to work it, besides other useful arts in which they were farther advanced than their conquerors."

The conquerors were known as Rangitane[33], a tribe originally Ngati Mamoe from the Wairarapa, and in their own Treaty of Waitangi settlement document[34] they acknowledge their intermarriage with the original inhabitants of New Zealand:

"A race of mythical people called Patupaiarehe, said to be the first occupiers of Aotearoa, lived in remote mountain areas not usually trodden by humans. They are said to have spirited away Māori women to take as wives, and the offspring of these unions were known as konako or korako: people of light complexion," explains the Treaty document.

"According to Rangitāne tradition two Patupaiarehe were captured on the Parororangi maunga [Mt Stokes in the Marlborough Sounds] by their tupuna. One was a man and one a woman. The man was killed and the woman became the wife of a rangatira. From them descended a line of beautiful women culminating in Kunari, the daughter of Tamahau, who had arrived in Te Tau Ihu[35] on the waka Te Awatea.

"For Rangitāne their descent from the Patupaiarehe people[36] represents a link between the spiritual and human realms; the 'upper realm' (te

---

33 The Rangitane themselves record their first tribal invasion into the area in the 1500s, when they crossed Cook Strait from their home territory in the Wairarapa. Rangitane were themselves hammered in the late 1820s when musket-wielding invaders from the North Island again crossed Cook Strait and forced the combined Rangitane and Ngati Mamoe remnant further into the bush at Nelson Lakes. See http://www.rangitane.org.nz/ourhistory.asp
34 Rangitane Deed of Settlement, http://nz01.terabyte.co.nz/ots/DocumentLibrary%5CRangitaneDocumentsSchedule.pdf
35 Te Tau Ihu was the name given to the prow of Maui's canoe, and to the top of the South Island where the original inhabitants, the first New Zealanders, are said to have decided to settle.
36 Given that an entire ancient forest had grown over the centuries, it's unlikely that the ancient Patupaiarehe people who met the first Maori were in fact the original vanished race from centuries earlier.

kauwau runga) and the 'lower realm' (te kauwau raro). These spiritual
links to the past form an integral part of Rangitāne identity today."

The *Encyclopedia of New Zealand* records that the original New Zealanders were skilled at net fishing and horticulture, capable of constructing
vast garden systems like those at Waimea. It seems the remnants of this
people captured by the Ngati Mamoe/Rangitane tribe had their engineer-
ing skills put to good use.

An example of the advanced technology of the first settlers can still be
seen at Cloudy Bay on the Marlborough coast, near Blenheim.

In 1912, the *Journal of the Polynesian Society* published details of an
archaeological discovery: nearly 20 kilometres of water canals connecting
a large raupo swamp (now reclaimed land at Riverlands) to the Upper

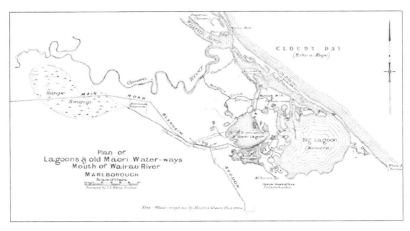

Lagoon and Big Lagoon at Cloudy Bay on the coast. An intricate network of carefully dug canals linked the two lagoons, while a longer feeder canal tailed back to the distant swamp. Presumably in ancient times the swamp was more of a lake. The Google Earth photo discloses near zero sea level rise over the past 100 years, sharp-eyed readers will note.

"The canals are still (1902-03) for the most part in a state of good repair, and navigable for small canoes. They have been constructed with great care, and many of them and 10ft or 12ft wide by 2ft or 3ft deep," reported.

"The big channel or canal that connected the Upper Lagoon with the raupo swamp, probably a lagoon at the time the canal was cut is a very heavy piece of work. It is over four miles in length, and from ten to twelve feet in width, with an average depth of cut of about eight feet. When it is considered that the whole of the excavation – over 60,000 cubic yards of soil – was made with the most primitive of tool, by means of the ancient wooden *ko* or spade, one begins to notice what an industrious and enterprising people the old time Maori was."

These huge earthworks were designed to attract waterfowl and allow easy capture for food, and as Google Earth pictures show, their canal handiwork from the early 1700s is still in full use today, under the protection of the Department of Conservation as a nature reserve.

There's one other reason that archaeologists may have difficulty finding traces of ancient human settlement of the Otago and Canterbury coasts in particular, and you won't find that reason discussed in the *Penguin History of New Zealand* or other usual history books.

At some point in the 1400s, a giant asteroid or comet (researchers believe it was most likely a comet) slammed into the sea near Stewart Island. The resulting explosion created a tsunami eclipsing anything ever seen anywhere in the world in the modern era. It struck at night, and "The impact fireball was seen by the [Australian] aborigines," reported one study.[37]

Researchers from America's Columbia University's Lamont-Doherty Earth Observatory and the University of Wollongong in Australia found beach sand deposited 220 metres above sea level at Stewart Island, and the tsunami threw beach flotsam 130 metres above sea level on the Australian coast and Lord Howe Island in the Tasman Sea. By triangulating the path of the tsunami the researchers located an undersea impact crater in waters 300 metres deep off the South Island of New Zealand, 20 kilometres

---

37 "Did a Bolide Impact Cause Catastrophic Tsunamis in Australia and New Zealand?", Abbott et al, 2003, see http://gsa.confex.com/gsa/2003AM/finalprogram/abstract_65239.htm

ABOVE, & RIGHT: Massive tracks of sand thrust inland at Stewart Island's Mason Bay, by the mega-tsunami caused by the Mahuika impact. Sand was found deposited up to 220 metres above sea level. Photos taken for Lamont-Doherty Earth Observatory study, you can also find images at Google Earth

across and with crater walls 150 metres deep.[38] The size of the incoming missile was between 500 metres and one kilometre in diameter.

The biggest known earthquake-caused tsunami can create 60 metre walls of water – around six times larger than the Japan tsunami. This New Zealand one created by what is now known as the Mahuika comet strike – after the Maori god of fire – was what scientists call a "mega-tsunami", 220 metres tall, 22 times higher than the Japanese tsunami, as it thundered up the South Island's east coast. Waves that high have been known to penetrate up to 45km inland in other parts of the world.[39]

To put this in perspective, if you were dining in the revolving restaurant at Auckland's Sky Tower, 190 metres off the ground, you would still be 30 metres (100ft) underwater.

You saw how much dirt and topsoil was churned up and sucked out to sea in Japan with a ten metre wave. Faced with a 220 metre high watery

---

38 The map coordinates for the crater are 48.3 S, 166.4E
39 "Missing in Action? Evaluating the putative absence of impacts by large asteroids and comets during the Quaternary Period", Masse et al, Los Alamos National Laboratory, 2007, see http://www.amostech.com/TechnicalPapers/2007/Poster/Masse.pdf

Armageddon, Moa and Maori alike, and maybe even those mysterious Mekosuchine crocodiles, were obliterated by the mega-tsunami's relentless tides, and with those surges the evidence of pre-1400AD human coastal settlements in New Zealand disappeared down an oceanic plughole. It is little wonder historians have been unable to find undisputed carbon-datings for moa hunting before 1400AD in the South Island.[40] Once again, it's a reminder that absence of evidence is not evidence of absence.[41]

At D'Urville Island in the Marlborough Sounds, the wall of water was still 40 metres high when it struck, despite being in a sheltered position. Australian tsunami expert Dr James Goff from the University of New South Wales says beach-level villages on the island simply disappeared off the map, and human habitation does not appear to have resumed until 1450AD there.[42]

The 40 metre tidal wave (possibly much larger given Wellington's line-of-sight to the impact) would have slammed into the Wellington[43], Wanganui and Wairarapa coasts, and the rollpast effect would have surged sea levels up right along the northern New Zealand coastlines. Seaside villages (as indeed most were) would have been drowned and sucked out to sea, along with evidence of earlier human habitation on the coast.[44]

Little wonder, perhaps, that a group of Moriori dwelling in the sounds

---

40 The Santorini eruption in Greece's Aegean Sea circa 1600BC – just slightly smaller than the Lake Taupo eruption – generated a tsunami wave between 35m and 150m high that's the prime suspect in the disappearance of the legendary Minoan civilisation on the nearby island of Crete. If one of the world's most advanced civilisations living in brick houses could be wiped off the map by a smaller tsunami, how much chance did a culture living in houses made of straw have facing waves half as tall again? The assumption by modern academics that because they can't find something now, that it can't have existed then, is an easy but dangerous mistake to make.

41 The Wairau Bar archaeological site, officially the country's oldest, is acknowledged to have been scoured by a tsunami, which emphasises the difficulties we have.

42 http://www.new-zealand-pictures.com/2011/07/tsunamis-and-taniwhas/

43 A large whale skeleton was found on the top of hills near Miramar in the late 1800s.

44 Intriguingly, Goff had earlier been a 2003 co-author, with bone person Keri Hulme and archaeologist Bruce McFadgen, of a Royal Society of New Zealand paper rejecting the idea of an asteroid strike off New Zealand. "In it the author links New Zealand evidence for widespread forest destruction and Maori place-names and legends with the 15th century timing of an apparent Tunguska-type meteor impact in the South Island of New Zealand, Chinese, and Japanese meteor sightings, comets, and "mega"-tsunamis in Australia. This paper critically reviews the lines of evidence used, and finds no evidence, either Maori or geological, for a 15th century meteor impact in New Zealand." See *Journal of the Royal Society of New Zealand*, Volume 33, Number 4, December 2003, pp 795–809. That article had already been committed to print when Abbott et al published their discovery of the impact crater and debris, including tektites created in the explosion, and then followed it up in 2005 with proof from Antarctic ice core samples that dated the asteroid impact to 1443 AD. See "Evidence from an Ice Core of a Large Impact Circa 1443 A.D", Abbott et al, American Geophysical Union, Fall Meeting 2005, abstract #PP31C-05, http://adsabs.harvard.edu/abs/2005AGUFMPP31C..05A

upped stakes and sailed off to the Chatham Islands around the same time, becoming the colonisers of that territory.

In his *History of New Zealand*, Michael King writes of this period:

"At some point in the last millennium, however, possibly around the fourteenth or fifteenth century AD, the era of widespread Polynesian voyaging ceased. This may have occurred because of the change in climate that produced colder, windier weather and rougher seas, or, possibly, because of a change in cultural priorities."

Sadly, King was killed in a car crash before news of the Mahuika impact was released. Knowing what we now know, the most likely reason that Polynesian exploration of the Pacific suddenly ended around 1400 is that the home islands got swamped by the same mega-tsunami that rocked New Zealand and Australia. The islanders would have been left licking their wounds and rebuilding their societies, and international travel was probably not a priority.

Maori, who have long been blamed for hunting giant moa and the giant eagle to extinction, probably played a lesser part than the asteroid strike. Without the washed-away moa to feed on, the Haast's Eagles would have faded away as well, and given they are believed to have become extinct in the 1400s, the timing fits.

So that's the story of early New Zealand settlement. What have we learnt?

Firstly, that New Zealand may have been settled sometime in the early first millennium AD, much earlier than historians currently believe. There are artefacts found five to six metres underground beneath ancient forests that clearly had to belong to people who existed much earlier than 1200 or 1300AD. The earliest artefacts are found in the South Island, which may have been the first colonisation point as it is a larger target coast for a New Caledonian canoe than the North Island is.

Secondly, that early South Island cave paintings depict creatures that existed in Melanesia, not Polynesia, once again raising questions about the identity of New Zealand's original settlers.

Thirdly, that Maori who met Captain Cook in the 1770s were able to describe and even draw pictures of pythons, in a country that has no snakes.

Fourthly, that modern historical assumptions and a continuing debate about the date of human arrival in New Zealand may be off-target because researchers have failed to factor in the evidence-destroying effects of the Mahuika asteroid strike and its mega-tsunami.[45]

45 Archaeologist Bruce McFadgen believes New Zealand was hit by another massive tsunami coming from north of New Zealand, around 1500AD, which would have cleaned out many of

Fifthly, that the original settlers, whether Melanesian or a Melanesian/ Polynesian mix, were either slaughtered or absorbed into a much bigger wave of Maori migration after 1200AD.

This then, is the early history of New Zealand. However, while it is important to know as much as we can about the first New Zealanders, it has absolutely no bearing on the legality or otherwise of the Treaty of Waitangi.

This is a really important point. It's fascinating academically, but it doesn't matter that modern Maori probably were not the first inhabitants (and in many of their Waitangi claims they actually admit the land was populated by someone else before them). Under international law, finders keepers and the rules of conquest, the first New Zealanders have long since been wiped out or intermarried or become slaves to the later Maori arrivals. Their lands became Maori lands. The Brits were not doing deals with the Patupaiarehe or the Waitaha or the Moriori, they were doing deals with the people who now controlled the land, the Maori.

As the first European contact begins, it's now the Maori story that becomes relevant.

---

the northern tribes. See "Tsunami wiped out historic knowledge", *DomPost* 12 Oct. 2009 http:// www.stuff.co.nz/dominion-post/comment/2953668/Tsunami-wiped-out-historic-knowledge
While McFadgen and Goff are adamant the tsunami was *not* impact related, and the US/ Australian research teams are adamant it was, both sides agree on the fact that there was a tsunami. Whether the wall of water was 220 metres high, 35 metres high or only 10 metres high (the size of the Japan wave) is irrelevant – most villages were close to the seashore, the effects of the big bad whoosh would have been fatal for most of the inhabitants sleeping in straw huts.

CHAPTER TWO

Me Tarzan, You James

Officially, the first Europeans to lay eyes on this country were those on board Dutch captain Abel Janszoon Tasman's two ships, the *Zeehaen* and the *Heemskerck*. "Towards noon we saw a large high lying land, bearing south-east of us", his journal from 13 December, 1642 records.

Although Tasman mapped part of the South Island and much of the west coast of the North Island, he failed to discover that he could sail through Cook Strait, and was fairly convinced he had therefore found the western edge of a rumoured great southern continent stretching all the way across the Pacific to South America.

His only interaction with Maori was an unfortunate one. When the ships anchored at Golden Bay to collect fresh water, they were greeted by Maori in canoes, blowing on pukaea – long timber horns. Correctly thinking this was an attempt at communication, but incorrectly assuming it was a friendly message, Tasman's men answered with their own horns, evidently indicating they were prepared to meet the military challenge that had just been blown their way.

Of course, they were unaware of the symbolism and were extremely surprised when a waka laden with warriors then rammed one of the *Zeehaen's* shoreboats, killing four of Tasman's crew before the startled Dutchmen could open fire and scare the attackers away.

Michael King writes, "We have only the accounts of the Dutch witnesses. Ngati Tumatakokiri, themselves originally invaders from the north, were attacked by waves of descending North Island tribes in the eighteenth and early nineteenth centurires and annihilated as an iwi. They left no descendants to transmit coherent versions of the first encounter between New Zealand Maori and European people whose beliefs and technologies had propelled them halfway around the globe."

Despite King's pessimism, there is a follow-up however, detailed by author John Tasker in his recent book *Sixteenth Century Portuguese Down Under*:[46]

"The story concerns an engine driver by the name of Frank Robertson who, together with his two sons, moved to Wainui in the Nelson Province and leased from Maori most of the flat land there. At Wainui, Robertson senior became very friendly with a Maori known as Paramena with whom he shared many a confidence, and endless hours discussing old times. The friendship blossomed to the extent that secrets were shared, and when one day a message reached Robertson that Paramena was dying, and wanted to see him quickly, Robertson hastened to the bedside of his old friend.

"Paramena disclosed that he was the last member of the Tumatakokiri tribe and that there was ancient information he wished to pass on before he died. He explained that when members of his tribe attacked the crew of a visiting European ship – which he supposed was that of the Tasman expedition…Maori prevailed to the extent that they were able to capture a quantity of arms which had been in the possession of the slain sailors.

"The victorious war party took the arms back to Wainui Pa where a dispute arose among the chiefs as to who should own them. The matter was referred to the tohunga who, Solomon-like, decided that nobody should. He placed a tapu on them and ordered that they be buried instead. Paramena knew where the burial had taken place and he explained to Robertson in great detail the exact location of the spot. But when Robertson arrived back home and discussed the matter with his family they all concluded that Paramena must have been delirious and had talked nonsense. And so the matter may have rested indefinitely. But some years later the paddock mentioned as the burial place was stumped and ploughed and to everyone's surprise two musket barrels were ploughed up by Frank's son Morris at the spot indicated. It was a great surprise.

"Robertson junior then remembered that Paramena had made specific reference to a 'cutlass,' and on digging around the area he found that also. The bronze handle and guard were in excellent repair but the steel blade was badly corroded and in trying to extract it from the ground the ancient relic broke in two."

It was 1910, and the items – which must have been weapons seized from Abel Tasman's men, were last seen in a local school museum, now long

---

46   *Sixteenth Century Portuguese Down Under*, by John Tasker, Kanuka Press, 2011

gone. At least we now know what the last surviving Ngati Tumatakokiri had to say about the encounter with Tasman.

There is growing evidence, however, that New Zealand may have been visited by Europeans or other explorers before Abel Tasman officially 'discovered' the place in December 1642.

Author John Tasker makes a reasonably convincing case in his book that certainly Portuguese explorers in the 15th and 16th centuries, and possibly even Arab explorers, had made it to the shores of New Zealand at one point or other in time. Of the latter, he raised the possibility that New Zealand's giant Haast's Eagle may have been the famed 'Roc' of Sinbad's Voyages claim. Of the former, he noted the Portuguese habit of leaving what they called 'Padroe', or priest-rocks, behind in the countries they visited. A couple of padroe stones appear to have been left at Aotea Harbour, west of Hamilton.

Authors Max Hill and Noel Hilliam, likewise, make the case in a recent book, *To The Ends Of The Earth*, that the Polynesian explorer Maui was actually a Libyan ship captain under the flag of Ptolemaic Egypt, accompanied by an officer named Rata. Maybe, maybe not. It's not a new claim, and actually hangs on assertions made by an ex-pat New Zealander based in the USA who has been trying to convince people since the 1960s of this. There are also suggestions in some quarters that

the ancient Celts, not known as the world's best seafarers, nonetheless
made it to New Zealand at some point in the distant past.

Perhaps. Perhaps not. As you saw in the previous chapter, someone was
certainly here, of whom we know very little.

However, once again it is fascinating but ultimately irrelevant to Treaty
issues whether Egyptians, Libyans, Greeks, Phoenicians, the Portuguese
or the Druid Getafix with his mates Asterix and Obelisk set foot on New
Zealand first – the important part is that they didn't get back to boast
about it or, if they did and they mapped it, they kept it very quiet and
didn't claim the land. Not even Tasman claimed New Zealand for the
Dutch. It was left to a British naval commander, Captain James Cook,
to be the first European to set foot on New Zealand soil and live to tell
the tale.

Official New Zealand history books state Cook raised the Union Jack
and claimed New Zealand for Britain's King George III on 15 November,
1769 at a ceremony on the Coromandel Peninsula.[47] While it's true that a
ceremony did take place, it's believed he actually claimed the country on
October 9th or 10th, only two days after first touching land here.[48] The case
for this is made by historian and missionary William Colenso,[49] who dug
out this passage from the journal of Sydney Parkinson, a draughtsman
assisting naturalist Sir Joseph Banks on the *Endeavour*.

"Early on the morning of the 10th," writes Parkinson, "the long-boat,
pinnace and yawl went on shore again and landed near the river where
they had been the night before."[50]

There was an interlude with the Maori on shore that left three natives
dead after they appeared to be preparing to throw their spears, but
Parkinson records the other Maori were more interested in taking the
possessions and weapons of their fallen comrades than revenge, and the
Maori "quietly departed".

47 "Today in History, 15 November", *British Flag flies for first time in New Zealand* http://www.
nzhistory.net.nz/timeline/15/11 As you can see above, the British Union Jack actually flew for
the first time in NZ at Poverty Bay on October 10.
48 There is a discrepancy of one day throughout the month of October between the journals
of Captain Cook, as published by his biographer Dr Hawkesworth, and those of *Endeavour's*
artist Sydney Parkinson and botanist Sir Joseph Banks. While events in the diaries match,
Cook's are always one day out. Whether that was a dateline error or a miscalculation by Cook's
London biographer, no one knows.
49 "On the Day in which Captain Cook took formal Possession of New Zealand", William
Colenso, *Transactions & Proceedings of the New Zealand Institute*, Vol 10, 1877, see http://rsnz.
natlib.govt.nz/volume/rsnz_10/rsnz_10_00_000760.html
50 *A Journal of a Voyage to the South Seas*, Sydney Parkinson, 1773, see http://www.nzetc.org/tm/
scholarly/tei-ParJour-t1-body1-d2-d1.html

"After having taken possession of the country in form for the King [emphasis added]," continues Parkinson, "our company embarked and went around the bay in search of water again."

So in the words of one *Endeavour* crewman's journal for 10 October 1769, formal possession of New Zealand was taken that day. Parkinson's version is backed up by Captain Cook himself in his journal entry for October 9th:

"In the morning we saw several of the natives where they had been seen the night before. As I was desirous to establish an intercourse with them I ordered three boats to be manned with seamen and marines and proceeded towards the shore accompanied by Mr Banks [and other officers].

"On the marines being landed they marched with a Jack [Union Jack] carried before them to a little bank about fifty yards from the water-side; here they were drawn up."

It had been Cook's practice elsewhere on the *Endeavour's* journey to plant the Union Jack on land as soon as practicable and claim the new territory for King George. Clearly, they'd followed the same procedure here in New Zealand.

So why do the official textbooks not record formal possession being taken until 15 November – six weeks after arriving here? Probably because the wording for Cook's 15 November journal entry as published by his biographer was more explicit.

"Before we left the bay [Mercury Bay on the Coromandel], we cut upon one of the trees near the watering place the ship's name and that of the commander, with the date of the year and the month when we were there; and after displaying the English colours, I took formal possession of it in the name of His Britannic Majesty King George the Third".

Commenting on this apparent confusion, William Colenso told the Hawke Bay Philosophical Institute in 1877:

"For several years I have been of opinion that all our colonial almanacs are in error on this subject. They all give the 15th of November, 1769, as the day in which Cook took possession of New Zealand in the name of the King. This they have always done, and in this they have been followed by other publications, both Colonial and British."

The error, according to Colenso, was relatively simple to explain and originated in Cook's suspicion that he had discovered the vast unknown southern continent, Terra Australis Incognita.

"The land became the subject of much eager conversation," records Cook in his journal, "but the general opinion seemed to be that we had found the Terra Australis Incognita."

While Cook knew, of course, that Tasman had discovered New Zealand, Tasman had only partially mapped the coast, and that squiggle sat on European maps for a century, taunting explorers. Was it just a tiny portion of the presumed massive coast of Terra Australis, everyone wanted to know. Terra Australis was supposed to be huge, and perhaps peopled by many kingdoms. Cook and his men, sure enough, found that it was possible several kingdoms existed along this new coast he was exploring, and each kingdom needed to be treated separately:

"As far as we had yet coasted this country from Cape Turnagain, the people acknowledged one chief whom they called *Teratu* [likely, Te Ratu]", records Cook's journal.

A little further on in his voyage:

"It is much to be regretted that we were obliged to leave this country without knowing anything of Teratu but his name. As an Indian monarch, his territory is certainly extensive. He was acknowledged from Cape Kidnappers to the northward and westward as far as the Bay of Plenty, a length of coast upwards of 80 leagues, and we do not yet know how much farther westward his dominions may extend.

"Possibly the fortified towns which we saw in the Bay of Plenty may be his barrier; especially as at Mercury Bay he was not acknowledged, nor indeed any other single chief," remarked Cook.

It is likely then, that, having planted the flag on Teratu's shores, Captain Cook decided to repeat the formality in the area where Teratu's influence did not extend – such as Mercury Bay. Cook, it seems, was a stickler for the flag-waving, as can be seen from his journal regarding Botany Bay in Australia some six months after his New Zealand visit:

"During my stay in this harbour [Sydney] I caused the English colours to be displayed on shore every day, and the ship's name and the date of the year to be inscribed upon one of the trees near the watering place." As William Colenso points out, Australia had well and truly been discovered and claimed already, but the bureaucrat within Cook saw no harm dotting the i's and crossing the t's a few times more than necessary. Maybe he sensed the natives might be sticklers for detail in negotiations at some point in the future.[51]

---

51 As if to prove the point, J B Condliffe's 1925 book, *A Short History of New Zealand*, revised 1953 with W G Airey, records at p16 that Cook again hoisted the Union Jack in the name of George when, cresting the top of a hill in the Marlborough Sounds whilst *Endeavour* was being repaired, "Cook first saw the strait that bears his name and realised that New Zealand consisted of two separate islands. He continued his voyage, after formally taking possession of the islands in the name of the King".

RIGHT: There's specula-
tion that this early attempt
to map Australia has actually merged part of NZ into
it. Is Cape Fremose on the
right really NZ's East Cape?
Likewise, is Saill Island
off the coast either North
Cape or the top of the South
Island? This map predated
Tasman by a century

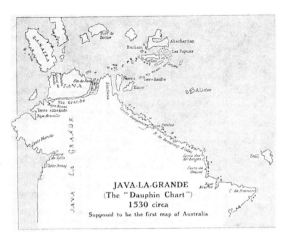

JAVA-LA-GRANDE
(The "Dauphin Chart")
1530 circa
Supposed to be the first map of Australia

Captain Cook's first week in New Zealand was a bloody one, as he and the Maori tested each other's mettle.

The usual routine in the more politically-correct New Zealand history books is to imply that Cook shot innocent Maori because he and his crew were unfamiliar with Maori haka and challenges. Cook may have been new to NZ waters, but he and his officers were not entirely stupid. They had, after all, spent a lot of time in the Pacific islands, and had on board the Tahitian chief Tupaea as their cultural advisor and translator.

Michael King reckons the first tragic meeting happened like this:

"Poverty Bay Maori paid a price for confronting the unknown visitors. When a Maori party approached the *Endeavour's* pinnace ashore on the bank of the Turanganui River and ceremonially challenged the crew, a sailor judged their intention to be hostile and shot one man dead."[52]

Readers can make their own minds up as to whether that's an overly simplistic paraphrasing of what follows, taken directly from *Endeavour's* diaries.

On Monday October 9, Cook and his men had gone ashore in several boats for the first time to make contact with the Maori, whom at that stage Cook called "Indians". With the language barrier, the Maori retreated into the bush, leaving Cook and his officers exploring the deserted Maori village while four cabin boys waited in the river by one of the smaller boats, a yawl. Suddenly, one of Cook's watchkeepers back at the beach saw four armed "Indians" running for the boat containing the cabin boys. The

52 *The Penguin History of New Zealand*, Michael King, p103

Coxswain yelled at the boys in the yawl to rapidly begin rowing down stream towards the beach, "which they did, being closely pursued by the Indians," recorded James Cook.

"The Coxswain of the pinnace[53] who had the charge of the boats," wrote Cook in his journal, "fire'd two musquets over their heads, the first made them stop and look round them, but the 2ᵈ they took no notice of, upon which a third was fired and killed one of them upon the spot just as he was going to dart his spear at the boat; at this the other three stood motionless for a minute or two, seemingly quite surprised, wondering no doubt what it was that had thus killed their comrade: but as soon as they recover'd themselves they made off dragging the dead body a little way and then left it."[54]

Hearing the gunshots, Cook and his men sprinted back to the beach, took one look at the dead Maori and another look back at the bushline where the rest were hiding, and the order was given to retreat to the safety of *Endeavour*.

Four armed warriors sprinting to a boat containing four young cabin boys doesn't sound like much of a "ceremonial challenge". Here's how Sir Joseph Banks recorded the incident:

"In the evening went ashore with the marines. March from the boats in hopes of finding water. Saw a few of the natives who ran away immediately on seeing us; while we were absent four of them attacked our small boat in which were only 4 boys, they got off from the shore in a river, the people followed them and threatened with long lances; the pinnace soon came to their assistance, fired upon them and killed the chief."[55]

The following morning, October 10, as previously recounted, Cook and his men were back on the beach with their Tahitian translator Tupaea in tow, hoping to get the message across, "we come in peace". The Maori gathered on

53 *Endeavour's* main tender vessel
54 Cook's journal, 9 October 1769, see http://southseas.nla.gov.au/journals/cook/17691009.html
55 Banks' journal, 8 October 1769, see http://southseas.nla.gov.au/journals/banks/17691008.html

the opposite bank of the river that cut down to the beach, and began a full-on haka. Now this *was* a ceremonial challenge, and was recognised as such.

"We called to them in the Georges Island Language, but they answered us by flourishing their weapons over their heads and dancing, as we supposed, the war dance."

Realising there was no Scotty to 'beam us up', Captain Cook did the next best thing, calling on a regiment of *Endeavour's* marines to take formation 200 metres behind the officers. Like a world cup rugby encounter, but with guns, the English team watched nervously as the haka was performed.

To their surprise, the "Indians" understood translator Tupaea perfectly, but naturally the events of the previous day had left everyone shaken. The Maori initially acted friendly, and first a handful then "20 or 30" swam across the river to meet the British. The first few were unarmed, but as more leapt into the water Cook's men noticed the latest arrivals were carrying weapons. The *Endeavour* officers handed out gifts to all, but what the Maori really wanted was to lay their hands on the strangers' mysterious weapons that seemed capable of killing people with a sound.

One Maori youth managed to snatch a British officer's cutlass and began waving it around, refusing to give it back despite Tupaea's pleas.

"Tupaea told us several times as soon as they came over to take care of ourselves, for they were not our friends," noted Cook, "and this we very soon found for one of them snatched M' Greens Hanger [cutlass] from him and would not give it up."

Cook realised his own *mana* was being tested, and with 30 mostly armed Maori at close quarters the situation could get fatal for the *Endeavour* if he wasn't decisive. "This encouraged the rest to be more insolent and seeing others coming over to join them I ordered the man who had taken the hanger to be fired at."

By the time the guns were

"A New Zealand Warrior in his proper dress and completely armed according to their manner." – Endeavour journals

silent, the original offender was confirmed dead and three others suspected so, although they were carried off by the tribe so their ultimate
fate was unknown.

Still hopeful he could win the tribe around, Cook and his men took to
the water again that afternoon, drawing their longboat close to a waka
containing half a dozen youths. Tupaea tried to ask them to come and
see *Endeavour*, but at that the paddlers just paddled even harder in the
opposite direction. Thinking he could scare them into stopping, Cook
ordered shots to be fired into the air. The reaction he got was unexpected
– the waka suddenly headed for their longboat and it looked as if the
paddlers intended to attack. This time Cook's men opened fire on the
canoe, killing three instantly and sending the others leaping into the surf.

"Three jumped overboard, these last we took up and brought on board,
where they were clothed and treated with all imaginable kindness and,
to the surprise of everybody, became at once as cheerful and as merry
as if they had been with their own friends; they were all three young,
the eldest not above 20 years of age and the youngest about 10 or 12."[56]

Later that night, with just candlelight to illuminate the parchment
of his journal page, Cook lamented his decision to open fire in the first
place, and kicked himself for not anticipating it.

"I am aware that most humane men who have not experienced things
of this nature will censure my conduct in firing upon the people in this
boat, nor do I myself think that the reason I had for seizing upon her
will at all justify me.

"Had I thought that they would have made the least resistance I would
not have come near them but as they did I was not to stand still and suffer either myself or those that were with me to be knocked on the head."

Cook was well aware of the fate that had befallen Tasman's crew back
in 1642.

After a night of good food on the British flagship, Cook's three Maori
guests were reluctant to leave, telling him through the interpreter that
they feared their enemies would catch them if he took them back to the
beach. Cook suspected it was the youths' sense of adventure and curiosity
getting the better of them, and was pleased to note the trio were greeted
by their own tribe when they returned that next morning.

News spread rapidly of the strange riches carried on *Endeavour*, and
on October 12 another waka full of Maori men pulled alongside. "The

---

56 Cook's Journal, October 10, 1769, see http://southseas.nla.gov.au/journals/cook/17691010.html

View of an Arched Rock, on the coast of New Zealand with an Hippa, or place of retreat, on the top of it.

people in this boat had heard of the treatment those had met with we had had on board before and therefore came on board without hesitation," noted Cook. In demand was cloth, made by the natives of Tahiti and stored on the *Endeavour*, and in return the Maori first traded their paddles and then tried to sell their canoe. When they finally departed, they voluntarily left behind three more Maori to stay on the British ship, and nothing Cook and his men could to would entice their guests to go back to the mainland.

When dawn broke the following morning, more canoes pulled alongside and translator Tupaea remarked to Cook the overnight guests were yelling over the rails to their friends, "It's OK to come on board, the white men don't eat people!"

"From which," Cook wryly and cautiously noted in his journal, "it should seem that these people have such a Custom among them."[57]

As *Endeavour* cruised south through Poverty Bay exploring, the ship grounded on a shoal briefly, long enough for four waka to be launched from a nearby beach. Not wanting his ship swamped by possibly hostile

---

"The head of a Chief of New Zealand, the face tattooed or marked according to their manner."
– Endeavour journals

strangers, Cook ordered warning shots to ring out.

"I ordered a musket shot to be fired close to one of them, but this they took no notice of. A four pounder was then fired a little wide of them. At this they began to shake their spears and paddles at us, but notwithstanding this they thought fit to retire."[58]

Monday 16 October saw the British again draw blood. A Maori fishing party wanted to sell "stinking fish" to Cook, who wrote that regardless of the state of the fish he was happy to trade with the locals "on any terms". The tribe seemed most interested in red cloth, while Cook was fascinated by what appeared to be a "bear skin" cloak being worn by one of the Maori. It ended with the tribe getting the red cloth, but Cook came out of the trade 'bear handed' as the mysterious cloak remained on the canoe.

Things turned nasty, however, when the Maori – on the pretence of offering more fish – managed to snatch hold of Tupaea's young Tahitian servant, Tiata. "They seized hold of him, pulled him into the boat and endeavoured to carry him off," wrote Cook. "This obliged us to fire upon them which gave the boy an opportunity to jump over board and we brought the Ship too, lowered a boat into the water and took him up unhurt.

"Two or 3 paid for the daring attempt with the loss of their lives, and many more would have suffered had it not been for fear of killing the Boy."[59]

The incident gave Cape Kidnappers its name.

Although Cook had now managed to kill more Maori than Abel Tasman's ill-fated sojourn, there was no sense of wanton tragedy. Both sides were continuing to test the other; Maori, with a strong warrior code and

---

58 Cook's journal, 13 October 1769, see http://southseas.nla.gov.au/journals/cook/17691013.html
59 Cook's journal, 16 October 1769, see http://southseas.nla.gov.au/journals/cook/17691015.html

sense of honour, wanted to know the mettle of the *Endeavour* and its crew and seemed to accept the previous skirmishes were policing actions rather than acts of outright hostility. To be frank, they couldn't keep away from the British.

"During our stay in this Bay we had every day more or less traffic with the Natives, they bringing us fish and now and then a few sweet Potatoes, and several trifles which we deemed curiosities. For these we gave them cloth, beads, nails. The cloth we got at [Tahiti] they valued more than anything we could give them, and as everyone in the Ship were provided with some of this sort of cloth I [allowed] everybody to purchase whatever they pleased without limitation, for by this means I knew that the natives would not only sell, but get a good price for everything they brought."[60]

By trying to ensure the Maori got value for their trade, Cook hoped they would be encouraged to trade a wider range of goods, including things the British were not yet aware of.

It has been speculated by modern historians that the mega-tsunami of the mid 1400s killed the craftsmen capable of building outrigger and full catamaran canoes. The Maori had emigrated to New Zealand from the islands in double-hulled waka with sails, which are much more stable for ocean use, but by the time the Treaty of Waitangi was signed there was not a double-hulled canoe to be seen.

In a *Dominion Post* article, columnist Bob Brockie directly attributes this to the tsunami:[61]

"In those days most Maori lived on the coasts of Northland, Auckland, Coromandel and Bay of Plenty – the very coasts that bore the full force of the tsunami.

"To fill out the picture, he [archaeologist Bruce McFadgen] draws on many traditional Maori accounts of disastrous seas rising to the height of cliff tops, overwhelming their lands, drowning communities and sweeping away their fleets of canoes about 15 generations ago.

"Dr McFadgen suggests the great wave would have carried away all canoes and fishing gear, gardens and stored food, buried shellfish beds and poisoned the soil with salt.

"He thinks many coastal Maori would either have drowned or died of their injuries and, with the wholesale loss of food, many survivors would have succumbed to starvation.

60 Cook's journal, 29 October 1769, see http://southseas.nla.gov.au/journals/cook/17691029.html
61 "Tsunami wiped out historic knowledge", *Dominion Post* 12 October 2009, see http://www.stuff.co.nz/dominion-post/comment/2953668/Tsunami-wiped-out-historic-knowledge

"The timing of the calamitous tsunami coincides with many changes that overtook Maori.

"Before the disaster Maori built two-hulled canoes, afterwards only single-hulled boats.

"The quality of stone adzes, fishing gear, ornaments and other artifacts declined after the tsunami, which Dr McFadgen attributes to the loss of many skilled craftsmen."

Yet a search of Captain Cook's journals, and those of ship's artist Sydney Parkinson, reveals some of those canoe techniques were still in existence in 1769.

"Several of the canoes had outriggers; and one of them had a very curious piece of ornamental carving at the head of it," noted Sydney Parkinson at Poverty Bay.[62]

Several weeks later, with *Endeavour* approaching Motuhora Island off Whakatane in the Bay of Plenty, Cook made this journal entry:

"At 7 was close under the first island from whence a large double Canoe full of people came off to us. This was the first double Canoe we had seen in this Country. They stayed about the Ship until it was dark then left us, but not before they had thrown a few stones: they told us the name of the Island which was Mowtohora."[63]

Clearly, not all the Pacific-style canoes had gone, and the catamarans were no slouches as Cook noted the following day:

"The Double Canoe which we saw last night followed us again today *under sail* [emphasis added], and kept abreast of the Ship near an hour talking to Tupaea, but at last they began to pelt us with stones but upon firing one musket they dropped astern and left us."[64]

Botanist Sir Joseph Banks writes of the same incident:

"A sailing canoe that had chased us ever since day break came up with us and proved the same double canoe as pelted us last night, which made us prepare for another volley of their ammunition, dangerous to nothing on board but our windows.

"The event proved as we expected for after having sailed with us an hour they threw their stones again; a musket was fired over them and they dropped astern not, I believe, at all frightened by the musket but content with having shown their courage by twice insulting us. We now begin to

62 Parkinson's journal, 13 October 1769, see http://www.nzetc.org/tm/scholarly/tei-ParJour-t1-body1-d2-d1.html
63 Cook's journal, 2 November 1769, see http://southseas.nla.gov.au/journals/cook/17691102.html
64 Cook's journal, 3 November 1769, see http://southseas.nla.gov.au/journals/cook/17691102.html

"View of a peculiar Arched Rock, having a river running under it, in Tolago Bay, on the East Coast of New Zaaland" – *Endeavour journals*

know these people and are much less afraid of any daring attempt from them than we were," exclaimed Banks.[65]

Banks' wry observations on the Maori propensity to talk tough showed again the following day.

"About dinner time three canoes came alongside of much the most simple construction of any we have seen, being no more than the trunks of trees hollowed out by fire without the least carving or even the addition of a washboard on their gunnels.

"The people in them were almost naked and blacker than any we had seen – only 21 in all – yet these few despicable gentry sang their song of defiance and promised us as heartily as the most respectable of their countrymen that they would kill us all."

Seeing that the waka paddlers were tiring as they chased the *Endeavour,* one of the English crew threw out a tow rope "to save them the trouble of paddling, this they accepted and rewarded the man who gave it by thrusting at him with a pike which, however, took no effect."

---

65 Banks' journal, 2 November 1769, see http://southseas.nla.gov.au/journals/banks/17691102.html

It was the beginning of a long and fruitful relationship between James Cook and the people of New Zealand. Some of his contemporaries, however, were not so lucky.

CHAPTER THREE

How Would You Like Your French Fried?

One of the things not often raised in New Zealand history books is the cannibalism. Michael King's 570 page opus, for example covers off in one sentence Abel Tasman's 1642 encounter:

"The body of one dead crewman was taken ashore by Maori, possibly to be cooked and eaten, a ritual means of absorbing the mana of a vanquished foe ('the first of many European imports consumed in New Zealand was a dead Dutchman', James Belich would write)."[66]

That's it. A brief mention to show you've acknowledged it, but nothing to give it real context. The exception to the rule has been the courageous Paul Moon at Auckland University of Technology, whose book *This Horrid Practice* detailing Maori cannibalism was published back in 2008.

Reading through the early accounts, however, it's clear that one of the reasons Maori eventually signed the Treaty of Waitangi and invited British rule was because they wanted an end to inter-tribal warfare and cannibalism. To understand the Treaty of Waitangi in its context, one actually has to confront some of these inconvenient historical facts.

None of Cook's men in that first voyage of 1769-70 ended up in a hangi, but some French explorers did. Michael King writes coyly:

"Marc-Joseph Marion du Fresne...brought two vessels around the Northland coast in April 1772. He put men ashore at Spirit's Bay and Tom Bowling Bay, and the proceeded to the Bay of Islands, where he and 26 of his crew were killed by Maori in June, apparently as a result of breaching tapu."

You will notice no mention in that paragraph of cannibalism. Michael

King knew about it, but he chose not to share it with you. Instead, he writes disapprovingly of the French:

"In retaliation, and in the process of repelling further attacks, the surviving crew members levelled a village and killed between 200 and 300 local Maori."

So what really happened to the French Naval Captain and his crew? Thanks to the wonders of modern technology, historians are no longer the sole gatekeepers of access to past knowledge. Documents that were once buried deep in special vaults in the basements of libraries behind doors with signs saying "Beware of the leopard", are now scanned, translated and available to anyone with a computer. Thanks to modern technology, you can if you wish now see if your favourite historians have been giving you all the relevant information or not.

The story of Marion du Fresne's misadventure is told in the pages of journals by two of his fleet officers, Lieutenant Jean Roux of du Fresne's vessel *"Mascarin,"* and Captain Ambroise-Bernard-Marie du Clesmeur of the sister ship *"Marquis de Castries".*

What Michael King called "breaking a tapu" was a throwaway line not sourced to anything. It may however have been based on a document written a century after the events in question, by a Pakeha who interviewed an unnamed Ngapuhi source about the actions of the Ngati Pou tribe who killed du Fresne. It is not first-hand testimony, and in fact it does not appear to have been published until 1965, 74 years after the Pakeha interviewer had himself passed on and almost 200 years after the massacre in question. A journalist would treat this as hearsay of the first order, but it passes muster as "authentic history" in modern academic circles, apparently.[67]

This alleged Maori version agrees that du Fresne and his ships came to Motu-arohia Island[68] in the Bay of Islands and had friendly relations with local iwi "for a long time. The Maoris were friendly towards them; they habitually ate together, and the foreigners slept in the Maori houses and the Maoris slept on board the ships.

---

67 "The story published here is one of many White manuscripts in the Alexander Turnbull Library, Wellington. John White lived at Hokianga from 1835 to 1850 (that is, from the age of nine until he was 24) but it is not known whether this account was collected during these early years. All that is known about his informant is that he was a member of the Ngapuhi tribe." See *Te Ao Hou*, No. 51 (June 1965), http://teaohou.natlib.govt.nz/journals/teaohou/issue/Mao51TeA/c7.html

68 This claim appears to be incorrect. Motu-arohia Island was little more than a rock. The ships anchored at nearby Moturua Island, which they named Marion Island, home to several Maori pa sites.

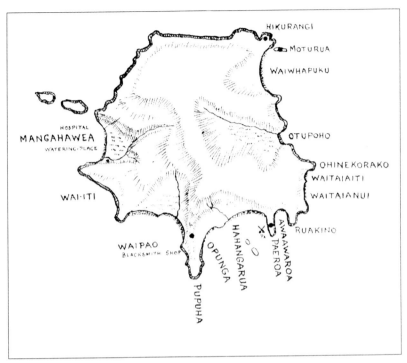

Moturua or Marion Island

"But there came a day when the foreigners rowed ashore in order to net fish on the beach at Manawaora. The Maoris scolded them for this, for the beach was tapu to some of Te Kauri's people (the people who lived at Whangamumu). Some men from there had been drowned in the Bay of Islands, and had been cast ashore on this beach. Although the people of Ngati Pou told them angrily not to do this (for they were afraid that Te Kauri's people would attack them in order to obtain recompense for the violation of their tapu), the foreigners took no notice, and persisted in drawing in their net on the beach. Then Ngati Pou became very sad, and no longer visited the ships and bargained for pieces of hoop-iron the size of a man's hand (these had been given in exchange for food, fish and birds, or for an entire day spent chopping firewood).

"Soon after this, some of the foreigners came on shore to wash their clothes. In the middle of the day, when it was time to eat, they sat down and had their meal, no longer watching their clothes, which were hung up on bushes in the scrub. Then the Maoris went and took some of the clothes, as a recompense for the foreigners having violated the tapu of

Manawaora by netting fish there, and eating those fish; it was this that made the desecration of the tapu such a grave offence.

"Marion's men went and told how their clothes had been stolen. Two chiefs of Ngati Pou were on one of the ships at the time, and Marion came and had them tied up with pieces of rope, intending to keep them prisoner until the stolen clothes were returned. But during the night the men managed to untie themselves, and escaped to land.

"When they arrived back, the Maori priests said that it was their gods which had parted the rope and allowed the chiefs to return alive. These two chiefs had not known the reason why they had been tied up, but when they returned they heard how the clothes had been stolen by Te Hikutu to give to Te Kauri's people as a recompense for the desecration of the tapu at Manawaora.

"One day soon after this, the foreigners rowed ashore to net fish again, and Ngati Pou learnt that it was Marion who had tied up their men. Marion and his men used their nets, and the fish were lying in their boat. When the foreigners were putting the net into the boat, the Maoris attacked them and clubbed them to death. All of them were killed; not one escaped.

"They took the bodies and cooked them, and Te Kauri and Tohitapu of the Te Koroa sub-tribe ate Marion, and Te Kauri took Marion's clothes. The bones of the foreigners who had been killed were made into forks for picking up food, and the thigh-bones were made into flutes."

That's the document that appears to anchor the *Penguin History of New Zealand*. As noted earlier, the bit about Du Fresne and his men being eaten was mysteriously sanitised from the 2003 book. However, here's how the actual journals taken on the days in question document the events.

The French anchored at Moturua Island to replenish supplies, and repair the ship. Relations with local Maori were initially good, with much trade and hospitality.

"As the natives are extremely intelligent, we were able to make them understand that the plantations we had made on Marion [Moturua] Island, of wheat, maize, potatoes, and various kinds of nuts, might be very useful to them. All these plants had grown very well, although it was winter. The natives seemed highly pleased, and informed us that they would take care of our cultivations, but I do not know whether they have preserved all these plants, which would be all the more valuable to them seeing that they have only the sweet potato and fern-root.

"Of the latter they make great use, and this is how they prepare it. Having torn up the fern, they expose it to the heat of the sun on branches of

"A New Zealand warrior and his wife, in the manner of that country." – Endeavour journals

trees, and as soon as it has faded in colour or dried, they place it in a fire, where they leave it for a little time. Then, having taken it out, they place it on a wide flat stone, and beat it with a kind of club until it becomes almost a paste. It is this paste that they chew, and, having extracted all the juice, they reject the skins or residuum. I have often tasted this paste, and always found the juice of the root very pleasant."[69]

Of their fishing skills, another French officer, Captain du Clesmeur, wrote:

"Fish is found in great abundance on these coasts, and is of excellent quality. I must not stop to enumerate the various species, which are almost the same as ours. The Natives fish with hooks and lines. The hooks differ in no way from those used in Tahiti. They are made out of mother of pearl, or of a root to which a piece of bone is very skilfully tied.

"The Natives soon recognized the superiority of ours, which we exchanged for their fish. Their lines are made of rushes, and knotted like ours. Instead of a cork they use a piece of spongy wood; and instead of a lead they use little pebbles, each tied separately."

---

69 Diary of Lieutenant Jean Roux of *Mascarin*. Quoted verbatim in *Historical Records of New Zealand*, Vol II, Robert McNab, see http://www.questia.com/PM.qst?a=o&d=91719029

One of the other things the French noticed was a strongly warlike culture, with little value on life.

"Each village of any importance has its own chief or its king, who exercises a complete and unquestioned authority over his subjects. These chiefs appear to me to be independent of each other. They declare war upon the slightest pretext, which wars are very bloody; they generally kill any prisoners they may capture.

"It seemed to me that they have a religion. First, I had noticed that each time these natives slept on board the ship they never failed to rise at a certain hour of the night, and commence to pray, muttering various words, amongst which they kept on repeating that of "Mathe" (*mate*), which signifies "to kill." This prayer lasted for about half an hour, after which they lay down again."[70]

In terms of social structure, Captain du Clesmeur wrote of apparent sexual freedom within the tribes:

"It appears, so I think, that they absolutely ignore the marriage ceremony and the marriage state. Everything is held in common amongst them, the women as well as the men observing this law."

Lieutenant Jean Roux saw this too:

"These natives are greatly given to embracing each other, but they display in these caresses a most noticeable ferocity. They are peculiarly fond of kissing each other, and this they do with great intensity."

Roux also spoke of women being offered as sexual gifts to the sailors by their menfolk:

"In the chief's handsome canoe there were four young women, by no means pretty, and rather badly built. The chief made them come on board, but he sent them away when he saw that we took no great notice of them."

The most surprising fact, Roux went on to say, "was the small regard they have for their women. They are not in the least jealous of them. The women have to do all the work, the men only occupying themselves with warlike preparations and exercises. They are continually engaged in these exercises, throwing darts and spears at each other. The women are always busy, either in making cloth, or cultivating the soil, or preparing food. Sometimes they even go fishing with very large nets, but, as a rule, the men do this work.

"These women appear to be completely subject to their husbands. I have never seen them eating with the men; on the contrary, they wait

---

70 ibid

upon them whilst the latter are eating. Indeed, I have even seen them push their servility to such a point as to actually place the food in their husbands' mouths. This custom of the women waiting on the men must be a rule amongst these people, for the men remain seated, and chat away with their fellows, without paying any attention to the women who wait upon them.

"This almost made me think the women were regarded as slaves. I have been able to get no definite information on this point. Despite the contempt in which the women are held, the population is very numerous. It seemed to me that each man had several wives, and they informed me that such was the case.[71]

"Time after time I have asked them why they so often made war upon each other, but I have never been able to understand the explanations they gave me. As to the way in which they treat their prisoners, they gave me a very clear explanation.

"As soon as the prisoners are in their power they are killed. From the demonstration they gave us on several occasions, there can be no doubt that they are cannibals, and that they eat their enemies. Several of our officers are of my opinion that this is the case, but what completely confirmed what I say on this subject is the fact that one of the chiefs, who well understood what I asked him, told me that after they had killed their enemies, they put them in a fire, and having cooked the corpses, ate them.

"Seeing that I was greatly disgusted with what he told me, my informant burst into laughter, and proceeded to reaffirm what he had just told me."

It was a harbinger of what was to come. While the Maori remained friendly, not everyone trusted them, especially given their inordinate amount of interest – naturally – in the superior French weaponry.

On one occasion a hapu chief at war with another hapu had arranged for a couple of French officers to march with them against their enemy, firing their muskets into the air. The mere sound made the rival tribe flee, awarding a "bloodless victory" to the chief with the French officers. Yes, the power of French weaponry was very seductive in the frequently conflict-ridden Bay of Islands.

Sixty of the French sailors from the two ships had developed scurvy

---

71   In the epic published in 1929 by Cambridge University, *The History of the British Empire*, they made this point about Maori society: "Among the Maoris, the family as we know it scarcely existed." There was no word, they pointed out, which uniquely meant 'Mum' or 'Dad', or which uniquely meant 'brother' or 'sister'. Instead the words that were used were equally used to describe Uncles, Aunts, cousins and friends. "Whanau", in the sense of extended family, was the closest early Maori society got.

during their Pacific voyaging and were disembarked to a hospital camp on the mainland, where a detachment of soldiers and sailors also worked on finding timber for new ships' masts.

The tapu-breaking document referred to earlier talked of chiefs being arrested over a fishing dispute. In the month leading up to the massacre, there were only two events that resulted in Maori being imprisoned for any reason. The first was this:

"The natives were already evilly disposed against M. Marion, who, having one day several of them on board his ship, had put into irons one of them who had stolen a sword – a treatment which frightened his comrades so much that they threw themselves in the sea and swam off to their canoes, threatening vengeance."[72]

It was also detailed here, taking place on 29 May 1772:

"One of these men, having seen through one of the port-holes of the gunroom a cutlass to which he took a fancy, took advantage of a moment when no one was looking to get into the gun-room and steal the weapon. He was seen with the cutlass as he was getting out of the port-hole, and M. Marion had him arrested simply to frighten him. Thereupon all the canoes made off, but shortly afterwards his countrymen came and begged that he should be pardoned, and at their request he was liberated."[73]

That was on May 29. The French had been there since May 12, anchored only a short distance from the beach allegedly declared "tapu". You may recall from a page back that Ngati Pou were supposed to have been controlling this beach and to have carried out the eventual massacre, in case Te Kauri attacked them for the tapu breach. But it's clear from the French journals that the beach was at the foot of Te Kauri's own village and controlled directly by him. He had numerous dealings with the French.

"This Tacoury, of whom I have just spoken, was regarded as one of the greatest chiefs of the district. Almost all the other chiefs paid homage to him, and were at the same time his enemies, often making war upon him. They wished to persuade us to do the same.

"This man often came to see us at our camp on Marion Island and on board our ships. It was easy to see that he took notice of everything he saw. His inquisitiveness and his boldness of manner made us distrustful of him at first, but M. Marion always believed in him."

---

72   Diary of Captain du Clesmeur, commander of the French naval vessel *Marquis de Castries* Quoted verbatim in *Historical Records of New Zealand*, Vol II, Robert McNab, see http://www.questia.com/PM.qst?a=o&d=91719029
73   Diary of Lieutenant Jean Roux, officer of *Mascarin*. Ibid

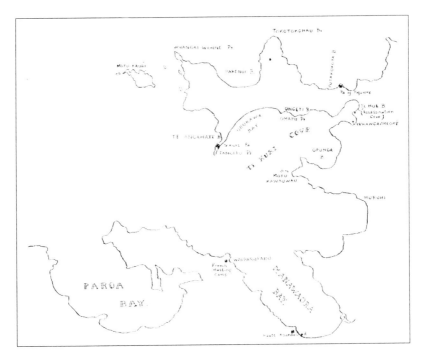

"TOP: Locality-map of activities of Marion. BOTTOM: Tangitu, fortified village of Te Kuri, burnt by French. Manawaora Bay in distance with hills behind where masts for French ships were obtained." – JPS journal

The journals record that Marion du Fresne frequently fished at this cove for sport during the three and a half weeks his fleet was anchored nearby, and there is no hint of any altercation with Maori over doing so although he did take an escort.

"M. Marion ... liked fishing, and often went to indulge in his sport in a cove which lies below Tacoury's village," wrote Roux. "This cove was out of sight of the vessels, and for this reason we persuaded him to always have with him a small detachment. He was therefore generally accompanied by two or three officers and some soldiers.

"On the 7th [June] I accompanied M. Marion to Tacoury's Cove, where we amused ourselves by gathering and eating some excellent oysters which were to be found in great quantities in this vicinity. It was this fact which induced M. Marion to go there so frequently, as to the pleasure of fishing he could add that of shooting, there being so many large birds, which allowed us to approach quite close to them."

Although the officers like Lieutenant Roux were becoming suspicious of Maori behaviour, Marion du Fresne would not hear any criticisms of the iwi, according to Roux' journal.

"Two chiefs came to see him on board our vessel. He was in his boat at the time with several of our company, and, as usual, there were several soldiers present. The chiefs took him on shore, and persuaded him to ascend a hill in the neighbourhood of Tacoury's village.

"Upon the hill there were a great many people gathered, who made him sit down with the officers who were with him. He was embraced by many of the natives, and at last they placed a sort of crown on his head, and pointing to the country all around, made him understand that they recognized him as their king. They went through several ceremonies, and treated him with great respect, making him presents of fish and of a stone upon which was engraved the figure of their divinity. On his part he made them several gifts, and made signs of friendship, and they then conducted him back to the ship."

Remember, this was well after the May 29 imprisonment incident. Turning to Lieutenant Roux, du Fresne added: "How can you expect me to have a bad opinion of a people who show me so much friendship? As I only do good to them, assuredly they will do me no evil."

There is not a hint, not a whisper, of any argument about tapu fishing grounds.

But trouble was brewing, in the form of a raid by local iwi on the French mast and hospital camp close to Te Kauri's village, where they succeeded in getting away with a gun and uniforms. It happened at night, and while a detachment of French sailors were giving chase, more Maori slipped in and stole an anchor being used in the repair of ships' masts. This is where the second imprisonment took place.

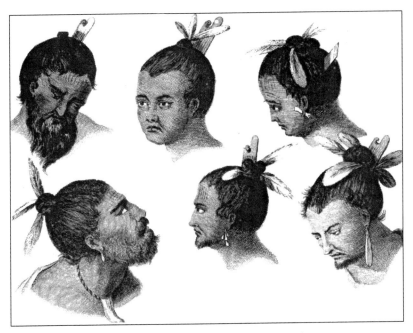

"The heads of six men, natives of New Zealand" – *Endeavour journals*

"At daybreak the forest was explored, with a view to finding the anchor, which, so it was supposed, could not have been carried very far away; but it could not be found. A detachment was sent to secure two Natives, and detain them as prisoners. The party secured a chief and a young man, who were taken to the camp. This chief wore a very handsome cloak, and his head was ornamented with the feathers worn in time of war. Someone took it into his head to declare that this chief was in command of the party which had committed the theft. Without making any further inquiry, the officer in command had the chief bound to a stake, and sent the young man under a strong guard to the mast-camp, where they made him understand what they had been looking for. Thereupon the young man declared himself guilty, and showed our people how the thieves had uprooted the anchor. The chief, who was kept bound up, accused Tacoury and Piquiore of this robbery.

"On the morning of the 9th M. Marion was informed of everything I have just recounted, and at first severely blamed the officer who had ordered the chief to be bound up, especially as he had given instructions that under no circumstances were these people to be ill-treated, only if it did happen that the Natives were clever enough to steal anything, he had ordered that an attempt should be made to make them restore the pilfered article, but without doing them any harm. These instructions were given to all who were in command, either at the camps, or at Marion Island, or in the boats. Our commander had given these orders, as he was convinced that if we did the Natives no harm they would never try to injure us."[74]

Du Fresne ordered the immediate release of the chief and the anchor thief, and reminded the camp commander that if his sentry team had kept a better watch, the Maori would never have been able to sneak in and steal the gun.

During the day of June 10, Roux stumbled upon a clearing where he saw two Maori men apparently play-fighting.

"At last I was so persuaded that they were not in earnest that I returned to the cover of the wood, so as not to interrupt them, and to hide myself from them, so as to enjoy the pleasure of seeing them. They displayed the greatest dexterity, and at the same time the most surprising agility. I had been watching them for about six minutes when all at once I saw each man throw away his weapons and draw his tomahawk from his belt.

"Immediately they rushed at each other with great fury, but missed each other. They then returned to the charge, whereupon I ran towards them; but it was too late, for in this one moment one of them had had his skull smashed in by a tomahawk stroke given him by his adversary, and had fallen dead on the spot.

"They were so excited that the victor only noticed me when I spoke to him. He was so astonished that he took flight at a great speed, and left me standing there by the side of his victim. I examined this unfortunate

---

74 If there was a tapu breach, arguably it was this seizure of the chief (but always bear in mind a chief was an ordinary, citizen-member of the tribe, as opposed to a slave) in response to the stolen musket, uniforms and anchor. Condliffe and Airey's *Short History of New Zealand* (Whitcombe & Tombs Publ, 1953, page 19) argues this was indeed the reason: "Marion's men, in binding a chief who had stolen an *axe* [an 1810 variation on the story], had insulted the chief's tapu and caused him to organise a drastic revenge." Perhaps. It's worth noting however that the captured chief blamed Te Kauri for the gun thefts the previous night that had led to the capture, and it was Te Kauri who organised the eventual massacre, not the supposedly insulted captured chief. The only other possible explanation for a tapu-breach was raised in Leslie Kelly's paper for the *Journal of the Polynesian Society* in 1933, which told of a Ngapuhi legend that Marion du Fresne had gathered some sacred wood for a fire (see JPS, Volume 42, No. 166, 1933, *In the path of Marion du Fresne*, by L. G. Kelly, p 83-96). In the author's view, however, there is so much evidence of premeditated attack that you can probably safely rule out a 'tapu breach' as anything other than a face-saving cover story told later to the missionaries; the Maori were not stupid, they were brilliant military strategists. As the dominant chief, Te Kauri wanted control of the French weapons and boats, which would have given him a decisive advantage in local and regional Maori conflicts. End of.

fellow, and saw that his head was cut down to nearly level with his eyes, as if by a single stroke of a cutlass. One-half of his skull hung down behind, and was still held by the skin, or at least it hung on by something. The brains had spurted out to a distance of three or four paces."

Later that afternoon Roux and his men noticed a party of armed Maori warriors approaching their camp as if about to make a challenge. The French officer knew the drill; he sliced off the green frond of a tree branch with his sword and offered the bough to the Maori, who responded with "Pai, haere mai," which Roux understood to mean "Let us have peace."

The leaders embraced and the Maori offered fish, while Roux responded with gifts from the French side. As Roux was preparing to return to the ships late that afternoon he caught up with du Fresne who'd been fishing at Te Kauri's cove again. When he told his commander of the strange behaviour he'd witnessed du Fresne wrote it off. "He said that everything the natives had done was only the result of tying up one of their chiefs, and this could be the only reason for their taking up arms, and that practically there could be nothing else which could have embittered them against us."

It seems clear from that conversation that no Maori had remonstrated with du Fresne about fishing or taking sacred wood. He would have mentioned it and probably would have modified his ways, given the fact he was so eager to please his Maori friends. The commander told Roux to leave the mast camp on the mainland and instead take charge that evening of the hospital camp on Moturua Island.

Slightly spooked, when Roux got to the island camp he found it virtually defenceless.

"I went to the island at 7 o'clock in the evening. So much confidence had been placed in the islanders that we were on this island without any defence. There were only four soldiers there who mounted guard; with these soldiers there was another officer, the surgeon-major, and myself – that is, in all, only seven persons in good health. The sick men could not be reckoned on, for as soon as they got well they were recalled to the ships."

The camp had six blunderbusses,[75] and Roux decided to haul them out of storage and mount them ready for use on their proper gun stands. Later that night his sentry reported scaring away six Maori who'd been scouting the perimeter of the camp.

In what turned out to be their final meeting the next morning, June

---

75 An early form of shotgun which, because of is funnel-shaped barrel, scattered shot in a wide arc. Described as the "French navy's weapon of mass destruction" in the 1800s.

11, du Fresne revealed Maori had been encircling the mast camp again overnight as well. "I told him that he ought not to place so much confidence in these men as he did, and that I was convinced they had some evil design," wrote Roux. "He would not believe me, and kept on repeating that all we had to do was to treat them with kindness and they would never seek to do us the slightest harm."

The French commander advised he was going fishing at Te Kauri's cove again that day, and that was the last Roux saw of him.

According to the "tapu document" modern historians are relying on in their version of events, after the tapu-breaking incident "Ngati Pou became very sad, and no longer visited..."

Yet in the French journals we read from Roux:

"During the afternoon the chief of the native village on Marion Island came to see me, accompanied by several other natives. They brought me some fish as a present, as is their custom when paying visits.

"They were very much astonished to see outside my tent the blunderbusses, which I had had put in good order the previous evening, and which were now all mounted on their carriages. As they had not seen this kind of arm before, the chief asked what they were, and how they were used.

"I explained the use of the weapons to them as well as I could, and made him better understand by taking eight or ten balls and loading a gun with them. He then understood quite well what I told him, and showed some alarm, making a sign to me that he considered them very dangerous. He went away shortly afterwards, but I noticed he was looking round and examining everything with much attention. He even asked me to let him go into the tent where the invalids were.

"Although I was beginning to be suspicious of all this inquisitiveness he was displaying, and the care with which he seemed to be taking stock of everything, I took him into the hospital tent, watching him very closely. He again examined everything in the tent very carefully, and then left me. All this convinced me that this man had some design.

"In the afternoon I went shooting with a volunteer, and as I wished to visit this chief's village, we went in this direction, proceeding to the village without any ostentation, and as if by accident. We were very well received.

"The chief asked me various questions as to the cleaning of our guns. He had seen me kill some birds, but he did not think a man could be killed in the same way. As there are a number of dogs in this country, he made signs to me to shoot one of them that happened to be passing by. I shot at it, and killed it, which completely bewildered the chief. He went

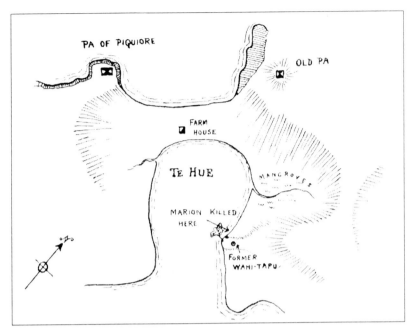

"Sketch of Assassination Cove" – JPS journal

and examined the dead animal with the greatest care, so that he could see where the dog had been hit, and then came back to examine the gun with the same minute attention.

"He then wanted to do what I had done, aiming at another dog, and blew upon the lock of the firearm, thinking that this was the right way to discharge the gun. I did not think it necessary to show him the right way to proceed. On the contrary, I was very glad he did not know in what way we made use of our weapons."

It was only a matter of time.

That night, June 11, more Maori on Moturua Island were discovered advancing on the hospital camp in the dark, but scattered into the night as Roux and his men emerged from their tents with muskets. The next morning, June 12, Captain du Clesmeur raised similar concerns regarding the mainland camp with du Fresne, but the commander again brushed them off and said he was going fishing with, as it turned out, some Maori friends who led him off like a lamb to the slaughter.

"That afternoon two chiefs came on board to seek Marion, and, at two o'clock, he went off in his cutter with them, with two armed officers and thirteen unarmed sailors. He had nets for fishing, and was going to visit

Tacoury's village. He did not return, but that was not altogether unusual, and the ship's company, though feeling a little anxiety, concluded he had gone to the masting camp to spend the night."[76]

The alarm was not raised when du Fresne and his men failed to return from fishing. Instead Lieutenant Roux was the first to become aware that hell had been unleashed when Maori on the island suddenly converged on the hospital camp in the night.

"At 1 o'clock in the morning [the sentry] came to tell me that the Natives were coming down the hill in great numbers. I was much surprised to see about four hundred Natives at a very short distance from our tents, and that they were advancing very rapidly.

"I immediately had the blunderbusses got ready, and arranged them in a square, into which seven of us entered. This was all of us who were not sick. As it was a fine moonlight night, the Natives could see our arms, and immediately they ceased to advance, and lay down in the fern. They were not more than a pistol-shot away from us, and it would have been easy enough, had we discharged our pieces, to have killed a good number; but seeing that they made no further advance, I did not wish to be the first to make attack, especially as M. Marion had particularly ordered me to do them no harm. I decided to let them be the first to begin a fight, but I resolved at the same time to make them pay very dearly if they dared to take this step."

Roux realised he and the French camp had narrowly avoided being massacred in their sleep. Clearly, the tribe had assembled a huge number of warriors, hoping for the advantage of surprise in the deep of the night. What he couldn't figure out was why. The answer came with the dawn.

"I soon had good justification for the mistrust with which the curiosity of the chiefs had inspired me, and for the careful precautions I had taken to safeguard our position. As soon as day broke we saw the hills surrounding us covered with Natives, who were all armed. I noticed they were making menacing signs. Soon I saw a chief whom I knew, and who belonged to the mainland, advancing by himself, and unarmed. I went up to him with only a pair of pistols in my pockets, in case he made up his mind to attack me. When he came up to me I saw he was weeping, whilst he uttered the words: 'Tacoury *mate* Marion', which signifies, 'Tacoury has killed Marion'."

Suddenly a warning was shouted and the Maori retreated. French long-

---

76 *From Tasman To Marsden: A History of Northern New Zealand from 1642 to 1818*, Robert McNab, 1914, Chapter 5, see www.nzetc.org/tm/scholarly/tei-McNTasm-t1-body-d5.html

boats were landing on the beach below the hospital camp. Reinforcements had arrived in the form of thirty men-at-arms, and a bearer of bad news.

A longboat with 12 men had been dispatched from the *Marquis de Castries* before dawn to collect firewood from Te Kauri Cove. The boat had not returned but at 7am observers on the ship spotted what appeared to be a man in the water, and they dispatched another boat to rescue him.

They pulled the hypothermic victim from the sea and found him bleeding from a spear thrust to the side. The survivor explained that the woodcutting crew had been welcomed onto the beach by local iwi, and even carried in on their shoulders. They were then shown which trees to take firewood from and while they were cutting, "a hideous cry" went up and a large crowd of armed Maori fell on them. Men were hacked down with clubs and spears, and this lone survivor explained he'd only escaped because his long handled axe allowed him to kill two of his assailants and escape into the bush, where he made his way back to the sea. In his flight, he recognised Marion du Fresne's empty longboat on the beach, and realised his captain and comrades had shared the same fate.

Historian Michael King dismissed what happened next in one line, "In retaliation, and in the process of repelling further attacks, the surviving crew members levelled a village and killed between 200 and 300 local Maori."

The real context is that the French came under sustained attack for days. As Lieutenant Roux explains, the first priority was to get reinforcements

Pohutukawa tree under which Marion du Fresne was killed. Te Hue (Assassination Cove). Ridge on the left of picture a wahi-tapu in former times)

and news of the attacks to the men at the mast camp on the mainland.

"The officer who was in command on board sent me word that he was arming the longboat with fourteen blunderbusses, four swivel guns, and twenty men to send and give the news of this unhappy event to the flag captain, who was in command at the mast camp, so as to prepare him to take such action as he might deem desirable."

Roux sent his by now 50-strong combat force on the island to digging trenches for their gun batteries and behind which the hospital patients could be sheltered from any attack. For their part, the 400 or so Maori warriors on Moturua Island retreated out of firing range, but they too were receiving reinforcements.

"At noon I saw ten to twelve canoes[77], which came off from the mainland, and which landed on our island, on the side of the villages. There must have been from three to four hundred men on board, who joined the others, so that at 1 o'clock there were about a thousand to twelve hundred natives surrounding us," wrote Roux.

"The natives began to shout insults at us, crying out that they had killed Marion, and would serve us the same way. So that we might understand what they said, they took their tomahawks, and showed us by signs how they had killed our commander.

"The latest arrivals had approached a little closer to us than the others, and amongst them I recognized the author of the massacre, who was at the head of the last comers; it was Tacoury himself."

Sensing that Te Kauri was the orchestrator, Lieutenant Roux ordered his men to target the chief when and if he came close enough. They got their chance half an hour later and seven French musketeers opened fire simultaneously, dropping Te Kauri like a stone. He was carried off by his tribe, and "never appeared afterwards".

By seven pm, word came through from the ships that "a great many more canoes, full of natives, had landed on the island." This was an all-out war involving, on one side, a battalion-strength team of Maori warriors drawn apparently from numerous tribes (about as many warriors as the current New Zealand Army can comfortably muster for any single military tour

---

77 A good description of the Bay of Islands waka is found in the journal of Captain du Clesmeur: "Their pirogues or canoes are of great beauty. I have measured some that were 70 ft. in length by 8 ft. in width, and made out of a single piece of timber. They are sharp at each end, and the keel is hewn out in such a way as to insure a good speed. They travel at a very rapid rate...There are usually about forty men in each canoe. The stern and the prow are ornamented with two pieces of carving; that on the stern is about 12 ft. in height."

at the moment), and on the other 50 armed Frenchmen, most of them sailors. One side, of course, had gunpowder. The other side desperately wanted gunpowder.

While this was unfolding on Moturua Island, back on the mainland by the masting camp, some "five or six hundred" warriors had advanced on the French base, but although raucous and confrontational, no fight of significance had broken out. Armed musketeers kept watch on both the camp and the mast crafting operation in the bay, and an armed escort accompanied sailors moving between both units.

When the heavily armed longboat arrived bearing news of the massacre, the French on the mainland decided to down tools and go to the assistance of the ships and crew on Moturua Island. No sooner had their boats pushed off from the bay than hundreds of Maori stormed the base camp and the mast unit, setting the camps ablaze and carrying off the tools and supplies left behind. There was no going back now. A brief discussion was held on the merits of trying to recover the two longboats beached at the massacre site. Monsieur Croizet, who by seniority had assumed command, decided no, based on the risk and an eyewitness account from one of the longboat crew who'd sailed past the site while bringing the news. He explained the Maori had tried to beckon them in as well.

"Several of these natives were wearing the garments worn by M. Marion the day he was killed, and by the other men of our crews who had suffered the same fate. They had passed quite close enough to the natives to recognize perfectly well the velvet waistcoat worn by M. Marion. A chief was now wearing it, and held in his hands the dead man's gun, which was silver-mounted, and which the savage held up so that it could be seen. Others of the savages imitated his example, exhibiting the uniforms of the two officers whom they had murdered with our commander."[78]

Some on the longboat felt her arsenal of swivel guns and blunderbusses was more than enough firepower to drive the Maori back and allow the longboats to be retrieved, and they were probably right. But it didn't happen.

Instead, everyone converged for the defence of Moturua Island. It was raining heavily that night, and the soldiers had two zones they needed to protect, the main camp and a blacksmith's forge about 300 metres away. A 12-strong detachment of men was sent to entrench themselves at the

---

78 Quoted in the diary of Lieutenant Jean Roux

forge, and as it turned out it was the first to be stormed just on 11pm. The gunfire from the French ran "hot" according to Lieutenant Roux, commander of the operation, and although the Maori were brave they eventually wilted as reinforcements arrived from the main camp to begin blunderbuss barrages. The sight of rocket flares – a signal to the fleet to dispatch reinforcements as well – would have added to the mystique in this first real clash on New Zealand soil between European firepower and sheer Maori muscle.

"Some of them attacked the forge for a time, but the fire was so brisk that they also took to flight. They had come very close to us, and we could see them carrying away some dead and some wounded. They rushed into the forest."

There was no further action that night, but it soon became clear who the extra canoes that arrived the previous evening belonged to. "At daybreak I found their numbers had greatly increased," wrote Roux. "They made menacing signs, showing us M. Marion's clothes and his gun."

It was, of course, the five or six hundred warriors who had burnt the mainland camp to the ground. This brought the total number of Maori warriors on tiny Moturua Island to somewhere approaching 1,500 men – close to the size of two modern infantry battalions.

Peering at the warriors gathering on the opposite hill, close to the nearest pa site, Roux decided valour, rather than discretion, might send a better signal in the face of such large opposition. After getting approval from Croizet, he assembled six volunteers and 20 soldiers, gave them each muskets, two side pistols and 40 rounds of ammunition, and then led them on a charge across the valley up the hill. Given the time it took to reload muskets, the Maori leaders could have made a killing if they'd been familiar with the business end of the weapons and their limitations. But they weren't. Instead, they reacted by abandoning the hilltop fortification and retreating towards the pa.

When Roux and his men finally crested the hill, below on the beach they could see women and children from the village being herded into the giant waka and evacuated, while the men poured into the pa, hundreds of them.

"It is situated on the extremity of a peninsula which projects into the sea, and is unapproachable on three sides by reason of the precipices which surround it," noted Roux in his journal. "For its better defence it has three rows of palisades. There is also a raised platform all round, which is made of long pieces of wood stuck up on their ends with planks on the top, supported by small poles, strengthened by cross-beams. The natives mount this platform by means of ladders, and on this can fight with much in their favour against an enemy armed in the same way as themselves.

"To the left there was a little path or track, where one man could pass along at a time by holding on to the palisades with one hand, so as not to fall into the moat. This track was so contrived as to lead to the gateway, which would be about 2 ft. square, and which was the only means by which the village could be entered.

"This gateway was at the far end of the village; there was no other means of entrance, as the other three sides were washed by the sea. As I was well acquainted with this village, I made up my mind very promptly, and we continued our march. We were not more than a musket-shot away when we saw two chiefs come out. I thought at first that they were going to sue for peace, but, on the contrary, they hurled darts from lashes. These are very dangerous weapons."

The first musket shot from the French in reply busted the thigh of one of the chiefs, who took another bullet in a second volley. His companion retreated back inside the pa.

"Before setting out, I told our men that as soon as they had entered on the pathway they were to march as quickly as they could, and that they should take great care to carry on a running fire, aiming as well as they could, so as not to waste their shots, and that they were to dodge as smartly as possible the darts, spears, and other weapons which might be thrown at them. I told them we should not stop until we had reached the gateway, in front of which was a small space of ground, where two men could stand abreast.

"Upon entering the track, we saw several natives, who ascended the raised platform of which I have spoken, but three or four of them who had got up having been shot the others were deterred from seeking to replace their comrades. The 300 paces which, roughly computed, we had to go to reach the gateway were soon traversed despite the spears that were hurled at us. What impeded us most was the water they had thrown on the track, but the palisade, which we took care to hold on by, saved us from slipping into the moat. We were lucky enough to reach the gateway without a single man being wounded, but we found it closed, and defended by two chiefs."

Here's where the French discovered the Achilles heel of 18th century Maori. It was acknowledged that rangitira ruled from the top down with absolute control, and indeed they had tight control on their subjects. But the flip side of that was a leadership vacuum: if you cut off the head the body becomes unsure of what it should do. The French identified senior chiefs by their headdress, cloaks and leadership skills. And then they picked them off, one by one.

"Having found ourselves in front of the gateway, and there being only the palisades to separate us from the enemy, we commenced a very sharp fire. First the two chiefs were killed, but another chief immediately took their place. I noticed that the palisades were hampering us by stopping our bullets, so I told our men to pass the ends of their muskets through the first row of palisades so as not to waste any shots. We had one great advantage over the natives, for when they stood up to throw their spears, darts, and other weapons they were obliged to expose themselves to our fire, and no sooner had they got ready to hurl their weapons than we fired at them. It was only their great numbers that could give them any advantage over us. When I got close up to the gate I had a full view of the chiefs, who were greatly protected by a sort of shelter. Nevertheless, this did not prevent five of them from being killed. These men fought with much courage, and kept on encouraging their people.

"The fifth chief, who came right up to the gate, displayed even greater daring than the others. He rushed up with a long spear, and gave a fierce enough thrust at the sergeant who stood by my side. The weapon caught him just above the eye, and the blow very nearly knocked him over into the moat. The chief was killed on the spot and he was apparently the last of them, for no others came forward. I noticed that the natives were now offering scarcely any resistance, and that very few spears were being thrown."

As the French busted into the pa, it was being evacuated simultaneously down to waiting waka below.

"I received a spear thrust, which wounded me in the thigh, and at the same moment a soldier was also wounded in the side. At the time my wound gave me no great pain, and we soon set off in pursuit of the fugitives, who we saw jumping into their canoes. Two large canoes had already been launched, full of natives, but those who were embarking did not escape us, for we poured several volleys into their midst. It was at this place that the most blood was shed, for there was nothing to prevent our men taking good aim, the natives at the foot of the rampart being either shot down or drowned. They had defended the entrance to the village for about forty minutes, and with great coolness, for no one could be heard speaking except the chiefs, who gave their orders, and who were always to be seen in the most dangerous places. But immediately the chiefs had been killed the natives displayed as much fear as they had previously exhibited courage so long as the chiefs were at their head, and they now took to flight."

When they later tallied the dead they found no children or youths had been involved in the fighting, the bodies were exclusively adult males, bar one elderly kuia who Roux praised for displaying "the greatest bravery" by handing weapons to the warriors during some withering French musket fire. She'd been shot.

Some 250 Maori warriors had died. Hundreds more escaped by canoe or into the bracken and bush that covered Moturua Island. Although many of the French had been wounded, no more had been added to the 27 killed and eaten in the massacre.

Having seen the damage that guns could do, local iwi chose not to provoke any further set piece battles.[79]

It wasn't until the 7th of July, nearly a month after the massacre, that Roux and his men were finally given permission to search Te Kauri's village on the mainland, close to the scene of the massacre. The pa was deserted, but inside what they knew was the paramount chief Te Kauri's house they found a sailor's cooked head on a stake, with signs it had been chewed on, and elsewhere in the village a human thighbone on a spit, with dried up flesh still attached in some places. The fate of Marion du Fresne and the 26 had finally been confirmed.

The decision was made to leave New Zealand, but not before claiming the country in the name of France – Captain Croziet being unaware Cook had already claimed it for Britain three years prior.

"On the 12th July we sent a bottle to be buried on Marion Island, in which were enclosed the arms of France, and a formal statement of the taking possession of all this country, which we named Austral-France. This bottle is 4 ft. under the earth, at 57 paces from the edge of the sea, reckoning from high-water mark, and at ten paces from the little stream. This bottle was buried with all necessary precautions."

The bottle, presumably, is still there. It has never been found.

Historians would later draw comparisons between Captain Cook's firm but fair approach, and du Fresne's perhaps naïve trust in the concept of the "noble savage".

---

79   An ambush attempt failed when a Maori raiding party of "sixty to eighty" was surprised in the bracken while coming up behind the French two weeks later, when a French sentry spotted one of them and opened fire, causing the remainder to break cover. The French gave chase, killing a further 25 warriors while the remainder escaped.

"In 1769 – little more than two years before – in this same Bay of Islands, Cook only escaped attack by the judicious use of "buckshot," followed by "ball," and ending with cannon from the ship (page 30). Had Cook been imbued with Marion's views he would never have returned on board the *Endeavour*. He resembled the Frenchman in being perfectly straight with the Natives, but he differed from the Frenchman in this, that when perfectly straight dealing did not avail he always gave a reminder – in buckshot, for preference – and this reminder, while it did not prevent him ending his career, like his French rival, in a South Sea oven, placed the two men very far apart as South Sea navigators and explorers."[80]

For the French, it was a time to lick their wounds and limp away from the country that had seemed so promising yet cost so much blood on all sides. With the French military assisting US rebels in the 1776 War of Independence, and then political introspection with France's own pending revolution and bloodshed in 1789, that country's attention was diverted away from New Zealand for some considerable time. For the Maori of the Bay of Islands, it was an incredibly steep learning curve that changed the course of New Zealand history.

Forget Cook's gunboat diplomacy that largely lobbed cannonballs safely over the heads of miscreants. With Marion du Fresne, New Zealand Maori had been confronted with everything the strangers could throw at them, from cannon to buckshot and all the weaponry in between. The Maori had been beaten but not crushed, and their experience at the hands of France is one of the reasons we speak English here today.

80 *From Tasman to Marsden*, Robert McNab, 1914. See www.nzetc.org/tm/scholarly/tei-McNTasm-t1-body-d5.html

CHAPTER FOUR

Wild South

When James Cook first arrived back in England and his journals were published, his reports of New Zealand wildlife captured the attention of sealers and whalers. The demand for blubber, oil, skins and other by-products in Europe was huge, and with the US about to undergo its war of independence traders were looking for new areas to harvest. For industrialists, reports of the New Zealand flax – suitable for linen and rope hemp – were promising, while the description of mighty Kauri and rimu forests suitable for tallship masts excited the interests of shipbuilders.

Coinciding with the events shaking up the Northern Hemisphere, Britain was just opening up Australia as a penal colony, taking delivery of its first fleet of convicts and settler families on January 26, 1788 at Sydney Harbour.

That decision, to turn Australia into a giant prison, had been influenced by the tragedies suffered by Abel Tasman, James Cook[81] and Marion du Fresne in New Zealand. Which of the two countries was most suitable

---

81 Ten crew from a cutter on Cook's consort vessel, the *Adventure*, were killed and eaten at Queen Charlotte Sound in 1773, apparently after shooting some normally friendly Maori during a mealtime dispute. There are conflicting views on who stole what, but the end result is that ten *Adventure* crew armed with only two guns shot two Maori, and before they could reload they'd been clubbed and hacked to death. A search party sent looking for them the following day discovered a Maori "throng...like a Fair" at the centre of which were flax baskets full of roasted human body parts belonging to the missing mariners. Unlike du Fresne's men, the rest of the *Adventure* crew resisted the temptation to slaughter, as they'd known the iwi for some years and figured there must have been a reason. Cook wasn't there at the time and didn't find out about the incident until he returned to the Sound a year later. Although other Maori hapu were urging Cook to take *utu*, as was his right, on the offender, a chief named Kahura, he let iwi off with a warning that a repeat occurrence would incur "the weight of my resentment". See "Cook: The 'Adventure' and misadventure in Queen Charlotte Sound, 1773–1777", John Davies, *Journal of the Nelson and Marlborough Historical Societies*, Volume 2, Issue 1, 1987 http://www.nzetc.org/tm/scholarly/tei-NHSJ05_01-t1-body1-d2-d1.html

for a penal colony? New Zealand Maori were perceived as too advanced and too battle-savvy, and that it would be too difficult for Britain to control both convicts and Maori at the same time if New Zealand was chosen. The aboriginal people of Australia on the other hand were far less organised and easily contained. Decision made.

Now officially on the map, New Zealand became a replenishment post for transports and merchant vessels en-route to and from Australia. A trickle of foreign explorers continued to visit, among them George Vancouver, who'd served with Cook and took the opportunity to return to New Zealand while heading to North America's northwest coast (yes, *that* Vancouver). His two ships, *Discovery* and *Chatham* anchored at Dusky Sound in 1791 before continuing their journey. During a massive storm after leaving New Zealand *Chatham* was blown off course and discovered the islands that now bear its name.

The first base station for the sealing industry in New Zealand had been established by 1792, only 20 years after Marion du Fresne's murder, and four years after the settlement of Australia. But there was no risk of those first sealers running into the militaristic northern Maori; Dusky Sound in southern Fiordland was about as far away from civilisation in this as yet uncivilised country as it was possible to get.[82]

The necessity of supplying and shipping product from that base station brought more familiarity, and more contact, with New Zealand, and some local Maori found themselves taken on as hired deck-hands on various vessels on the South Pacific trade routes. Sometimes, as in the case involving the British warship *Daedalus* in 1793, the Maori weren't so much 'hired' as kidnapped – in this case supposedly to teach convicts on Norfolk Island how to dress flax to make linen and rope. The order had been given by the Governor of New South Wales, so two chiefs were lured on board and didn't realise the vessel had set sail until it was well out to sea. When the kidnapped chiefs ended up in Norfolk and "found they were expected to do women's work, their disgust and their anger were great."[83] The Governor of the Norfolk penal colony eventually took pity and repatriated the pair to New Zealand, but he received a boot up the rear from the Governor of New South Wales for spoiling the convict flax industry plan.

It was a Bay of Islands local named Te Ara, however, whose alleged

---

82 New Zealand's first officially-sanctioned commercial exports – seal skins from Dusky Sound – were sold to the Chinese in exchange for tea, marking the beginning of a long trading relationship between both countries.

83 *A Short History Of New Zealand*, J B Condliffe & W T G Airey, Whitcombe & Tombs, 1953

ill-treatment as a hired deckhand[84] by a merchant master led to an even bigger massacre of Europeans than the French incident.

The ship involved was the *Boyd*, skippered by Captain John Thompson, carrying at least 75 passengers and crew from Sydney to South Africa and England via a cargo stop at Whangaroa Harbour in the far north in early December 1809 to pick up timber spars for sailing ships.

The first report of what happened to the *Boyd* came from Alexander Berry, an officer of the whaling vessel *City of Edinburgh*, who stumbled upon the carnage three weeks later, on December 31st 1809.

"During our stay in this harbour [Bay of Islands by Kororareka] we had frequent reports of a ship being taken by the natives in the neighbouring harbour of Wangarawe [Whangaroa][85], – and that the ship's crew were killed and eaten."

The *City of Edinburgh* dispatched "three armed boats" to the area (close to what is now Kaeo) where they quickly discovered "the miserable remains of the ship *Boyd*...which the natives (after stripping of everything of value) had burnt down to the water's edge."

Under the guidance of a distinguished Bay of Islands chief named Metenanagh, Berry and his three boatloads of musketmen found the local village where Maori were wandering around in European clothes taken from the wreck. Of the 70 or so Europeans who'd been on board there was no sign, except four: passenger Ann Morley and her baby, a 15 year old cabin boy with a deformed foot, named Thomas Davis, and a little two year old girl named Betsey Broughton. Betsey's mother Anne had perished in the massacre and been eaten, but the little girl's father, New South Wales government official, Commissary William Broughton, had not joined his wife on this voyage and remained back in Sydney.[86]

After bargaining for the release of the remaining captives by trading axes, Metenanagh and Berry sat down with their source, a young chief

---

84 Historian Paul Moon writes, "An experienced sailor, he had signed on as a crewman but when at sea, he refused to work, giving sickness and his chiefly status as reasons. After refusing orders three times, he was flogged." See *The Treaty & Its Times*, Paul Moon & Peter Biggs, Resource Books, 2004, p31

85 The Ngapuhi dialect didn't have the 'F' sound in 'Wh' that's become the current fashion, and the early attempts by Europeans to phonetically spell the Maori place names in the far north reflect the silent H as it then was. The earliest Maori dictionaries and pronunciation guides disclose no 'F' sound in Maori, and given they were spelling the language phonetically [Fonetiklee] you can bet they would have used an 'F' if such a sound existed. Memo to Radio New Zealand, it wasn't 'Fukkatane' but W-hock-a-tane, as in the gentle 'Wh' in 'Whoosh'. Having said all that, language is a living thing and Maori now has an 'F'. As they say in Old English, cnāwan is bēn scēawian, or, as you would recognise to today, "to know is to be shown".

86 See http://adb.anu.edu.au/biography/broughton-william-1831

who Berry called "Tarra", who explained what had happened.

It was all, said Tarra,[87] a plan hatched "by that old rascal Tippahee [Te Pahi]" – a well known chief in the district. Te Pahi, he said, had turned up with a lot of canoes wanting to trade with the Boyd while anchored in Whangaroa Harbour. They boarded the boat under the pretence of doing so and mingled with passengers on the decks. The *Boyd's* captain and some of his men, meanwhile, had been scheduled to go and examine timber onshore that might be suitable for spars. After they left on this mission, "Te Pahi, waiting a convenient time, now gave the signal for massacre. In an instant the savages, who appear'd sitting peaceably on the deck, rushed on the unarmed crew, who were dispersed about the ship at their various employments. The greater part were massacred in a moment, and were no sooner knocked down than cut to pieces while still alive.

"Five or six of the hands escaped up the rigging. Tippahee now having possession of the ship, hailed them with a speaking trumpet, and ordered them to unbend the sails and cut away the rigging, and they should not be hurt. They complied with his commands and came down. He then took them ashore in a canoe and immediately killed them. The master went on shore without arms, and was of course easily dispatched. The names of the survivors are Mrs. Morley and child, Betsey Broughton, and Thomas Davis, a boy."

There are a few things that are a dead giveaway in this account, and one of them is the claim that the half-dozen sailors who escaped up the rigging would come down and give themselves up to the supposed ring-leader of the massacre, Te Pahi, on a promise that out of the whole 70 passengers, they alone would be let go unharmed.

Really? Would you be that gullible?

"The natives of the Spar district in this harbour have behaved well, even beyond expectation, and seem much concerned on account of this unfortunate event; and, dreading the displeasure of King George, have requested certificates of their good conduct in order to exempt them from his vengeance; but let no man (after this) trust a New Zealander," wrote Berry and Captain Pattison before adding:

"We further certify that we gave Tarra, the bearer of this, a small flat-bottomed boat as a reward for his good conduct and the assistance of getting us a cargo of spars."

---

87 As retold to Berry, see *The Historical Records of New Zealand*, Vol. 1, Robert McNab, letter from Captain Simeon Pattison and Alexander Berry, January 6 1810 http://www.nzetc.org/tm/scholarly/tei-McN01Hist-t1-b7-d4-d1.html

This first official account of the massacre of the *Boyd* essentially was built on the word of one "Tarra". Could Tarra in fact be this person referred to by Paul Moon?:

"On board were 70 people including some Maori and Te Ara (known as George) the son of a Maori chief at Whangaroa."[88] It was this Te Ara who was allegedly flogged and who, after displaying his wounds to his iwi, exacted revenge. The 'Tarra' who told Alexander Berry that it was all the plot of the "old rascal Tippahee" made no mention of why Te Pahi would have done it and, more significantly, how – as Te Pahi's tribe lived 60 kilometres away. The survivors were found in a different tribe's village, not Te Pahi's. It appears "Tarra" had successfully covered his backside and shifted blame for the entire cannibal feast onto a visiting chief. In the process, he'd been rewarded with a boat.

Archbishop Henry Williams, in his memoir, wrote that news of the *Boyd* tragedy made missionaries delay their arrival in New Zealand for five years.

"Intelligence had been received of the massacre of the crew and passengers of the "Boyd," in Whangaroa harbour, in revenge, as was generally understood, for the flogging of a chief (Te Puhi, of Ngatiuru, commonly called George,)[89] on board during the voyage. Also of certain reprisals, as they were called, by the crew of a Sydney whaler – misled, it is alleged, by false information."[90]

That false information, of course, was the claim of Te Pahi's guilt. A whaling ship from Sydney led an attack on Te Pahi's home village at Rangihoua, east of KeriKeri, killing sixty Maori and wounding Te Pahi who – fleeing for his life – ended up in the hands of Whangaroa Maori again who allegedly killed him.[91]

So what did Te Pahi actually do? A second version of the *Boyd* massacre was published in the *Sydney Gazette* in September 1810.[92] Whilst the first version had been based on the claims of one "Tarra" who may in fact have been the aggrieved chief who caused the massacre, this second version

---

88 *The Treaty and Its Times*, Paul Moon & Peter Biggs, 2004, p30
89 This appears to be a misidentification. McNab sources from an 1807 ship's document the following: "when Captain Wilkinson sailed away, there accompanied him as a sailor a young Native chief called Tara, to whom the name of George was afterwards given by the sailors." *From Tasman to Marsden*, page 115
90 *The Life of Henry Williams*, Vol. 1, by H Carleton, 1874 , page 25, see http://www.enzb. auckland.ac.nz/document?wid=1040&page=0&action=null
91 See *From Tasman to Marsden*, Robert McNab, 1914, p 143 http://www.nzetc.org/tm/scholarly/tei-McNTasm-t1-body-d11.html
92 *Sydney Gazette*, 1 September 1810

was anchored in the testimony of a Tahitian islander who had been at Whangaroa at the time of the incident but was not affiliated to any of the NZ Maori tribes. These are his words, as told to a Captain Chace:[93]

"When the *Boyd* went from hence [Sydney] she had on board four or five New Zealanders, who made part of her crew. These people were displeased at their treatment on the passage, and determined on revenge.[94] On their arrival they communicated their complaints to their friends and relatives, who were of the Whangaroan party, and frequently at war with Tippahee [Te Pahi] and his subjects; and the design of taking the ship was formed in consequence."

Realising they had to get the captain and a number of his men off the ship and away from their weapons stores, the Whangaroa iwi told Captain Thompson they had found suitable spars upriver, but he and his men would have to come and see them.

"The Captain was thereby prevailed on to leave the vessel, accompanied by his chief officer, with three boats manned, to get the spars on board.

"The boats were conducted to a river, on entering which they were out of sight of the ship; and, after proceeding some distance up, Captain Thompson was invited to land, and mark the spars he wanted."

According to the Tahitian source, the iwi waited until the longboats had been left high and dry by the ebb tide, before suddenly turning on the *Boyd's* captain and crew with "clubs and axes, which the assailants had till then concealed under their dresses; and although the boat's crew had several muskets, yet so impetuous was the attack that every man was prostrated before one could be used. Capt. Thompson and his unfortunate men were all murdered on the spot, and their bodies were afterwards devoured by the murderers, who, clothing themselves with their apparel, launched the boats at dusk the same evening and proceeded towards the ship, which they determined also to attack."

Captain Thompson did manage to fire off his own weapon – a hunter's "fowling gun" – once, before he was killed, the shot hitting and killing a Maori child watching the massacre from the perimeter.

---

93 *From Tasman to Marsden*, p144, http://www.nzetc.org/tm/scholarly/tei-McNTasm-t1-body-d11.html
94 An alternative version of motive is recorded in an 1833 Church Missionary Society document written by the Bishop of Waiapu. "I learned to-day [at Pupuke, Ururoa's place,] that the "Boyd" was cut off, not, as has been stated, on account of ill-treatment from the Captain to the chief George; but because that chief, on his return from Port Jackson, found his parents dead through sickness, which was attributed to the influence of Europeans."– "Church Missionary Record," November, 1833. See http://www.enzb.auckland.ac.nz/document?wid=1040&page=0&action=null#note11

Under cover of darkness, the Maori managed to fool the *Boyd's* watch into assuming it was their crewmates returning in the longboats, "and the officer was knocked down and killed by those who first ascended the ship's side. All the seamen of the watch were in like manner

The Explosion of The Boyd, by Louis John Steel

surprised and murdered. Some of the assassins then went down to the cabin door, and asked the passengers and others to go on deck to see the spars, and a female passenger obeying the summons was killed on the cabin ladder. The noise occasioned by her fall alarmed the people that were in bed, who, running on deck in disorder, were all killed as they went up except four or five, who ran up the shrouds, and remained in the rigging the rest of the night.

"The next morning Tippahee [Te Pahi] appeared alongside in a canoe, and was much offended at what had happened, but was not permitted to interfere or to remain near the ship. The unfortunate men in the rigging called him, and implored his protection, of which he assured them if they could make their way to his canoe."

The men leapt from the rigging into the water, scrambling for the protection of Te Pahi's canoe. He landed them onshore but couldn't prevent them being captured by the pursuing Whangaroa iwi.

"The pursuit was continued on shore. They were all overtaken, and Tippahee [Te Pahi] was forcibly held while the murder of the unhappy fugitives was perpetrated. A female passenger and two children, who were afterwards found in the cabin, were spared from the massacre, and taken on shore to a hut, in which situation Mr. Berry and Captain Pattison, of the *City of Edinburgh*, found when they rescued them.[95] Tippahee [Te Pahi] was afterwards permitted by the Whangarooans to take three boat loads of any property he chose out of the ship, fire-arms and gun-powder excepted; and the bulk they divided among themselves.

95   Apparently the only reason the life of 15 year old cabin boy Thomas Davis (sometimes referred to as Davison) was spared was because of a deformity: "The boy Davison...owed the preservation of his life to his being club-footed, the natives taking him for a son of the Devil!" remarked Alexander Berry. See *Historical Records of NZ, Vol. 1*, http://www.nzetc.org/tm/scholarly/tei-McN01Hist-t1-b7-d35.html

"The salt provisions, flour, and spirits they threw overboard as unpalatable; the carriage guns they did the same with, considering them useless; the muskets they prized very much; and one of the savages, in his eagerness to try one, stove in the head of a barrel of powder, and filling the pan of the piece snapped it directly over the cask, the explosion of which killed five native women and eight or nine men, and set part of the ship on fire."

And that's how Berry and his men had found the ship, gutted to the waterline and, on the shore nearby, he wrote, "we had seen the mangled fragments and fresh bones of our countrymen, with the marks even of the teeth remaining on them."[96]

The village chiefs are said to have explained their actions quite nonchalantly, even proudly, to Berry.

"They showed no hesitation about referring to the massacre, nor secrecy about its details, regarding it as a British tar would regard 'some successful attempt against an enemy's ship of superior force.' The reason given for the attack was that one of their chiefs [ordinary tribe member] had secreted a carpenter's axe, and had been detected before leaving the ship, with the result that he was tied up to the capstan, where he was kept for several hours and threatened with flogging. This indignity to their chief could not be forgiven, hence the massacre. They admitted there were several who had not been killed.[97]

"Berry now commenced negotiations for the release of these survivors. He put down a number of axes, and mustered his men; to the Natives he offered the axes, if the survivors were handed over peaceably; but told them, that if that proposal was not accepted, war would be declared against them by the forces they saw in front of them. After a moment's hesitation the reply came that 'trading was better than fighting' and the captives would be given up for the axes. It was the old story of Cook's superiority over Marion, when dealing with the Natives always to keep buckshot in reserve."

Despite invitations from their now seemingly over-eager hosts to have Berry and his men dine with them and sleep in the confines of the village that night, Berry thought better of it, glancing at the remains of the cannibal feast. "It certainly could not be agreeable to pass the night by the side of their devourers."[98]

---

96 *From Tasman to Marsden*, Robert McNab, p130, http://www.nzetc.org/tm/scholarly/tei-McNTasm-t1-body-d10.html
97 Ibid, page 129
98 With good reason, potentially. Berry later discovered the chiefs had lied to him about the whereabouts of the captives initially, and that they had secreted tribesmen armed with muskets

The next day, after trading axes for the release of the four captives, they heard the survival stories, and mercy shown by some of the tribe.

"The boy Davis escaped into the hold, where he lay concealed until the Natives were fairly glutted with human flesh. Ann Morley was discovered by an old savage who was so moved by her tears and embraces that he took her to Te Pahi and obtained permission to spare her life. At that time the deck was covered with human bodies which were being cut up. A few minutes after Te Pahi sent the sailors ashore, the woman went ashore with her deliverer, and the first thing she saw was the dead bodies of the sailors lying on the beach. When she landed several made to come towards her to kill her also, but her life was saved by the interposition of some women who rushed in between them and covered her with their clothes. The second mate begged his life, and was kept alive for about a fortnight, when he also was killed and eaten."[99]

Berry had to wait a little longer to recover two year old Betsey Broughton, who'd been taken by a chief further up the harbour.

"After an hour's delay, little Betsy Broughton was brought down to the boat, clad in a linen shirt which had belonged to Captain Thompson, and in a very emaciated condition. As the poor little girl saw the white people round about her she feebly cried out for her "mamma," who had, alas, perished at the hands of the human brutes of Whangaroa."[100]

There was an irony of history taking place here as well, recorded in dispatches at the time:

"The Natives of the Bay of Islands told Mr. Berry that the Whangaroan Natives were the remnant of the tribe which had killed Marion and his men in 1772, and that they had fled from the Bay after the terrible punishment the French had inflicted upon them for the death of their leader."[101]

The *Boyd's* passengers weren't the only Europeans to find their goose was

in the mangroves to shoot at the Europeans as they rowed back to a small island in the harbour. The attempted ambush was thwarted, however, by Berry's forethought in insisting that two of the chiefs share the boat ride with them in good faith. When the Maori musketeers realised their chiefs were also coming under fire the attack ceased.
99 See *From Tasman to Marsden*, Robert McNab, p133, http://www.nzetc.org/tm/scholarly/tei-McNTasm-t1-body-d10.html
100 Ibid, see p131. The survivors were taken on board the *City of Edinburgh* which, after leaving New Zealand, became disabled in a southern ocean storm and eventually drifted onto the coast of South America. The mother, Ann Morley, died during the voyage, leaving the crew to look after two infant girls as best they could. While the ship underwent repairs at Lima, Betsey was cared for by a Spanish couple and ended up speaking "Spanish like a native". Such was the roundabout nature of ship voyaging that Betsey was free before she was eventually reunited with her father in Sydney, having travelled halfway across the world and back.
101 See Ibid, page 136. The tribe at Whangaroa Heads was Ngati Pou – one of the hapu that had the run-in with the French, but the tribe that actually burnt the *Boyd* was Ngati Uru.

cooked on a New Zealand visit, however, and some of them appeared to have well and truly asked for it. In 1806, the sailing ship *Venus* had been commandeered by Australian convicts and a mutinous ship's mate, and the pirates decided to make a break for New Zealand. The men anchored in Northland, kidnapping and raping a group of Ngapuhi women to satisfy their desires, killing a number of Maori in the process. The surviving Maori Ngapuhi women were traded as slaves or – worse – food to rival tribes along the way, causing Ngapuhi to seek utu against those tribes. The ten or so men on the *Venus* eventually met their comeuppance, and history records they had escaped the long arm of British law only to end up "in the mouths of New Zealand justice" – captured and eaten somewhere south of East Cape.[102]

In 1808, the 11-strong crew of the *Parramatta* learned the hard way that dealings with Maori needed to be honourable.

"She had, in distress, put into the Bay for provisions and water. The Natives supplied them with pork, fish, and potatoes, as much as the *Parramatta* could stow away. After the schooner had received her refreshments, the Natives naturally wanted their pay, but, on making application, were thrown overboard and fired at by the crew, who immediately thereafter weighed anchor and sailed away. Besent[103] saw three who had been wounded with small shot in the fight. A heavy gale of wind came up immediately and blew the vessel on shore not far from Cape Brett, where her remains lay for several years. The New Zealanders naturally took advantage of the wreck to have their revenge, the shipwrecked sailors were cut off to a man, and the fate of Marion and his companions was theirs."[104]

By 1809, then, anywhere between 90 to 120 Europeans had been killed and eaten since Abel Tasman's visit in 1642, while several hundred Maori had been killed in clashes with Europeans over the same time. The New Zealanders had shown they could give as good as they got, and that was to have a major bearing in the lead-up to the Treaty.

102 Ibid, page 110
103 Witness John Besent, who talked to local iwi in 1812 and was the first to discover *Parramatta's* fate
104 *From Tasman to Marsden*, Robert McNab, 1914, p115, see http://www.nzetc.org/tm/scholarly/tei-McNTasm-t1-body-d9.html

CHAPTER FIVE

Ghost Chips

By the early 1800s, thanks to trade with whalers and sealers, and the capture of European ships and shipwrecks as already detailed, Northland Maori in particular were beginning to amass quite a collection of captured weaponry, from the tempered steel of cutlasses and swords to the power of the mighty musket. The cardinal rule – never bang a casket of gunpowder – had been tested and learnt by the Ngati Uru of Whangaroa – and Maoridom's inevitable catch-up with European technology and power was well underway.

There was, however, an even more potent force sailing over the horizon: missionaries.

As Britain began to show signs of serious empire building in the late 1700s, a group of Christian MPs, like the man who succeeded in later abolishing slavery, William Wilberforce, joined forces with evangelical Anglican clergy like the Reverend Josiah Pratt in London, with the aim of spreading the Gospel where Britain went around the globe. From its establishment at Aldersgate in April 1799, the group raised funds and resources to send missionaries to new frontiers in Oceania, Asia, Africa and South America.

The opportunity to visit New Zealand arose when a Rangihoua chief named Ruatara (written as 'Duaterra' in the early correspondence) ended up as deckhand on a whaling ship, whose travels took him as far as England. On the return journey back to Sydney, Ruatara met and was befriended by a middle-aged preacher named Samuel Marsden. Initially, Ruatara was emaciated and near suicidal, and Marsden wanted to know why. It turned out Ruatara hadn't been paid for his last voyage, had not been allowed to spend one night ashore in London despite being in

Marsden's Parramatta residence

the River Thames for two weeks, and hadn't been allowed to fulfil his greatest wish, meeting King George III.

"He stated that the hardships and wrongs which he had endured on board the *Santa Anna* were exceedingly great," wrote Samuel Marsden, "and that the English sailors had beat him very much, which caused him to spit blood, and finally that the master had defrauded him of all his wages, and prevented him from seeing the King. I should have been most happy, if there had been time, to call the master to account for his conduct, but it was too late. I endeavoured to soothe his afflicted mind by assuring him that he would now be protected from insults, and that his wants should be supplied. By the kindness of the surgeon and master, and by administering proper nourishment to him, he began, in a great measure, to recover his strength and spirits, and got quite well before we reached Rio-de-Janeiro. He was ever after truly grateful for the attention that was shewn him. As soon as he was able he did his duty as a common sailor on board the *Ann* till she arrived at Port Jackson, in which capacity he was considered equal to most of the men on board."[105]

Ruatara stayed with Marsden at his New South Wales property (pictured), learning horticulture, animal husbandry and other skills to take back to his people, as well as the basics of Christianity from his host.

In late 1810, the opportunity arose for Ruatara and three other Maori in Sydney to return home. The Reverend Samuel Marsden personally arranged for their passage to New Zealand on the whaler *Frederick*.

"I applied to the master of the *Frederick* for their passage, who agreed to take them on condition that they should assist him to procure his cargo of oil, while the vessel remained on the New Zealand coast, and when he finally left it he would land them at the Bay of Islands. They were four very fine young men who had been a good deal at sea, and were therefore a valuable acquisition to the master; and, on his promising to be kind to them, I agreed that he should take them on his own terms. They all left

105 *Memoir of Duaterra*, Samuel Marsden, Historical Records of NZ, Vol. 1, page 340, see http://www.nzetc.org/tm/scholarly/tei-McN01Hist-t1-b7-d39.html

Port Jackson in the *Frederick* in November, with the gratifying hope of soon seeing their country and friends.[106]

"When the ship reached the North Cape of New Zealand, Duaterra went on shore for two days to procure supplies of pork and potatoes, as he was well known, and had many friends among the natives. As soon as the ship had procured her necessary supplies, she proceeded on her cruise, and, in little more than six months' time, procured a cargo, and was ready to depart from the coast."

But chief Ruatara was about to become the victim of yet more dishonourable behaviour from a Pakeha skipper. The *Frederick* was moored in the Bay of Islands, less than three kilometres from Ruatara's whanau.

"Duaterra, finding that the master intended to sail for England, naturally requested that he and his companions might be put on shore, on the specific terms of their engagement with the master, made by me on their behalf," reports Marsden.

"The ship lay (at the time) in the mouth of the Bay of Islands, where the residences of all their relatives then stood, and Duaterra had got everything ready to put into the boat, expecting they would be immediately put on shore. The master, however, on his being urged to land them, said he would do so by-and-by, when they had caught another whale, and the vessel then bore away from the harbour.

"Duaterra felt great distress on this occasion, as he had been away from home about three years, and was most anxious to see his wife and friends. He earnestly solicited the captain to land him on any part of the coast – he cared not on what place – as all he wished was to get put on shore, and he would find his way home. The master was deaf to all his entreaties, and told them he would proceed to Norfolk Island, and from thence direct to Britain, and that he would be landed as they passed New Zealand on their way to England.

"When the *Frederick* arrived off Norfolk Island, Duaterra and his three companions were sent on shore for water, and were all nearly drowned in the surf,

Rev Samuel Marsden

106   Ibid, p341

Hongi Hika

having been washed under some hollow rocks (with which that shore abounds) which placed him in such danger of his life, as he emphatically observed to me afterwards, that 'on reaching the surface of the water, his head was full of sea.' It is generally very dangerous for a boat to land at Norfolk Island on account of the great surf among the breakers.

"When the *Frederick* was sufficiently supplied with water and wood, so that the master had no further occasion for the services of Duaterra and his countrymen, he had the cruelty to inform them that he would not again touch at New Zealand, but proceed direct on for England. This occasioned great distress to Duaterra, who reminded the captain of his violated promises – the cruel usage to which he had been subjected by not being put on shore while the ship lay at the Bay of Islands (within two miles of his home), and being subsequently-prevented from leaving the vessel when off the North Cape; that it was a great addition to his misery to be left with his companions in a destitute situation on Norfolk Island, after all the assistance they had rendered him (the master) in procuring his cargo. Nothing, however, which Duaterra could urge had any effect on the callous mind of the captain, who proceeded on board his ship, and left the New Zealanders to provide for themselves as they best could."

In another twist of ironic divine justice, the *Frederick* was captured soon after leaving Norfolk by an American privateer, and *Frederick's* captain and first mate were killed in the battle. For his part, Ruatara was found naked and friendless on the Norfolk Island shoreline by the skipper of the *Ann*, the vessel he and Marsden had sailed together on from London two years' previous. The *Ann* took Ruatara on board, fed him, clothed him and gave him passage to Sydney.

Not only had Ruatara been robbed of his homecoming, having travelled right around the world to within two miles of a friendly village before being abducted again, but he and his Maori companions had also been robbed of their share of the whale oil, roughly £100 each (NZ$30,000 in today's money). The agricultural tools and seeds Samuel Marsden had given him to take back to his village all remained on the *Frederick*. So when Ruatara got back to Sydney, he was overjoyed to see the friendly face of the Christian missionary once again.

Another ship followed, and another promise of passage to New Zealand if he worked the decks. This time, however, the captain kept his promise and it was a highly relieved Ruatara who arrived home with sacks of wheat seed to share around and plant.

The poor guy who had endured so much, however, was set to endure even more, this time at the hands of his wider whanau who accused him of giving them New Zealand's first recorded example of "ghost chips":

"The people to whom Duaterra had given seed wheat put it properly into the ground, and it grew well, but before it was ripe many of them became impatient for the produce, and as they expected to find the grain at the root of the stems, like their potato crops, and finding, on examination, that there was no wheat under the surface, they all, with the exception of Shunghee[107] [Hongi Hika], pulled it up and burnt it.[108]

"The chiefs ridiculed Duaterra about his wheat speculation very much, telling him that because he had been a great traveller he thought he could easily impose on their credulity by telling them fine stories, nor could anything in his power to urge serve to convince them that wheat would make bread.

"Shunghee's crop and his own came in due time to perfection, and were reaped and threshed, which convinced the natives that the grain was produced from the top, and not from the bottom, of the stem, as they had supposed, yet they could not be persuaded that bread could be made from it."

After all that effort to grow grain, Marsden had forgotten to include for Ruatara a small grinder so that grain could be milled for flour. If the proof of the pudding was ultimately in the eating, in this case there was to be no eating. Not, at least, for several months.

Efforts to send milling equipment initially foundered because Marsden was forced to rely on unscheduled and unreliable commercial shipping,

107 As a sign of how living languages change, when the first Europeans arrived in New Zealand northern Maori pronounced 'H' as 'Sh'. Hongi Hika would not have immediately recognised his name if you called it out the way you just read it, but he would have responded to "Shongi Shika". Likewise, if newsreaders want to be really PC and pedantic, the Hauraki Gulf is actually the "Shauraki Gulf". See the *Cambridge History of the British Empire* by Rose & Dodwell, 1929, page 10
108 *Memoir of Duaterra*, Samuel Marsden, Historical Records of NZ, Vol. 1, page 343, see http://www.nzetc.org/tm/scholarly/tei-McN01Hist-t1-b7-d39.html

so the solution was to purchase his own ship, a brigantine[109] named the *Active*. This gave the Sydney branch of the Church Missionary Society a guaranteed line of transport and communication to and from New Zealand, and it meant Rua "ghost chips" Tara could finally prove he'd learnt something from his travels.

"Duaterra was greatly rejoiced by the receipt of the mill. He quickly set to work and ground some wheat in the presence of his countrymen, who danced and shouted for joy at seeing the flour. He told me that he made a cake, baked it in a frying-pan, and gave it to the people to eat, which fully satisfied them of the truth of what he had repeatedly told them – namely, that "wheat would make bread." The chiefs then begged some more wheat, which they received and sowed, and there can be little doubt but they will soon learn to appreciate the value of wheat," wrote Samuel Marsden.[110]

Marsden wasted no time putting his new brig to use. The Church Missionary Society had sent young evangelicals Thomas Kendall and Thomas Hall and their families out to New South Wales to assist Marsden, who took the opportunity to dispatch them on the journey that took the mill to Ruatara.

They returned with Ruatara several months later, bringing with them the young chief's uncle, the famed Ngapuhi leader Hongi Hika on his first visit to the bright lights of Sydney – by that stage a city of some 30,000 people. Marsden was anxious to know, both from his juniors and from the chiefs, whether New Zealand was a safe place to visit in light of the local taste for European takeaways highlighted by the *Boyd* massacre.

Hongi assured him he and his tribe would protect the missionaries if they established churches in New Zealand, and on Monday November 28, 1814, the *Active* finally left Australian waters destined for the Bay of Islands and a new era in New Zealand history.

"The number of persons on board (including women and children)

---

109 A small two masted sailing ship similar in style to the ill-fated *Mary Celeste*
110 *Memoir*, p345

were thirty-five. Mr. Hanson, master, his wife and son, Messrs. Kendall, Hall, and King, with their wives and five children, eight New Zealanders, two Otaheitans [Tahitians], and four Europeans belonging to the vessel, besides Mr. Nicholas, myself, two sawyers, one smith, and one runaway convict (as we found him to be afterwards). We had also on board one entire horse, two mares, one bull, and two cows, with a few sheep and poultry of different kinds – intended for the island. The bull and cows had been presented by Governor Macquarie, from His Majesty's herd."

It's not unusual to bump into a neighbour while out shopping, but to have done the equivalent in an uncharted country in 1814 was quite the feat. Nonetheless, as the *Active* rounded North Cape on December 15 the ship received a visit:

"A large war-canoe came off to the vessel. She was very full of stout, fine looking men, and sailed very fast, though the sea was rather rough, and we were at some distance from the land. It was pleasing to behold with what ease she topt the rising waves. One of the principal chiefs was in the war-canoe with a number of his attendants, and a young Otaheitan known to Europeans by the name of Jem, whom I had known some years before, as he had resided a considerable time with Mr. McArthur at Parramatta. This Otaheitan had married the chief's daughter, and his wife was in the canoe. He was much surprised to see me, and I was no less so to meet him there, so very unexpectedly. He had been in the habit of calling at my house when at Parramatta, and was well acquainted with my situation in New South Wales, and he could speak English exceedingly well."[111]

Likewise, in the less than 50 years since Cook's visit the level of Maori contact with Australia was such that when another waka pulled up Marsden records:

"I told them my name, with which they seemed well acquainted, and immediately enquired after a young man belonging to that place who had lived with me [in Sydney] some time previously; [it turns out] his brother was in the canoe, and greatly rejoiced he was to see me!"

As the *Active* sailed south, Marsden decided to call in at Whangaroa, scene of the *Boyd* tragedy. Ruatara had explained that the Whangaroa tribes and the Bay of Islands tribes had been at war ever since it happened, each blaming the other for the ill-fortune the massacre had brought the Maori people. Marsden wanted to put an end to the war over the *Boyd*, and found himself on a marae in Whangaroa.

111 *Memoir of Duaterra*, Samuel Marsden, Historical Records of NZ, Vol. 1, page 350, see http://www.nzetc.org/tm/scholarly/tei-McN01Hist-t1-b7-d39.html

"We accordingly mended our pace, and soon came in sight of the Whangarooa people, who had stopped to receive us. A line was formed on each side for us to pass through them. An old woman, whom I took to be a priestess, made a very great noise, and waved a flag in her hand as we advanced. The chiefs were all seated on the ground, according to their custom, and their warriors standing up, with their spears fixed in the ground uprightly. These instruments were from 15 ft. to 20 ft. in length. They were also armed with patooes."[112]

"Duaterra, with a pistol in his hand, stood at some distance from the chiefs, and, on my coming up to them, he fired off the pistol, and directed those who had muskets to do the same. This being done, the Whangarooa party returned the compliment by discharging their firearms, which I considered a favourable omen to the success of my mission. One of the principal chiefs (who had cut off the *Boyd*) had been at Parramatta and knew me; he had also acquired tolerable English from being on board of whalers. He was known to Europeans by the name of George [Te Ara]."[113]

And that's how Marsden heard, direct from the horse's mouth, why the *Boyd* passengers had been butchered:[114]

"George (their head chief) had fallen sick while on board, and was unable to do his duty as a common sailor, in consequence of which he was severely punished – was refused provisions, threatened to be thrown overboard, and many other indignities were offered to him, even by the common sailors. He remonstrated with the master, begged that no corporal punishment might be inflicted on him, observing that he was a chief in his own country, which they would ascertain on arrival at New Zealand. He was told he was no chief, with many abusive terms which he mentioned, and which are but too commonly used by British seamen.

"When he arrived at Whangarooa his back was in a very lacerated state, and his friends and people were determined to revenge the insult which had been offered to him. He said if he had not been treated with such cruelty the *Boyd* would never have been touched.

"From the accounts which these people and their chiefs gave of the destruction of the *Boyd*, Tippahee [Te Pahi] had had no hand in this melancholy affair – it was wholly their own act and deed. This appeared to be strictly true, for I saw no reason to disbelieve their declaration that

---

112   Patu's, the wooden or stone clubs.
113   *Memoir*, p356
114   This version, for the record, contradicts the version the same tribe had given Alexander Berry five years earlier, which centred on a chief stealing an axe and being threatened with a flogging.

Tippahee and his people suffered innocently, and that their death was the cause of much bloodshed, for many men since that rash act was committed have been cut off belonging to the Bay of Islands, as well as to the Whangarooa Tribe, with whom the affair originated. I never passed Tippahee's island without a sigh – it is now desolate, without an inhabitant, and has been so since his death. The ruins of his little cottage, built by the kindness of the late Governor King, still remains, and I hope that those Europeans who were engaged in that fatal transaction were ignorant at the time that they were punishing the innocent."

Samuel Marsden's first night on New Zealand soil was spent with the tribe who, only five years earlier almost to the day, had murdered a shipload of men, women and children in revenge for the unjustified flogging of one man. Over the course of that five years, more than a hundred more people had died as a direct result of that incident. Marsden knew he needed, and he desperately wanted, his first night in this new country to herald a new beginning, to bring peace to the warring tribes once and for all. So, when George and his warriors invited the priest to stay the night, Marsden realised what he had to do.

"I then addressed them on the subject of peace; pointed out to him how much more it would be for their interest and happiness to turn their attention to agriculture, and the improvement of their country, than continue to fight and murder one another, and particularly now, as the Europeans were about to settle amongst them, through whom they would obtain wheat to sow their land and tools to cultivate it. I assured them that every assistance would be given by the Europeans to promote the improvement of their present situation; and that if they would only attend to the cultivation of their land, and lay aside all sorts of war and murder, they would soon become a great and happy people. George replied that he did not want to fight any more, and was ready to make peace.

"As the evening advanced the people began to retire to rest in different groups. About 11 p.m. Mr. Nicholas and I wrapped ourselves up in our great coats, and prepared for rest also. George directed me to lie by his side; his wife and child lay on one hand, myself on the other, and Mr. Nicholas close by the family. The night was clear, the stars shone brightly, and the sea in our front was smooth. Around us were numerous spears stuck upright in the ground, and groups of natives lying in all directions like a flock of sheep upon the grass, as there were neither tents nor huts to cover them.

"I viewed our situation with new sensations and feelings that I cannot express – surrounded by cannibals who had massacred and devoured our

Landing of Marsden, at Rangihoua

countrymen, I wondered much at the mysteries of Providence, and how these things could be. Never did I behold the blessed advantages of civilisation in a more grateful light than at that moment."

Marsden's courage helped him achieve his aim. The enmity between Te Pahi's hapu and the Whangaroa hapu ended that day.

From the cannibal village at Kaeo, the next stop for Marsden and his crew of missionary migrants was Ruatara's home pa at Rangihoua,[115] a tiny bay on the Purerua Peninsula just east of Kerikeri. Today, nothing remains of that pa except its earthworks and shell middens, but in 1814 it was already nearly 500 years old.

It was December 22 when Marsden first disembarked there, at the site of what was to be New Zealand's first church.[116]

"The *Active* was soon surrounded by canoes from all quarters. On going ashore Duaterra and Shunghee found all their friends and relatives well, who wept for joy at their return, and the women cut themselves, in a similar manner to those of the Cavalles, with shells and flints till the blood flowed down. It was in vain to attempt to persuade them not to do this, because they considered it the strongest proof of their affection."

As the horses and cattle came ashore, for many of the Maori inhabitants it was their first exposure to large animals.

"No New Zealander, except the few who, like Duaterra, had been on foreign travel, had even seen either cows or horses, for the largest quadruped yet naturalized in the island was the pig, and even that had been introduced recently. Duaterra had often told his countrymen of the horse and its rider, and in return was always laughed at; but when the horses were now landed and Mr. Marsden actually mounted one of them, they stood in crowds and gazed in astonishment."[117]

115 Rangihoua can now be reached by the road north from KeriKeri. For a more detailed guide to the area's significance as the first base of significant British settlement in New Zealand, see the Historic Places briefing paper, http://www.historic.org.nz/TheRegister/RegisterSearch/RegisterResults.aspx?RID=7724&m=advanced

116 Some history books erroneously date his landing at Rangihoua to Monday, December 19, 1814, but the date above is taken directly from Marsden's journal. See *Memoir*, p360, www.nzetc.org/tm/scholarly/tei-McN01Hist-t1-b7-d39.html

117 *The Life And Work Of Samuel Marsden*, J B Marsden, Whitcombe & Tombs 1913, see http://

It was now Saturday, December 24th. Christmas was not only one day away but this year it just happened to fall on the Sabbath as well. Unprompted by Reverend Marsden, chief Ruatara took it upon himself to make the necessary preparations for what was to be the first reading of the Gospel on New Zealand soil.

"He enclosed about half an acre of ground with a fence, in the centre of which he erected a pulpit and a reading-desk, and covered the whole with either black native-made cloth or some duck which he had brought with him from Port Jackson," writes Marsden. "He also procured the bottoms of some old canoes, and fixed them up as seats for the Europeans on each side of the pulpit, intending to have Divine service performed next day.

"These preparations were made of his own accord, and in the evening he first informed me that everything was ready for public worship. I was much pleased with this singular mark of his attention. The reading desk was about 3 ft. and the pulpit 6 ft. from the ground. The black native cloth covered the top of the pulpit, and hung over the sides. The bottom of the pulpit, as well as the reading desk, was made of part of a canoe, and the whole was becoming and had a solemn appearance.

"He had also erected a flagstaff on the highest hill in the village, which had a very commanding view. On Sunday morning, when I went upon deck, I saw the English flag flying, which was a pleasing sight in New Zealand. I considered it the signal for the dawn of civilization, liberty, and religion in that dark and benighted land. I never viewed the British flag with more gratification, and I flattered myself they would never be removed till the natives of that island enjoyed all the happiness of British subjects."

The Maori may not have understood any of the words Samuel Marsden uttered on that first Christmas morning, or their significance, although Ruatara did translate. However, they were certainly aware of the solemnity of the occasion, as their own chiefs were wearing British military uniforms.

"When we landed, we found Koro Koro, Duaterra, and Shunghie, dressed in regimentals, which Governor Macquarie had given them, with their men drawn up, ready to be marched into the enclosure to attend Divine Service. They had their swords by their sides, and switches in their hands.

"We entered the enclosure, and were placed on the seats on each side of the pulpit. Koro Koro marched his men, and placed them on my right hand, in the rear of the Europeans: and Duaterra placed his men on the left. The inhabitants of the town, with the women and children, and a number of other chiefs, formed a circle round the whole. A very solemn silence prevailed – the sight was truly impressive.

"I rose up and began the service with singing the "Old Hundredth" Psalm; and felt my very soul melt within me when I viewed my congregation, and considered the state they were in. After reading the service, during which the natives stood up and sat down at the signals given by Koro Koro's switch, which was regulated by the movement of the Europeans, it being Christmas Day, I preached from the second chapter of St. Luke's Gospel and tenth verse, 'Behold, I bring you glad tidings of great joy,' etc.

"The natives told Duaterra that they could not understand what I meant. He replied, that they were not to mind that now, for they would understand by-and-by; and that he would explain my meaning as far as he could. When I had done preaching, he informed them what I had been talking about.

"Duaterra was very much pleased that he had been able to make all the necessary preparations for the performance of Divine worship in so short a time, and we felt much obliged to him for his attention. He was extremely anxious to convince us that he would do everything in his power, and that the good of his country was his principal consideration. In this manner, the Gospel has been introduced into New Zealand; and I fervently pray that the glory of it may never depart from its inhabitants till time shall be no more."

The first European settlers who'd accompanied Marsden, including John Nicholas, certainly felt awed. They had brought their wives and children with them, to live amongst the Maori, in a land with no British presence beyond their own and the occasional ship.

"I do not believe," Nicholas writes, "that a similar instance can be shown of such unlimited confidence placed in a race of savages known to be cannibals. We are wholly in their power, and what is there to hinder them from abusing it? Next to the overruling providence of God, there is nothing but the character of the ship, which seems to have something almost sacred in their eyes, and the influence of Mr. Marsden's name, which acts as a talisman amongst them. They feel convinced that he is sacrificing his own ease and comfort to promote their welfare."[118]

---

118 *The Life and Work of Samuel Marsden*, See http://www.nzetc.org/tm/scholarly/tei-DruMars-t1-body-d1-d6.html

Although they were a Church Missionary Society outpost, their first aim was not to forcibly or immediately convert Maori to Christianity, but to lead them gently into civilisation. Some historians have damned the Rangihoua mission station as a failure because it had not made "one conversion"[119] by 1822. All this time, however, it had been laying the groundwork, starting with that first visit by Marsden.

Although the ghoulish habit of cannibalism scared the proverbial out of the Europeans, Marsden, the missionaries and even British fleet officers like Cook had seen something else. The Maori, for all the terrible habits, were an advanced, intelligent, civilised people. They traded, they had a strong code of honour and justice, they could interact as equals with Europeans and hold their own in battle. The Maori people (for the most part) were not randomly stalking the countryside looking for people to eat – the practice of cannibalism was ritualistic and strongly tied to the warrior code; providing a final insult to a slain enemy.[120]

Looking beyond the bad, the missionaries saw the good, and tried to work with that to effect change.

"Mr. Marsden, in his conversations with the natives, explained to them the nature of our government, and the form of trial by jury; he discoursed with them upon the evils of polygamy, and showed his marked abhorrence of their darling vices, theft and lying. A chisel being lost from the *Active*, a boat was sent on shore, manned by Duaterra and other chiefs, to demand restitution; the culprit was not found, nor the implement restored; but a whole village was aroused from its slumbers at midnight, and the inhabitants literally trembled with fear of the consequences when they saw the angry chiefs, though no harm was permitted to ensue."[121]

Marsden's lectures about British justice were soon put to the test. On Thursday, January 12 1815, a Maori man, Weri, had beaten his wife after finding her in possession of a ship's nail, which she said a European man from the *Active* had given her as a present. Weri figured no woman could have gained something as sought after as a nail (iron was extremely pre-

---

119 *Penguin History of New Zealand*, Michael King, 2003, p142
120 Some historians (King, Belich and others) have suggested cannibalism was about "absorbing the mana", others like Paul Moon have criticised that analysis as too romantic – it was about excreting the mana. By eating an enemy and digesting him with its logical endpoint, Maori were making the ultimate insult possible. It was a battle-rage, bloodlust behaviour, similar in sentiment if not substance to indignities practiced on the bodies of dead Iraqi or Afghani fighters by young and rash western troops.
121 This incident took place on the Cavalli islands and is recounted in *The Life And Work Of Samuel Marsden*, J B Marsden, 1913, see http://www.nzetc.org/tm/scholarly/tei-DruMars-t1-body-d1-d6.html). However, in his own words in *Memoir*, Marsden says the thief was eventually found, but he decided to let the matter rest.

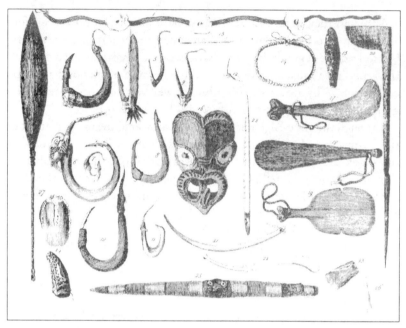

"Various kinds of instruments and utensils of the inhabitants of New Zealand, with some ornaments of the people of Terra del Fuego and New Holland" – Endeavour journals

cious to the tribes, being a vast improvement on wood and stone for cutting) from a man unless she had given him something 'special' in return.

Marsden interceded, saying he would confine the nail-giver to the brig if it was established anything improper had taken place, and he arranged for the Rangihoua chiefs to hear the woman's story and sit in judgement. Although a European suspect was brought before the court as well, the woman refused to ping him as the nail-giver.

"She defended herself very warmly, but said she could not identify the man who had given her the nail, affirming, however, that she had received it as a present. After a long examination she was acquitted by the unanimous voice of the chiefs, to the satisfaction of all parties."

Marsden was unconvinced, however: "Though I could not but entertain suspicions of the lady's chastity from her hesitation to point out the person who had given her the nail, I took this opportunity to assure them that if any person belonging to the *Active* either insulted or injured any of their people he or they should be punished."[122]

---

122 *Memoir of Duaterra*, p371

Ghost Chips

The missionaries wasted no time making their presence felt. By mid January they had ventured deep into the heart of Northland to visit Hongi Hika's pa, befriending numerous tribes on the way, and in late January Marsden took the *Active*, with only seven Europeans and 28 Rangihoua Maori warriors, down past what would later become Auckland to the Firth of Thames. Even there, local iwi had become aware of him and his mission. Nor were the Europeans the only ones trading in trinkets. Marsden recounts how one chief convinced another chief's wife to disrobe, all for the sake of a few feathers.

"Several of the natives of the Bay of Islands had brought with them a little trade, some a few nails, others small pieces of iron-hoops, some a few feathers, and some had fishing-hooks, with a variety of articles of no value to Europeans but of much value to themselves.

"The village was all in motion. They crowded together like a fair from all quarters. Some of the inhabitants brought their mats to sell and various other articles, so that the whole day appeared a busy scene, and many things were bought and sold in their way of trade.

"When the fair was over the ladies entertained us with several dances and songs. One of them had on a very fine upper garment, which a chief from Rangheehoo (who had come with us) wanted to procure for his wife. He had brought a box of feathers, neatly dressed, the pithy part of the quill having been all cut off, and only the external part remaining, to which the feather was attached. He made the feather wave gracefully with the smallest breeze when placed in the air. He opened it in presence of the ladies, many of whom wanted these feathers. He on the other hand wanted the fine garment.

"After placing them very tastefully, two or three feathers in each of the ladies' hair, she that had got the fine garment beheld how elegantly they appeared on the heads of those who wore them, and became seemingly impatient to possess such an ornament. He asked her to sell her garment. She hesitated for some time. At length he laid a certain number down at her feet. This proved a temptation she could not resist, and she instantly threw off the fine garment and delivered it to him for his feathers. The chief intended this article as a present to his wife, and he presented it to her on his return."[123]

As Marsden notes in his journals, everywhere he went he was welcomed warmly. The theme running through his writings time and time again:

123 Ibid, p376

treat the Maori honourably, and you shall be treated that way by them. And everywhere, they were keen to know how the rest of the world lived.

On an excursion to Kawa Kawa, Marsden found himself embroiled in an enlightening discussion about justice, which two hundred years later provides insight into the problems the Treaty of Waitangi was trying to solve:

"On passing up the River Koua Koua I observed upon the summit of a very high hill a Roman cross, and asked the natives what it was for. They told me it was to hang thieves on, whom they first killed and then hung up their dead bodies till time or the vultures destroyed.[124]

"During our stay at Koua Koua I had many interesting conversations with the chiefs relative to the nature of crimes and punishments, and I pointed out to them that there was no comparison between a man who would steal a potato and another who committed murder. And yet their punishment (in New Zealand) was the same, for they will as soon kill a man for stealing potatoes as for murder. The chief has the power of life and death over his people.

"They appeared much astonished when I told them that King George had not the power to put any man to death, tho' a much greater king than any in New Zealand. I explained to them the nature of a British jury – that no man could be put to death in England unless twelve gentlemen had examined into the case of the accused prisoner on any alleged offence, and if they pronounced him guilty of a crime deserving death then King George could put him to death, but if these twelve gentlemen said he was not guilty King George could not put him to death; and even when a criminal is condemned to die King George has the authority to pardon him if he wishes to do so.

"They remarked that such a law was very good, and one of them asked what Governor we should send them. I replied that we had no intention of sending them any, but wished them to govern themselves.

"I mentioned some crimes which were punished with death, and others which we punished with banishment; and observed that punishment should be regulated at all times by the nature of the offence. I told them if a man had two wives in England, tho' he was a gentleman, yet he would be banished from his country. One of the chiefs said he was of opinion that it was better to have only one wife, for where there are many there will always be quarrelling; others said that their wives made the best overseers, and that they could not get their grounds cultivated if it was

---

124 Ibid, p381-382

not for the industry of their wives; and for that reason only, they thought to have more wives than one was good policy.

"These conversations sometimes passed while the women were present, and they were generally of opinion that a man should have no more than one wife. Some of the chiefs thought there were too many kings in New Zealand, and that if there were fewer they would have fewer wars and be more happy. I told them there was only one king in England; at the same time there were more gentlemen than in New Zealand, but that none of these gentlemen could put a man to death nor dared they go to war with one another. King George would not allow it, and they could not do this without his permission, on which account there was no fighting with nor murdering of one another in England, as there were among them."

These trips were also a chance to get a first hand look at how ordinary Maori lived. European contact was still almost non-existent in most of the interior villages, and Marsden describes arriving at one, up the Waikare river, in the middle of a teeming rainstorm on a bitter autumn night.

"When I came up to this hut I had to creep into it through a small doorway about 2 ft. high and 18 in. broad. A number of women and children and a few of Weevea's servants composed the inmates. There was about a handful of fire in the centre of the hut (made of a few small sticks), round which were the children, all naked. Sometimes a little fire blazed for a moment and then went out, and the hut was full of smoke (as there was no vent for it to get out except at the small doorway already mentioned)."

The floor of the whare was dirt, and down the centreline had been laid a 10 metre long log, "and the natives lay on each side of the log with their heads reclined on it. When they sleep they lie upon the ground, have little covering, and some none at all."[125]

Marsden's host, the chief 'Weevea', could not remain in the hut because of the choking smoke, but Marsden needed the warmth of the fire to dry him out. What followed is an example of the housing conditions and tapu beliefs concerning the sick, that undoubtedly hugely escalated Maori death rates when European diseases hit them. It may not have been that the diseases were exponentially more deadly to Maori, but that Maori methods of treating the seriously ill were far more likely to kill their patients:

"About midnight Weevea came to the hut and informed me that one

125 *Memoir*, p384, see http://www.nzetc.org/tm/scholarly/tei-McN01Hist-t1-b7-d39.html#n384

of his wives was very ill, and her little child – that he was afraid she would die – and requested I would pray with her in the morning, which I promised to do. He appeared much concerned about this woman. I had heard a person moaning very much for some time, as if very weak and in great pain, and I also heard a child cry occasionally.

"Early in the morning I rose to see the poor woman, and found her lying with a child about three days old by her side in the open air, sheltered only by a few reeds placed in the direction from which the storm of wind and rain blew. She had been exposed all night in this manner, notwithstanding the stormy weather, and looked very ghastly, as if death was near.

"I talked to her for some time. She could scarcely speak, but smiled feebly, and seemed pleased with my attention to her. I knelt down by her side, along with Weevea and some of his people, and offered up my supplications to the Father of Mercies on her behalf. She well understood the meaning of prayer, tho' not the language in which it was then offered, as the New Zealanders consider that all their afflictions come from some superior Being, whom they are much accustomed to address while in trouble.

"The poor woman wanted nourishment. I presented her with a piece of biscuit, but she gave me to understand that she was forbidden to eat anything except potatoes. I spoke to Weevea, who told me God would be angry if she ate the biscuit. He took the bread, and, after repeating many petitions over it, placed it under her head and told me the presence of God would be in the biscuit, but his wife must not eat it.

"I lamented that the poor woman had been in the open air all night, which was enough to occasion her death, and learned that it was the prevailing custom among the New Zealanders when people were sick to carry them out of the huts into the open air lest the huts should be defiled. These people neither eat nor drink in their houses, but always in the open air, for the above reason.

"They suffer much in times of sickness from their superstitions, being compelled to lie in the open air, and to refuse food and water for days together, under an impression that if either be administered to the sick they will surely die. I had often been struck previous to my present visit to Wycaddee [Waikare] with the weakly and aged appearance of young women who had borne children, which I now attribute to the colds and other complaints caught, no doubt, by exposure whilst giving birth to their offspring," writes Marsden.

There is no record of whether mother and newborn lived, as Marsden left the village later that day. It was, he wrote, an example of how their ancient spiritual beliefs were killing them, softly but surely. One can only imagine how influenza must have later ravaged tribes with a policy of kicking the sick out into the rain, without food, water or shelter to strengthen them.

On his way back to Rangihoua, Marsden was forced to intervene in a standoff between a local tribe and the crew of a whaling ship, the *Jefferson*. It transpired that a young crewman on the whaler, armed with a sword, had struck the wife of a chief with the flat of the blade and attempted to stab the chief as well, simply because he was in a bad mood. The chief, seeing Marsden arrive, pointed at the mast and indicated he wanted the offender to hang. Given the large number of Maori who had gathered and who could have taken control of the entire whaling ship in an instant, Marsden saw this decision to wait for justice as progress.

"Previous to this time I had frequent conversations with the chiefs respecting the loss of the *Boyd*, and pointed out to them the injustice of putting to death the innocent with the guilty, as the people of Whangaroa had done in that instance. They readily admitted that the guilty only ought to suffer. I was pleased to find that Tupee was strongly impressing upon the minds of the natives the same idea, and instructing them not to injure any person on board the *Jefferson* except the man who had given the offence."[126]

Despite not being a British territory, Marsden defused the crisis by hauling the young sailor in front of the Rangihoua missionary and deputised Magistrate, Thomas Kendall, in a process agreed to by the iwi and the ship's captain. Marsden also warned the ship about the dangers of insulting Maori, and explained to the *Jefferson's* captain that his ship had narrowly dodged a one-way invitation to a hangi on this occasion.

Whether that advice was properly taken was a moot point, as the *Jefferson's* crew continued to play with fire:

"While the *Active* was taking in her cargo at Koua Koua a number of native women came on board every day. I told them I could not allow any of them to remain on board at night unless their husbands were with them. Accordingly, in the evening the vessel was searched, and if any women were found they were sent on shore (sometimes not very well pleased).

"During my stay on board the *Jefferson* I saw many of my old female acquaintances, who laughingly said they were not now on board the *Active*, and that the *Jefferson* was not *tabooed* when the evening came like

---

126   *Memoir*, p389, see http://www.nzetc.org/tm/scholarly/tei-McN01Hist-t1-b7-d39.html#n389

the *Active* – there was no *iriauta* (meaning there was no command to be off). I replied that I was angry with the master and crew of the *Jefferson* for suffering them to remain all night in the vessel, and that these were all very bad men. The women smiled, and expressed their confidence that they would not be molested."[127]

Marsden, however, had more immediate tasks on his mind, like returning to the settlement at Rangihoua. When he got there, however, he was stunned to find his friend and mission protector, Ruatara, "dangerously ill".

"This was a very distressing circumstance to me. I called to see him, but the superstitions of the natives would not permit me for several days to do so. Having at length gained admission, I found Duaterra lying on his back facing the sun, which was exceedingly hot, in a high fever, his tongue very foul. He complained of violent pains in his bowels, and from every appearance he was not likely to survive long."

Just as back in the Waikare village, traditional Maori healing methods were a killer, and despite Ruatara's recent Christian beliefs, the cultural ones ran deeper.

"All the utensils used for conveying meat or drink to the sick chief were detained by his relations, who said if they [the relatives] were removed Duaterra would die, and he was himself of the same opinion! So strongly rooted is superstition in the human mind when once admitted."

With Ruatara on his death-bed, the two men reminisced over what had been, and what might yet be. Ruatara, even then, still had faith he would beat the illness.

"He said with joy and triumph in his eyes, 'I have now introduced the cultivation of wheat in New Zealand. It will become a great country; for, in two years more, I shall be able to export wheat to Port Jackson, in exchange for hoes, axes, spades, and tea and sugar.'

"Under this impression he made arrangements with his people for a very extensive cultivation of the land, and formed a plan for building a new town, with regular streets, after the European mode, to be erected on a beautiful situation, which commanded a view of the harbour's mouth, and the adjacent country round.

"He mentioned his intention to me, and hoped he would recover in time to have the town properly marked out before I sailed. I told him I should be ready to attend him, but hoped to see him better first, and recommended him to take what nourishment he could.

---

127 Ibid

"The streets were to have been all marked out before the brig sailed for Port Jackson; but at the very time of these arrangements being made Duaterra was laid on his dying bed.[128] I could not but look on him with wonder and astonishment, as he lay languishing under his affliction, and could scarcely bring myself to believe that the Divine Goodness would remove from the earth a man whose life was of such infinite importance to his country, which was just emerging from barbarism, gross darkness, and superstition. No doubt he had done his work, and finished his appointed course, though I fondly imagined that he had only begun his race."

Marsden had a deadline to return to Sydney on the terms of Governor Macquarie's orders, and brief him on the establishment of the mission. He was mindful he had not yet purchased the land the Church Missionary Society needed. Together with a couple of senior chiefs at Rangihoua, they measured out roughly 200 acres, and agreed on a price: twelve axes. A Deed of Settlement – the first ever drafted in New Zealand for a land purchase – was executed by copying the facial moko (tattoos) of each chief beside their X on the paper. In this way, with the moko performing the role of fingerprints, the document was signed and witnessed.

The price might seem trivial by today's standards, but iron axes were a lot more useful and durable than anything Maori technology offered. With Marsden refusing point blank to trade muskets and ammunition for anything, the tribe's need for iron was the biggest bargaining chip they had.

In the final days of February, his initial work done, Marsden looked back on the tiny village receding in the distance as *Active* pulled away, bound for Australia. Little did he know how important that first settlement was in charting the course of New Zealand's future.

Over the next few days, in the sanctity of his cabin, the reverend had cause to reflect and jot down his general feelings about what he called "the New Zealanders".

"The only profession of the chiefs may be said to be solely that of war. It is no uncommon occurrence for the people of the North Cape to travel throughout the country to the East Cape, a distance of two hundred

---

128   The town Ruatara planned never really got a chance to take shape. While Rangihoua was eventually home to 200 Maori and British migrants, its influence in the Bay of Islands dwindled as that of Kororareka (Russell) grew. The Department of Conservation is currently trying to locate the archaeological remains of what small European settlement did exist at Rangihoua, in time for the bicentenary of New Zealand's first authorised British settlement in December 2014.

miles,[129] to make war. This is a great undertaking when it is considered that there are no regular roads, no bridges over rivers, and little means of subsistence in an uncultivated country like New Zealand.

"Jem, the Otaheitean, told me he had been three times within the last five years at the East Cape to war, accompanied by a thousand men each time. When, with all this travel and toil, they get to the territory of their supposed enemies, the spoils to be gained consist of nothing more than a few mats and the prisoners who may be taken in battle."

Little wonder, perhaps, that as early as 1814 the chiefs could see the advantage of uniting under one sovereign authority with the power to stop tribes from going to war all the time. Then, of course, there were also the things best not spoken of in polite company.

"The New Zealanders are all cannibals, and appear to have no idea that it is an unnatural crime. When I expressed abhorrence at their eating one another they said it had always been customary to eat their enemies. I could not learn, however, that they ever eat human flesh merely to satisfy hunger or from choice, nor in cool blood, but solely from a spirit of retaliation and revenge for injuries sustained, and, as far as I could form an opinion of this horrid custom, I am inclined to believe that these people consider the eating of their enemies in the same light as we do the hanging of a criminal (condemned by the laws of his country), and that the disgrace reflected on the surviving relations of the victim is nearly the same as that reflected on a family in Europe by the public execution of one of its members.

"When I informed them that this was a custom unknown in Europe, and considered there as a great disgrace to the nation which practises it, they seemed surprised, and Shunghee, tho' a man of great authority, has since told me that he thought it was wrong, and that his people would never be guilty of it again. A few others made a similar promise. I took opportunities as occasion offered to convince them of the inhuman nature of this practice by picturing the horror it excited in the bosoms of all good men of other nations, in whose opinion they were disgraced and dreaded on its account.

"It may be proper to remark here that altho' we met a friendly reception on every part of the coast at which we stopt or touched, I should recommend masters of vessels who may visit New Zealand to be very cautious unless they can depend upon the proper behaviour of their respective

---

129   Actually, a journey of around 800 kilometres, or 500 miles.

crews. The New Zealanders will not be insulted with impunity, nor be treated as men without understanding, but will assuredly resent and revenge an injury as soon as opportunity permits."

CHAPTER SIX

Reverends, Guns & Money

Few Maori had seen the outside world, but those that had were among the most instrumental in bringing the winds of change to tribal life in New Zealand. Ruatara's death may have robbed the country of a visionary, as Marsden liked to put it, but it had not robbed the vision.

Marsden was cultivating visits of New Zealand Maori, including youth as young as ten, to Sydney so they could see for themselves where the future would lie.

"Their minds are enlarging very fast," Marsden wrote. "Beholding the various works that are going on in the smiths and carpenters' shops, and spinning and weaving, brickmaking and building houses, together with all the operations of agriculture and gardening, has a wonderful effect on their minds and will excite all their natural powers to improve their own country."[130]

Hongi Hika, in particular, realised that a lot of money could be made if his tribe produced goods that the British desired. But there was also a dark side to the British settlement of New South Wales, and it had haunted Ruatara in his final months. The fact that he rose above it, built the first church enclosure and welcomed the settlers shows the measure of the man, but as Marsden was to later reveal, Ruatara had been told by someone that the British would eventually take over New Zealand:

"I observe in Mr. Kendall's letter, when speaking of the death of Dua-terra, that he remarks that Duaterra had imbibed strong prejudices in his mind against the missionaries. These prejudices originated at Port Jackson, just before I sailed with him to New Zealand, from some person

---

130   Extract of a Letter from Rev Mr Marsden, reprinted in *Evangelical Magazine*, June 1816, see www.nzetc.org/tm/scholarly/tei-McN01Hist-t1-b8-d5.html

Hongi Hika (centre) with Chief Waikato and the Rev Thomas Kendall

or persons, with the most dark and diabolical design, telling Duaterra not to trust us, as our only object was to deprive the New Zealanders of their country, and that as soon as we had gained a footing there we should pour into New Zealand an armed force and take the country to ourselves.

"To make the impression the deeper, they called his attention to the miserable state of the natives of New South Wales – deprived by the English of their country, and reduced by us to their present wretchedness. This suggestion darted into his mind like a poisoned arrow, destroyed his confidence in Europeans, and alarmed his fears and jealously for the safety of his country, for which he had the most unbounded love.

"On our sailing from Port Jackson I perceived him to be dejected, with a constant melancholy on his countenance. I often enquired what was the cause of his grief, but he cautiously concealed the matter from me, and always evaded giving me a satisfactory answer. I repeatedly pressed him to tell me; and. a little before we arrived in New Zealand, he informed me that he was told at Port Jackson that it was our intention to take his country from him, and that the New Zealanders would be very angry with him if he should be the author of their country being taken and given to the English. I pressed him much to inform me who had told him these things, but no argument that I could use would induce him to tell me. I concluded that he was bound by some solemn promise not to reveal the author of this mischief. I frequently endeavoured to remove his fears, but to no purpose. The poison infused into his mind was too subtle and active ever to be destroyed.

"Mr. Kendall mentions Warrackie [Waraki] also as having the same fears. He is the chief of whom the settlers purchased the last piece of land. This chief was Duaterra's uncle. Warrackie is since dead, and I hope these groundless fears will die with them; and that the persons who thus intended to give a fatal blow to the mission will, by the overruling providence of God, be disappointed, and their wickedness be brought to an end."[31]

Maori fears cannot have been eased by the frequent escape of Australian convicts from passing ships.

"I am sorry to observe that the five prisoners who were left here… have all made their escape from this settlement," wrote magistrate and missionary Thomas Kendall to the New South Wales governor's office, "and must either be gone into the interior of the country or otherwise have secreted themselves…"[32]

The missionaries lacked any means of enforcing the law or restraining escapees as, "the leg-irons and handcuffs mentioned in his Excellency's letter are not received," complained Kendall.

Despite the occasional convict, and rather than troops, as Ruatara had feared however, Australia's main exports to the tiny New Zealand settlement at Rangihoua remained peaceful and wealth-creating. "Several horned cattle" were now producing "Milk, butter, beef and labour" for the settlers and Maori, while "fruit trees of various kinds have also been sent over by Mr Marsden. The settlers have peaches in perfection," reported a briefing paper to the Church Missionary Society in London.[133]

Perhaps just as sweet was the news that a school for the Maori children had taken off, being well supported by parents:

"Mr. Kendall and Mr. Carlisle have paid every attention to the education of the native children which circumstances would allow. The school was opened in August, 1816, with 33 children; in September, there were 47; and in October, 51. In November and December, there being no

---

131 Letter from Marsden to Rev. Josiah Pratt, CMS London, 26 October 1815, see http://www.nzetc.org/tm/scholarly/tei-McN01Hist-t1-b8-d8.html
132 Letter from Kendall to Secretary Campbell, 23 October 1815, see http://www.nzetc.org/tm/scholarly/tei-McN01Hist-t1-b8-d7.html
133 Report to the Church Missionary Society, London, delivered at AGM, 4 May 1819, see http://www.nzetc.org/tm/scholarly/tei-McN01Hist-t1-b8-d24.html

provisions for the children, they were scattered abroad in search of food. In January, 1817, the number was 60; in February, 58; in March, 63; and in April, 70. There are the latest returns of numbers which have arrived.

"At first the girls were double in number to the boys, but latterly they became nearly equal. The age of the children was generally from 7 to 17. Among them were 17 orphans, and six slaves which had been taken in war. Several sons of chiefs were among the scholars, and one of them, Atowha, son of the late Tippahee, began, after a few months, to act as assistant in the school."[34]

Samuel Marsden sent a questionnaire to the Rangihoua settlers in late 1819, hoping to hear things had improved in the first five years of life there. Of native mortality rates, he asked:

"Have the deaths of the natives for the last three years been in the same proportion to the first two years you lived amongst them?", to which the settlers responded, "They have not. During the first year in particular there was a great mortality among the natives, but we now seldom hear of the death of a native. The natives live better. Many of them were formerly very much afflicted with boils, but since they have lived upon more wholesome food they are free from them and at present appear healthy and well."

On the life expectancy front, Maori could expect to enjoy a longer life if they turned their swords into ploughshares, wrote the settlers:

"They are still very fond of war, but manifest a greater desire to promote agriculture. The means now afforded them to purchase hogs, potatoes, corn, mats, fish, lines etc, with axes, hoes and other European articles has awakened their native industry exceedingly…and have far exceeded our expectations. They have enlarged their field, as they have procured implements of husbandry, and the comforts of life have increased accordingly."[35]

But life in the tiny town of Rangihoua was about to get messy.

Village patron and protector, Hongi Hika, desired to visit England. Thomas Kendall, on the pretext of correcting his Maori dictionary manuscript (which became the basis of the written Maori language as we know it today), sailed to London with Hongi and his fellow Ngapuhi chief Waikato.

Their visit coincided with a surge of surplus military weapons onto the British and world markets in the wake of Napoleon's defeat at Waterloo in 1815, following the subsequent demobilisation of the British Army. "Cheap

134 Ibid
135 Mr Marsden's Queries to the Settlers of the Bay of Islands, 5 November 1819, see http://www.nzetc.org/tm/scholarly/tei-McN01Hist-t1-b8-d28.html

military muskets such as the Brown Bess flooded onto the market," notes historian Paul Moon.[136] The Bess was sought-after as a much more powerful and accurate weapon (up to 100m in the right conditions), than the common garden variety of musket (range of around 50m).

The missionaries at Rangihoua had been under Marsden's orders never to sell guns and ammunition to the Maori, lest it set off an arms race. But that horse had well and truly bolted – whalers, sealers and everyone down to old Tom Cobley and his dog had figured out they could trade their guns for land and goods. Some tribes were building a decent collection of firearms. Hongi Hika wanted in, and sensing an opportunity in London he did what every great wheeler-dealer does – flicked off an asset to raise cash.

By chance, Hongi's path in the UK crossed that of French nobleman Baron Charles Hippolyte de Thierry, who'd fled to Britain after the French royal family were beheaded, and the Ngapuhi chief sold off to him a whopping great 40,000 acres of tribal land at Hokianga for somewhere between eight hundred and eleven hundred pounds cash[137] (roughly $300,000 in today's money), and 36 axes for the tribe back in New Zealand.[138]

De Thierry wasn't the first Frenchman to be taken for a ride by Northland iwi, but this land purchase and the implications of it played another massive role in the later acceptance of the Treaty of Waitangi.

Cashed up, Hongi Hika had some minor things to attend to in the British capital, such as an audience with King George IV who gave the warrior a suit of chainmail armour to wear in battle. Together with Rev. Kendall and chief Waikato, their next stop was Sydney and a meeting with an arms trader. Using the cash he'd received from "selling" a Hokianga acreage, Hongi Hika bought 400 mostly Brown Bess military muskets and set sail for home.

Kendall knew he'd done it, and he knew what the upshot was going to be. He also later tried to claim he had no option. But Kendall himself was having a midlife crisis, abandoning his wife and eight children to shack up with a Maori schoolgirl he'd once taught – Tungaroa, the daughter of the Rangihoua tohunga. Evidently under her spell, Kendall began to write that Maori spiritual beliefs were "sublime" – forgetting for a moment that

136 *The Treaty & Its Times*, Paul Moon & Peter Biggs, p42
137 *The Treaty & Its Times*, p45
138 Formal Deed of Sale and Purchase was drawn up by Kendall and executed back in New Zealand. Hongi Hika appears to have requested that his share of the deal - the cash - was not mentioned to the tribe back home, see http://www.nzetc.org/tm/scholarly/tei-TurEpit-t1-g1-t1-g1-t2-g1-t4-g1-t2.html

those same spiritual beliefs had banished the merely sick to catch their death of cold outside, or that those same spiritual beliefs drove the cannibalism that remained rife in the Maori community even at this stage.

Kendall certainly knew of the practice, as he was a contributor to this article that appeared in Britain's *Evangelical Magazine* in 1821, recounting Wesleyan missionary Samuel Leigh's recent experiences at Whangaroa:[139]

" 'While I continued in the Island', says Mr. Leigh, 'one day, as I was walking on the beach, conversing with a chief, my attention was arrested by a great number of people coming from a neighbouring hill. I inquired the cause of the concourse, and was told that they had killed a lad, were roasting him, and going to eat him. I immediately proceeded to the place, in order to ascertain the truth of this appalling relation. Being arrived at the village where the people were collected, I asked to see the boy.

" 'The natives appeared much agitated at my presence, and particularly at my request, as if conscious of their guilt; and it was only after a very urgent solicitation that they directed me towards a large fire at some distance, where, they said, I should find him. As I was going to this place, I passed by the bloody spot on which the head of this unhappy victim had been cut off; and, on approaching the fire, I was not a little startled at the sudden appearance of a savage-looking man, of gigantic stature, entirely naked, and armed with a large axe. I was a good deal intimidated, but mustered up as much courage as I could, and demanded to see the lad. The cook (for such was the occupation of this terrific monster) then held up the boy by his feet. He appeared to be about fourteen years of age, and was half roasted.

" 'I returned to the village, where I found a great number of natives seated in a circle, with a quantity of coomery (a sort of sweet potatoe) before them, waiting for the roasted body of the youth. In this company were shown to me the mother of the child. The mother and child were both slaves, having been taken in war. However, she would have been compelled to share in the horrid feast, had I not prevailed on them to give up the body to be interred, and thus prevented them from gratifying their unnatural appetite.

" 'But notwithstanding this melancholy picture of New Zealand, I believe they are very capable of receiving religious instruction, and a knowledge of the arts in general. They are very ingenious and enterprising, and discover a surprising willingness to receive instruction. I did

---

139 "New Zealanders Cannibals", Samuel Leigh et al, *Evangelical Magazine*, London, 1821, see http://www.nzetc.org/tm/scholarly/tei-McN01Hist-t1-b9-d23.html

not visit any one village, where the principal chiefs did not strongly urge my residence among them; and I believe that God is preparing them to receive the ever-blessed Gospel of peace'."

Perhaps Kendall's endorsement of native beliefs, and decision to sell weapons and ammunition to Maori was simply a case of giving up the fight – he felt overwhelmed by the enormity of the situation he found himself in. Certainly, he told the Church Missionary Society in his defence, the tiny European mission did not have the strength to dictate to local Maori what 'they must receive in payment for their property & services. They dictate to us! …It is evident that ambition and self interest are amongst the principal causes of our security amongst them."

Just before he had sailed for England with Hongi Hika, Kendall had a run in with Samuel Marsden on arms-dealing, recorded in one of Marsden's letters.

"Their bartering with the natives and shipping for muskets and powder excited their avarice, and avarice excited jealousy, and both together destroyed all Christian love, and carried them so far out of their duty that they could not even meet at last to read the service of the Church on the Sabbath day together," lamented Marsden.[140]

"When I visited them in August last I found them all in a state of confusion. I saw these evils to be exceeding great, but the difficulty was to find a remedy. I had for a long time been remonstrating with them by letter against the nefarious traffic of muskets and powder with the natives, and against all private traffic; but notwithstanding the direction I had given, and the resolutions which they entered into against this barter, I found it was still continued and productive of every evil.

"I had a string of resolutions or rules drawn up, which were read one by one in the committee, and approved by the signature of them all. When these resolutions were past I hoped a death blow was struck to this abominable and disgraceful evil. Not many days after one of the old settlers purchased a quantity of hogs with a musket. I now despaired of ever preventing this evil, without all the missionaries who were concerned in this wickedness were dismissed from the service of the mission."

Samuel Marsden was furious a couple of years later when he discovered that Kendall had gone so far as to ask the Church Missionary Society to send out a gunsmith for the mission – the CMS being unaware there was a sinister reason.

---

140 Letter Marsden to Pratt, CMS, 24 April 1820, see http://www.nzetc.org/tm/scholarly/tei-McN01Hist-t1-b8-d48.html

"When remonstrating with Mr Kendall on the impropriety of his conduct in bartering muskets with the natives, he attempted to justify the measure by informing me that the Society was going to send out to Shunghee [Hongi Hika] a gunsmith named Mr Clark. I told him Mr Clark would not be allowed to come to New Zealand on those terms."[141]

When Clark and his wife duly turned up from London at the Sydney wharf, Marsden indeed intercepted them and kept them in Australia to work for the CMS there.

"I am persuaded it will be better for the present," wrote Marsden, "to keep him here until I write to New Zealand and inform Mr Kendall and Shunghee that Mr Clark must not come to New Zealand if they expect him to be employed making muskets."

Marsden, however, was having a real problem with Reverends, guns and money.

"I found the Reverend Mr Butler had shot three of my heifers and two bulls, and also one cow in calf," complained Marsden at one point. The reason for shooting? "He said he wanted to get them into the settlement, and finding he could not he shot five of them and Shunghee shot one."

Describing himself as "hurt" by this "wanton, thoughtless act" that had wiped out cattle costing him "considerable trouble and expense to get them into the country", Marsden noted that the settlers had shot the cattle beasts that should have been breeding and providing milk, butter and beef with a decent sized herd by this stage. It seemed he couldn't even trust the clergy with guns. Yet everywhere Marsden looked, someone was selling guns to the tribes.

"The whalers are likely to ruin the whole country by importing such quantities of firearms and gunpowder. How this evil can be remedied, I know not. It is a very great one..."[142]

Indeed it was. Armed with his 400 military muskets, surplus from the Napoleonic wars, Ngapuhi's Hongi Hika led strike forces throughout the upper North Island, seeking utu for past tribal differences and almost wiping out tribes like Ngati Whatua and Ngati Paoa in the Auckland region.

They did it in war canoes and spells of carrying the massive waka overland between streams and harbours, leading "war parties of 500 to 1000 warriors on fleets of war canoes to almost every part of the North

141 Letter, Marsden to Pratt, CMS, 15 January 1823, see http://www.nzetc.org/tm/scholarly/tei-McN01Hist-t1-b9-d40.html
142 Letter Marsden to Pratt, CMS, 21 March 1821, see http://www.nzetc.org/tm/scholarly/tei-McN01Hist-t1-b9-d5.html

Island. In one Nga Puhi invasion of the Waikato, up to 5000 men were said to be involved in the fighting," wrote Paul Moon and Peter Biggs.[143]

"But nowhere was the slaughter more concentrated than in the area alongside the Tamaki river estuary that today houses the suburbs of St Heliers, Glen Innes, Panmure and Mt Wellington, then home of the Ngati Paoa: two attacks in 1821 effectively wiped out or captured almost all Ngati Paoa. The death toll has been estimated between 1000 and 3000 and the feasting on the dead went on for days."

Other writers have described these events as the beginning of "an arms race", and indeed they were. Hongi Hika's first major land deal had funded weapons of mass destruction that were used to devastating effect against tribes armed with wooden clubs and spears. The French crew of Marion du Fresne's ill-fated mission had described how chiefs in their own battle tried to hold up their cloaks to ward off the musket balls, and failed miserably against the new and mysterious western weapons. One can only imagine the horror for the other North Island tribes as they found themselves confronted with the full force of firearms.

Marsden, of course, had foreseen it back in 1820:

"I condemn the barter because its natural tendency is to defeat the grand object of the Society. It arms one tribe of natives against another, who are unarmed, for a man with a club has not the same means of defence that one has with a musket.[144]

"The morning Kendall sailed, I believe not less than 40 canoes came into the harbour from a war expedition, with prisoners of war, and the heads of a number of chiefs whom they had slain in battle. I went onshore and saw the prisoners and the heads when they landed. The sight was distressing beyond conception.

"Arms and ammunition tend to inflame their warlike spirit, and to urge them to blood and slaughter. No man can, upon Christian principles, defend such a barter. Satan could not have had a more powerful instrument to overthrown the mission than this barter."

From an ideological and moral point, Marsden was correct, but in practical terms, he wasn't. History (and the musket wars are a classic example) has repeatedly shown that when the balance of power is upset, carnage ensues. It is one of the reasons that gun-control might sound like a great idea in principle, but it never works in practice: once criminals,

143 *The Treaty and Its Times*, Paul Moon & Peter Biggs, 2004, p 47
144 Letter, Marsden to Pratt, CMS, 24 April 1820 http://www.nzetc.org/tm/scholarly/tei-McN01Hist-t1-b8-d48.html

who never bothered about licences in the first place, are the only ones left with weapons, violent crime in the community rises exponentially. Those US states that allow private citizens to carry concealed weapons have far lower crime rates than those that ban guns, because the crims fear being pinged by armed members of the public acting in a citizen's defence capacity.[145]

In 1820, much of New Zealand's heartland remained unseen by Europeans and unexplored, in the map category of "Here be dragons…". Those heartland tribes did not have access to the guns that would have saved their lives, and they were slaughtered. The only thing that could have made it any worse for them was if Hongi Hika had managed to purchase warhorses as well and come crashing through the bush with guns, on the backs of beasts the other tribes had never even known existed.

As it was, Hongi Hika went into battle wearing the suit of chain mail armour that King George had given him. The suit meant greenstone meres, wooden taiaha spears and the like had no impact on Hongi – simply bouncing off the armour and adding to fears that he simply couldn't be killed. That idea only ended, ironically, when a rival tribe, who'd finally managed to lay their hands on a gun, shot Hongi Hika through the chest, causing an infected wound he died a slow and painful death from. Live by the musket, die by the musket, is the paraphrased and most obvious Bible verse that more than one missionary must have lectured on during the Sunday services that followed.

There are those who blame the settlers and traders for selling the guns in the first place, and certainly there's an element of truth in that. But Hongi Hika had purchased his armory not in New Zealand in a beads-and-blankets deal but Sydney. Nor should it be forgotten that the first muskets had not been traded, but plundered from wrecked or captured ships. The arms race began while Marion du Fresne was slow-cooking back in 1772.

A "holocaust" it might later have been, as Michael King labelled it, but in terms of apportioning blame you could be tempted to argue it was an inevitable and tragic trajectory that owed its origins to the collateral damage of human progress. Just as the Maori had arrived in New Zealand and wiped out whoever was living here first, so too was Europe on a mission to explore the planet and settle new lands. There was no way New Zealand was going to remain in a sheltered South Seas protective

---

145   For statistical validation of the claim that personal gun ownership leads to a drop in violent crime, see http://www.thebriefingroom.com/archives/2007/08/the_gun_debate.html

bubble; the world had arrived and it was a world of pirates, privateers, ponces and plunderers. Adapt or die, or, as Darwin was so fond of saying, eat or be eaten.

It's also unfair to paint a picture of Europeans flagrantly selling guns just for the sheer amusement of it. Guns, even to sailors, were valuable items back in the day. When the *Parramatta* crew tried to buy supplies from Maori, the tribe offered 150 buckets of potatoes "and eight hogs" in return for one musket.[146] By 1822 with more guns available, the value of a musket in the Bay of Islands was only seventy buckets of potatoes and two pigs.[147]

If the Europeans could have kept getting away with offering glass beads and blankets in exchange for provisions, they would have, but by this time the larger Maori population had wised up to the value of British goods offered by small groups of settlers. Novelty items were now appreciated as novelties, and while blankets certainly kept you warm they were infinitely more difficult to use as weapons on the battlefield, where much of Maori political 'discussion' was still done. Power was invariably perceived as emanating from the barrel of a gun, and those who refused to trade food for weapons went hungry.

While the Musket Wars were consuming the attention of iwi and to some extent the settlers, behind the scenes in London and Sydney the talk of the power cliques was New Zealand and its political future.

The French nobleman, Baron Charles de Thierry, who'd paid a small fortune to Hongi Hika for a 40,000 acre [16,000 hectare] plot in the Hokianga now wanted – naturally – to visit his lifestyle block. He sought clarification from the Colonial Office in London, essentially trying to figure out what Britain's interests in New Zealand were.

"Will land purchased from the natives be considered the property of the purchaser in case the island is taken possession of by the British Government; and in case such lands are again sold, will the sale of them be lawful and binding?"[148]

The response was brief:

"As the questions which you have proposed to his Lordship respecting

---

146 Although *Parramatta's* captain agreed to the trade, he then kidnapped a chief and tried to ransom him off for a further 170 buckets of potatoes and five more hogs. Little wonder the tribe thought Christmas dinner had come early when the *Parramatta* was shipwrecked in a storm within view of the village, and the obvious consequences that followed.
147 See Diary of Reverend John Gare Butler, 12 February 1822, *Earliest New Zealand: The Journals and Correspondence of the Rev. John Butler*, http://www.nzetc.org/tm/scholarly/tei-BarEarl-t1-body-d7.html
148 Letter, Baron Charles de Thierry to Earl Bathurst, Colonial Secy., 2 December 1823

the Island of New Zealand are founded upon the assumption that that island is considered as a possession of the Crown, it seems necessary to apprise you that you have been misinformed on the subject."[149]

In other words, New Zealand is not a British possession, what are you bothering me with this for? In fact, the good Baron had made it clear in his original letter that he realised it was not yet a "possession", but like everyone else he strongly suspected it would become so and he wanted to ensure his property purchase would be valid if the Brits sailed in and claimed the country.

Perhaps sensing he had not been heard or understood, the Baron wrote again, noting that he had "an estate of 40,000 acres in New Zealand, with the means of adding considerably to its extent, and is desirous of sending off a colony of a large number of useful persons who are anxious of going to settle there with their families."[150]

Always one with an eye for the main chance, Baron de Thierry wondered aloud whether the 500 pound grant paid "to each person going to settle in New South Wales" would also be payable to his own settlers, on which basis the Baron wanted an "advance of eight to ten thousand pounds" from His Majesty's treasury coffers so that he could send "off a colony to New Zealand."

One of the Baron's former employees, a "Captain Stewart of the whale trade" was, sniffed the Baron, now seeking the rights to an island "which bears his name, on the southern extremity of New Zealand," yet this same Captain Stewart was a man who had "deserted from His Majesty's Royal Navy", and had become "a privateer" (an officially-sanctioned pirate allowed to raid foreign ships). Surely, exclaimed the Baron, a French nobleman loyal to the King of England should have first dibs at New Zealand above the claim of a pirate.

God, as they say, loves a tryer.

The Baron wasn't the only one snooping around trying to get certainty on the status of New Zealand. A group of merchants, traders and ship owners petitioned the Colonial Office on the "great advantage and expediency of forming a settlement in New Zealand, for which purpose they most respectfully solicit that a military force may be stationed in those islands for the security of the various British interests which are springing up therein, and which must rapidly increase under its protection."

The merchants told Earl Bathurst their fleets of ships were mindful

---

149   Letter, Under-Secy. R Wilmot Horton to Baron Charles de Thierry, 10 December 1823
150   Letter, Baron Charles de Thierry to Earl Bathurst, Colonial Secy., 16 January 1824

of the "dangers frequently attending their intercourse with the natives, between whom and the crews of European and other vessels fatal quarrels have arisen, from the wanton outrages offered in many instances by them to the New Zealanders."[151]

At least it was a recognition that Maori had been badly provoked by ill-disciplined sailors and traders, but the merchants felt the safety of everyone was being compromised by the lack of a security force capable of keeping the peace, because the Maori, "although easily managed by good and judicious treatment, are a high-spirited and intelligent people, and extremely susceptible of injury and insults."

Despite the potential for fatal misunderstandings, the merchants nonetheless sang the praises of local iwi, telling the Colonial Office, "The natives of New Zealand are a robust and enterprising yet docile race, and when [our] vessels are deficient of hands they readily volunteer their services, and prove orderly and powerful seamen, and that at the present time there are no less than twelve New Zealand men on board one single whale ship."

With seals, whales, flax and timber increasingly being purchased from New Zealand, they said, it was inevitable that trade with the South Pacific nation would grow, bringing with it increasing opportunity but also increasing risk of bloodshed. This, they argued, was why Britain needed to establish a military presence in New Zealand, whether they liked it or not, purely as a police force.

"That such a force, restrained from every attempt at conquest or aggression and acting solely for the defence of persons and property, would be equally advantageous to the natives as to His Majesty's subjects, inasmuch as, while it secured British subjects frequenting these islands from being assailed and plundered by the natives, it would protect the latter from the insults and outrages which the crews of European vessels have sometimes perpetrated, and which have proved the occasion of exciting the natives to murderous and indiscriminate retaliation.

"A British protecting force, which several of the most intelligent chiefs have expressed a strong desire to obtain, while it gave security to persons and property, as between His Majesty's subjects and the native inhabitants, would have a powerful tendency to check that barbarous warfare which the several independent tribes are perpetually waging against each other."

---

151 Memorial [Memo] from Samuel Enderby et al, to Earl Bathurst, Colonial Office, London 24 April 1826, see http://www.nzetc.org/tm/scholarly/tei-McN01Hist-t1-b10-d40.html

Historians Michael King, Angela Ballara[152] and others acknowledge that this state of intertribal warfare had existed long before European contact. What King argues, probably quite justifiably, is that the presence of muskets made existing wars much more bloody and one-sided. Lawyers reading this will probably equally make the point that people have to take responsibility for their actions. A man who picks up a club to kill, and a man who picks up a gun to kill have both formed the intent to commit murder. Their choice of weapon may affect their chances of success, but the intent is the same. It is that ongoing intent to murder each other that really lay at the heart of the wars, and to which the idea of an independent military force to keep the peace was meant to appeal. For the tribes, there were too many conflicting interests; too many chiefs and not enough Gandhi's. The idea of a new overlord to keep and enforce the peace – the essence of what later followed at Waitangi in 1840 – was forged during the carnage of the 1820s.

There was one final parting shot in the letter from the merchants to the British Colonial Office in London – a veiled reference to Baron Charles de Thierry:

"Above all, your memorialists [petitioners] are exceedingly desirous that the important British interests connected with New Zealand should, as soon as may be found practicable, be placed under the formal protection of His Majesty's Government, because ... the French have it in contemplation to establish themselves there, and that it would be a most valuable colony for France."

The "safe and capacious harbours, with the naval stores and powerful [Maori] seamen" would give France, they warned, "a complete ascendancy in the eastern seas and South Pacific ocean" and could potentially cut off access to Britain's colonies in Australia.

The merchants were supported in their pitch by Colonel Robert Torrens, a British MP and former Marines commander, who told Downing Street a force of "two hundred marines would be amply sufficient, and they might be stationed in New Zealand as cheaply as they are now stationed at Portsmouth or Plymouth."[153] Torrens hoped that if the British

---

152 Ballara, and James Belich, have also pointed to that other introduced Pakeha weapon of mass-expansion, the potato, as the fuel behind tribal wars. Potatoes provided more sustenance and were easier to grow than kumara, freeing up manpower for other activities, like warfare. Of course, as we saw in chapter one, there was also plenty of warfare long before potatoes arrived. Even without muskets, one intertribal stoush in the Waikato in the late 1700s reportedly saw 8000 people killed in hand to hand combat in what became known as the Battle of Hingakaka, or 'fall of the parrots', in reference to the huge numbers of chiefs who died.
153 Letter, R Torrens to Downing Street, 27 June 1826, Historical Records of NZ Vol 1,

government approved, he might be given command of such a garrison.

His only reason for asking, he said, was that he could "give practical application to those sound principles of colonisation which I conceive to be of vast and growing importance to this country."

It wasn't to be. Colonel Torrens' destiny lay in Australia, where a river in Adelaide carries his name, as London simply wasn't interested in colonising New Zealand.

Australian convicts, on the other hand, had no such qualms and continued to nurse fantasies of escaping into the New Zealand bush. On a hot January day in the Bay of Islands in 1827, crew on board the whaling vessel *The Sisters* were surprised to see the sailing ship *Wellington* call into port.

McNab, 1908, see http://www.nzetc.org/tm/scholarly/tei-McN01Hist-t1-b10-d39.html

CHAPTER SEVEN

Of Pirates And People-Eaters

"I don't like the looks of that brig, sir," remarked the whaler's chief mate, Mr Tapsell, noting a whole lot of men on the *Wellington's* deck who did not look entirely like sailors.

Knowing the *Wellington's* owner, the master of *The Sisters*, Robert Duke, decided to pay a courtesy visit but was told "that she was proceeding with troops to make a settlement in the River Thames, in New Zealand."[154]

That couldn't be right, thought Duke. Every man and their dog knew London kept turning down requests for troops to police the lawlessness in New Zealand.

Tapsell, meanwhile had heard from missionary Henry Williams that sailors from the *Wellington* had been purchasing gunpowder in Kororareka, and word had been slipped to the reverend that 65 convicts being shipped from New South Wales to Norfolk Island had captured the vessel and had the captain and crew locked up below decks, with the intention of murdering them once they were back out in the open ocean.

"I'm going to prevent that damned rogue from going to sea," Tapsell told Captain Duke.[155] The crew of another nearby whaling vessel, the *Harriet*, were brought into the plan, and at dawn the next morning they hatched it. The British ensign was suddenly run up the masts of the two whaling ships, indicating the vessels were now in combat mode for what became New Zealand's first recorded ship to ship naval battle.

"Mr Tapsell saw that all his guns were loaded and more ammunition

---

154   Letter, Robert Duke to Lieutenant-General Ralph Darling, New South Wales Governor, 19 February 1827, see http://www.nzetc.org/tm/scholarly/tei-McN01Hist-t1-b10-d47.html
155   "The Pirates of the Wellington Brig", by James Cowan, *Hero Stories of New Zealand*, Tombs, 1935, see http://www.nzetc.org/tm/scholarly/tei-CowHero-t1-body-d4.html

ready. Then he carefully laid and fired the swivel gun on the poop. It was well aimed. The nine-pound round shot struck the *Wellington's* foretopmast, and so damaged it that it presently carried away.[156]

"A cheer went up from the crew of *The Sisters*. Tapsell and his gun crew reloaded the long swivel and fired another shot. This too was a lucky one. The cannonball struck the brig's mainmast and cut it half through, two feet above the deck.

"The main-deck guns now were fired. Tapsell ordered the gunners to fire at the masts and rigging, to avoid injury to the soldiers and crew in the hold.

"Now the Harriet took up the firing, and delivered four or five cannon shot. Altogether the two ships fired about a dozen rounds."

There was no sign of anyone on *Wellington's* deck – they'd all dived for cover or jumped in the water as the cannonballs began whistling past and the timbers splintered and crashed to the decks around them. The whalers' crew found most of the prisoners cowering below decks.

At the same time, local Maori in Kororareka had rounded up a number of the runaway convicts who'd been in town or swum to it, and paddled them back out to the ships. "They had tied them up like pigs, with thongs of flax," reported writer James Cowan of the event. Several more of the convicts had taken to the hills, with Maori in pursuit.

Of the 59 prisoners captured, five were hanged in New South Wales, the balance were sent "to the Norfolk Island hell".[157]

Politician and historian William Pember Reeves colourfully summed up the makeshift policing action as "a triple alliance of missionaries, grog-sellers and cannibals [who] combined to intercept the runaways." Local Maori, he noted, were rewarded with their efforts in the capture "by an official payment at the rate of a musket per convict".[158]

Pressure continued to build for some kind of expeditionary force to be stationed in New Zealand with a view to long term colonisation, and Colonel Robert Torrens was in the thick of it. In an 1827 letter to the Secretary of the British Navy he suggested that a large fleet vessel, "having on board one hundred families, estimated at five in each family, beside the crew, should touch at New Zealand on the voyage to New

---

156 Ibid
157 For the other side of the story, an engaging account of why the convicts seized the ship in the first place, see http://www.darkmatter101.org/site/2009/12/20/%E2%80%98liberty-or-life%E2%80%99-the-convict-pirates-of-the-wellington/
158 *The Long White Cloud* by William Pember Reeves, 1898, Allen & Unwin, London, chapter eight, see http://www.nzetc.org/tm/scholarly/tei-ReeLong-t1-body-d1-d8.html

South Wales". The logic, explained Torrens, is that the colonists bound for Australia could be employed chopping down "cowdie trees" for use as ships masts for the British Navy.

The Admiralty wasn't as impressed at the plan as Torrens was, pointing out that the biggest kauri trees grew some considerable distance away from the beaches and getting the massive logs prepared and down to harbours was a massive task. The costs of New Zealand timber as a result were considerably higher than buying masts from the American state of Virginia.

Secondly, explained the Admiralty, if your ship was full of five hundred settlers, there plainly was not going to be room for 100 kauri ship masts as well.

There was, however, a third reason the Navy rejected the idea:

"The natives of New Zealand are exceedingly apprehensive that their island will be taken possession of by the English, and the arrival of a ship with so many people would, we fear, excite unfriendly feelings."[159]

There are some things against which the tides of history beat relentlessly, and the colonisation of New Zealand was one of them. No matter how honourable Britain wished to be, and how differently it wished to handle the New Zealand question, all of England was now aware that this country existed.

Papers in the New South Wales Governors' collection include an unsigned letter to the Governor in April 1828 setting out "many other important advantages" of colonising New Zealand, whose islands are described as "the best in the South Pacific ocean, in soil, climate, timber, trees, rivers."

As for local Maori, they are "a population of intelligent natives, brave, active, and, I believe, partial to the English…many of the minor chiefs wishing to put themselves under the protection of Great Britain. The natives are an enterprising and powerful race of people."

More to the point, explained the letter writer, if Britain didn't snap up New Zealand, someone else would.

"I feel considerable anxiety into whose hands New Zealand will be placed, as I am satisfied that the possession of the islands of New Zealand by Great Britain, France or America will give that Power the command of the South Pacific, and if in the hands of either of the latter Powers will soon disturb the peace of our colonies in New Holland [as Australia was still known at that stage][160].

159 Letter, Navy Commissioner to Secretary Hay, 6 June 1827, Historical Records of NZ Vol 1, see http://www.nzetc.org/tm/scholarly/tei-McN01Hist-t1-b10-d50.html
160 The name 'Australia', coined by Matthew Flinders, was not legally agreed to until 1824, and in fact the British Colonial Office continued to refer to the territory as New Holland right up until 1837.

"If France takes possession of New Zealand, which she appears disposed to do, from the number of her cruisers which we see by the public papers are continually visiting all parts of that ocean, it will be almost impossible to retain for any length of time New South Wales as a colony."

Just when the Aussies thought it might be safe to send some migrants across, however, came through more news that – like the *Boyd* massacre two decades earlier – reminded them that New Zealand's Maori population were a far different kettle of fish from the comparatively docile aboriginal tribes of Australia.

A merchant ship, the brig *Haweis*, ended up anchored off Whakatane in March, 1829. The ship had been plying the Bay of Plenty coast for several days, and several days earlier its captain and crew had been greeted and invited onto the marae in the fortified pa at the top of the hill overlooking modern Whakatane. There'd been trade and friendly discourse, so when the *Haweis* anchored again nearby on March 2, and purchased 20 pigs from the tribe that morning, everyone seemed to be in good spirits.

Everyone, that is, except John Atkins, second officer on the brig. His captain and most of the crew had gone ashore to a hot spring near the beach, leaving Atkins and three deck-hands to mind the ship at anchor. Also on board, a chief Ngarara – named after the mythical giant lizard of the cave paintings – and ten men from his tribe. It was early afternoon when Atkins felt something about Ngarara's body language wasn't good. He and his men were in "earnest discussion" and Atkins knew enough Maori to realise they were talking about the ship.

"Suspecting some treachery, I desired the steward, who was an Otaheitian [Tahitian], to hand up the cutlasses, keeping a strict watch on the chief who I saw cock his piece and put it under his kakahoo (or upper garment). His men at this signal sprang in the main chains, each having a musket, which they had secreted in their canoes."[161]

Unfortunately for Atkins, there were no pistols on deck, and it dawned on him fairly rapidly that the Maori outnumbered and outgunned his skeleton crew. The ship was theirs for the taking. Atkins' crewmates hadn't seen the guns, however, and thought the second officer was being paranoid when he asked them to locate a musket and shoot the chief.

"They each positively refused, not being so convinced as I was of the designs of the savages."

"Damn this," muttered Atkins, "I'll do it myself." He gave his men

---

161 "A Narrative of the Sufferings and Most Miraculous Escape of Mr John F Atkins...", *Historical Records of NZ* Vol 1, see http://www.nzetc.org/tm/scholarly/tei-McN01Hist-t1-b10-d61.html

strict orders to keep a sharp lookout in his absence, "which they unfortunately paid but little attention, telling me I was meditating the life of an innocent man."

Unbeknownst to Atkins, his captain and most of the crew had already been ambushed when they reached the beach that morning – discovering most of their weapons had been stolen while they inspected the hot pool. Seeing Maori in the distance carrying the loot they gave chase but realised discretion might be the better part of valour. Dragging their longboat back into the surf they rowed for the brig in the distance, coming under gunfire as they tried to leave.

Back on the brig, however, the die had already been cast. When chief Ngarara saw Atkins with a musket on the top deck, he didn't stop to ask questions but simply whipped his pistol from beneath his cloak, already cocked, and shot one of the *Haweis* deckhands in the back of the head from just a few paces away. The remaining crew, except for the Tahitian, were quickly picked off. Within a minute of the gunshots, writes Atkins, "three large war canoes were alongside, which had been laying concealed behind the rocks", and "then began the plunder of the ship."

The Tahitian had run to Atkins to try and grab a musket in self defence, but the advancing iwi fired a volley that shattered bones in Atkins' arm just as he was about to return fire. The two survivors were swiftly captured and bundled into one of the canoes for the journey back to shore.

The big canoes, Atkins noted, were being filled with supplies from the ship, particularly the muskets, pistols and gunpowder barrels. That decision to overload the waka with plunder came back to bite the Whakatane iwi on the backside as they ran into heavy surf approaching the beach – many of the weapons were lost when the waka overturned.

Atkins and the Tahitian were separated, but the Pacific Islander's fate was worse. "On the third day of my capture…a native brought me the head of one of my unfortunate shipmates; it was the Otaheitian steward." He had, Atkins learned, been shot five times the following day and beheaded, with the skull kept for shrinkage and preservation as a trophy.

"The practice of preserving heads is universal among the New Zealanders," he remarked, "they bring them as trophies from their wars, and in the event of peace restore them to their families, this interchange being necessary to their reconciliation."

Necessary, perhaps, but evidently not compulsory. "They now frequently barter them with Europeans for a little gunpowder."

Convinced his own head would be dished up on a plate in the near future, Atkins was pleasantly surprised to find himself still alive next morning and the tribe distracted by a rumour that Tauranga Maori had heard of the insult to the Pakeha ship and were coming to avenge it.

Chief Ngarara himself approached Atkins and asked him to prophesy on the problem, using a ship's sextant which had belonged to the *Haweis* captain. The second officer decided to play the game, using the sextant to stare earnestly into the sky, then hastening to examine one of the ship's books that had been plundered. Finally, drawing in his breath, Atkins looked Ngarara in the eye: "I told him the Towrenga people would come against him with hostile intentions. He inquired, 'when?' with much agitation, and, scarcely knowing what I said, I replied, 'Tomorrow'."

The chief seemed happy with the answer and immediately ordered his tribe to bring their fortifications up to scratch. None was more surprised however than John Atkins when, at dawn the next morning, he heard the sound of muskets.

"In a few minutes Ngarara came running to my hut, informing me of the attack of the Towrenga people as I had predicted."

The Tauranga tribe were prevented from crossing the river by fierce gunfire, and afterwards Ngarara was calling Atkins an "Attoah" [atua], or 'god'. Atkins was forced to watch however as captured Tauranga warriors were "embowelled and cooked, and, from the satisfaction displayed by both sexes at this horrible repast, I am persuaded they prefer human flesh to any other food."

During his time in the Whakatane encampment, Atkins got a chance to see village daily life first hand, particularly the role of the women.

"In complexion they are as fair as Italians, are generally short, but well made and handsome. They are subject to great brutality from their husbands, which they bear with exemplary fortitude and patience.

"They are faithful and affectionate wives, and regard the children they rear with the greatest fondness. An appalling practice, however, prevails among them: that of destroying their female infants should they exceed in number the male issue.

"This is done by the mother herself at the birth of the child, and is effected by pressing her finger on the opening of the skull."[62]

Atkins didn't know it, but freedom was near.

---

[62] This is believed to be one of the big causes of the so-called "Maori holocaust": by killing off their female (ergo, child-bearing) offspring, the Maori population was not well placed to repopulate after many of their fertile men and women were killed in the Musket Wars. See also Dr John Robinson's article on this point at http://www.investigatemagazine.co.nz/Investigate/?p=2717

After fleeing the beach under gunfire, the *Haweis* captain and crew had soon realised their sailing ship had been captured, and instead rowed their longboat furiously up the Bay of Plenty coast, eventually being picked up by another vessel and rescued.

The captain of the rescue ship decided to recapture the *Haweis* from the Maori, but when they arrived the boat was deserted.

"On boarding her," wrote Atkins in his report, "they were shocked with the appalling spectacle of fragments of human flesh scattered about the decks, with the remains of a fire, from which they immediately concluded their shipmates had been all of them massacred and devoured."

Saddened, it was they who had sailed back to Tauranga and raised the alarm, which had in turn prompted Tauranga iwi to declare war on Whakatane. One of the Tauranga tribe had learnt from his Whakatane contacts that Atkins was still alive and being held hostage, which was a further incentive for the military action. After the abortive raid, the *Haweis* captain decided to trade two muskets with Chief Ngarara in return for the life of John Atkins.[163]

It was, again, a salutary lesson that even in 1829 you could take nothing for granted in New Zealand.

Nonetheless, change was afoot. As the musket wars raged in the interior and death rained down on a scale not normally seen, Maori who had initially been reticent about the Gospel suddenly flocked to it, finding comfort in the Bible as a spiritual refuge from the hell all around them. The ideas of a life after death, and a God who healed wounds on the inside, freed the slaves and forgave sin, these were powerful messages that resonated with a people struggling to reconcile their own long-established cultural practices like cannibalism, head-hunting, slavery, utu and war, with the obvious abhorrence that white settlers were showing for it.

To Maori, eating one's enemy as an act of revenge and disgust had a strong political element, yet they were becoming increasingly embarrassed as they realised others didn't share the same view of it. What had once been acceptable within monocultural Maori society was not in a bicultural one, and Maori had seen enough of European culture to know it was technologically and socially advanced and they wanted more of it. Those who had seen the bright lights of Sydney and London, or served on ships plying ports like Rio de Janeiro and Cape Town, and seen beasts

---

163 Chief Ngarara, evidently fancying himself as somewhat of a pirate, apparently tried to pull the stunt on another sailing ship just a few months later, and got shot dead for his troubles by a Ngapuhi warrior on board who realised what was going down.

like elephants and lions, had come back with stories of wonder to share with their tribes in front of flickering campfires.

There were still big cultural clashes, however, and responsibility for those fell on Pakeha and Maori alike.

One such incident was the wreck of the brig *Harriet* – the ship involved in the capture of the *Wellington* in the Bay of Islands. In the early 1830s the *Harriet* was shipwrecked on the Taranaki coast. Under prevailing Maori cultural law, local iwi did not come to rescue the helpless crew of the *Harriet* but to plunder the stricken ship. This wasn't especially aimed at Pakeha; the Maori treated their own shipwreck survivors exactly the same.[164] The *Harriet's* crew, naturally upset at this turn of events, got into a scrap with Maori who were following their cultural traditions, and it didn't go well. Several of the *Harriet's* crew were killed, and the skipper's wife and children and some of the crew ended up as hostages at the local pa.

The skipper travelled to Sydney to plead for military intervention to rescue his family.

"As a matter of fact," noted historian William Pember-Reeves,[165] "it was the misconduct of his own men which had brought on the fighting, and even to his Sydney hearers it was obvious that his tale was not wholly true. But the main facts were correct. There had been a wreck and plunder; there were captives."

The Man-o-War HMS *Alligator* was dispatched to Taranaki to effect a rescue, along with the skipper and one of his mates from Kororareka. It was the latter two who went ashore to negotiate for the return of the hostages, and the price they agreed to was a keg of gunpowder.

When the *Alligator's* captain came onshore to oversee the hostage release, Harriet's skipper 'forgot' to mention that he'd bargained a keg of the *Alligator's* gunpowder as part of the deal. All of the crew members were released into *Alligator's* care on the beach, but the wife and children were held back until the ship agreed to keep to the agreement.

Alligator's captain was having none of it, and instead seized the tribe's chief negotiator as a hostage and took him back to the warship where he was beaten to within an inch of his life. The tribe agreed to release the wife and one child to secure their negotiator's release, but the other

---

164 One missionary was stunned one day to see a tribe's canoes, while making a friendly visit to another tribe, overturn in the tide. Immediately, the hosts swooped on the visitors, not to save them from drowning but to plunder their possessions under the rules of tikanga.
165 *The Long White Cloud* by William Pember Reeves, 1898, Allen & Unwin, London, chapter eight, see http://www.nzetc.org/tm/scholarly/tei-ReeLong-t1-body-d1-d8.html

child remained in tribal custody until the gunpowder was brought to the beach, as originally promised.

"Again," writes Pember-Reeves, "a strong-armed party was landed, and was peacefully met by the natives, who brought the child down but still asked, naturally, for the stipulated ransom. The sailors and soldiers settled the matter by shooting down a chief, on whose shoulders the child was sitting, and firing right and left before the officers in charge could stop them. Next day, these men made a football of the chief's head.

"Before departing, the *Alligator* bombarded a pa, and her crew burnt villages and destroyed canoes and cultivations…[exciting] disgust by these doings even as far away as England.

"The whole proceeding was clumsy, cruel and needless. A trifling ransom would have saved it all. The Maori tribal law under which wrecks were confiscated and castaways plundered was, of course, intolerable. Whites again and again suffered severely by it. But blundering and undisciplined violence and broken promises were not the arguments to employ against it.

"So long as England deliberately chose to leave the country in the hands of barbarians," wrote Pember-Reeves with just a hint of cultural snobbery, "barbaric customs had to be reckoned with."

Taming the "barbarian" was a tough job, however, and the historian reckons it was purely down to the missionaries' hard work that progress was made during the 1830s:

"Missionaries were labouring along the coasts and in many districts of the interior, and as the decade neared its end, a large minority of the natives were being brought under the influence of Christianity."[166]

Pember-Reeves also reinforced the point made earlier – that the quickest way to end the musket wars was in fact to give everyone muskets:

"The tribal wars were dying down. Partly, this was a peace of exhaustion, in some districts of solitude; partly, it was the outcome of the havoc wrought by the musket, and the growing fear thereof.

"Nearly all the tribes had now obtained firearms. A war had ceased to be an agreeable shooting party for one chief with an unfair advantage over his rivals. A balance of power, or at any rate an equality of risk, made for peace.

"But it would be unjust to overlook the missionaries' share in bringing about comparative tranquillity. Throughout all the wars of the musket, and the dread slaughter and confusion they brought about, most of the teachers held on. They laboured for peace, and at length those to whom

166   *The Long White Cloud* by William Pember Reeves, 1898, Allen & Unwin, London, chapter eight, see http://www.nzetc.org/tm/scholarly/tei-ReeLong-t1-body-d1-d8.html

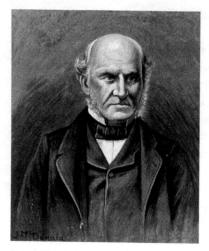

British Resident James Busby

they spoke began to cease to make themselves ready unto battle."

Yet still New Zealand lacked an effective justice system. Broadly speaking there were four subgroups of Pakeha now living in New Zealand: missionaries; traders; whalers and sealers; and lastly the so-called 'Pakeha Maori' – Europeans who had 'gone bush' or married into Maori tribes. The largest settlement in the country was Kororareka, now evolved today into picturesque Russell, famously described by Charles Darwin as "the hellhole of the Pacific" who also remarked that "the majority of the British there were the refuse of society".

With up to a thousand Pakeha in residence at any one time, mostly low-rent seafarers and traders peppered with freed convicts from New South Wales, Kororareka had a taste for wine, women and song, fuelled by men who "found among the rum shops and Maori houris of Kororareka a veritable South Sea Island paradise," wrote Pember-Reeves.

"The Maori chiefs of the neighbourhood shared their orgies, pandered to their vices, and grew rich thereby. An occasional murder reminded the whites that Maori forbearance was limited." When justice needed to be done, he says, "they arrested certain of the most unbearable offenders, tarred and feathered them, and drummed them out of the township. When feathers were lacking for the decoration, the white fluff of the native bulrush made a handy substitute."

There were still people alive in 1831 who'd been children and young adults when French Captain Marion du Fresne had met his end in a Bay of Islands oven. These Maori well remembered French justice – the full firepower of two ships and their crews that obliterated a Maori pa. The stories of the French reaction had spread far and wide over the years, and every time the French flag flew into New Zealand waters local iwi became increasingly twitchy. The Brits, they'd become used to. The French? Not so much. So when a French naval vessel appeared off the coast in 1831, thirteen northern chiefs – acting on advice from the missionaries – sent a letter to Britain seeking protection.

Britain's answer was not guns and marines, but the international man of mystery, Busby. James Busby. Britain's agent in New Zealand. Johnny English without the humour or, as Pember-Reeves like to call it, "a farce without laughter". Busby had once escaped an assassination attempt at his Waitangi home when a disgruntled chief lurking on the verandah one evening shot Busby's shadow on the curtains, rather than Busby himself.[167] Described by the same writer as "well-meaning, small-minded", and like "a man-of-war without guns" because his position was largely symbolic, Busby was nonetheless the bureaucratic glue that held the fledgling state of New Zealand together in the decade leading up to Waitangi.

Like the Maori and the missionaries, he too was worried France, in the form of Baron Charles de Thierry or worse, would take formal possession of New Zealand in the absence of any clear British intention to do so.

One of his first opportunities to pounce came in late 1835 when strong rumours circulated that the Baron was finally planning to establish a French colony on the 40,000 acres in Hokianga that he'd purchased from Hongi Hika in London all those years ago. De Thierry had written to Busby from his current perch in Tahiti, saying that he planned to arrive in New Zealand soon and hoped to become "Lord and Governor" of New Zealand. Busby swiftly organised a meeting of northern chiefs at his home, where he had hammered out a Declaration of Independence for them to sign.

Essentially, the Declaration recognised New Zealand as a sovereign state in its own right, where sovereignty vested in the hereditary chiefs of the "United Tribes" of New Zealand. By declaring their own sovereignty, the Chiefs were effectively telling France, "go away, this land is spoken for".

While the Governor of New South Wales, who was not overly enamoured of Busby, dismissed the document as a "silly and unauthorised act...a paper pellet fired off", nonetheless the deed was done.

Busby, however, knew he was pushing his luck but told the Baron in a letter that he had no choice:

"I have acted on the discretion which...I have considered it my duty to exercise, under circumstances of so extraordinary a character. But even had I been entrusted with no powers at all in this respect, I should have thought it my duty upon the broad principles of common justice

---

167   Busby was not entirely disliked. Charles Darwin recounted a story of a group of young Maori men reading the bible late one night by candlelight. "Afterwards they knelt down and prayed. In their prayers they mentioned Mr Busby, and his family, and each of the missionaries." Darwin's Letter on New Zealand and Tahiti, *South African Christian Recorder*, 1836

and humanity to have used whatever influence I possessed to prevent the occurrence of so much mischief as would be the inevitable result of an attempt upon the liberties of a free people."[168]

Historians have generally regarded Busby as overreacting to the de Thierry letter and its ambitions. That's probably fair comment, but hindsight is a wonderful gift to the cynical. The facts as Busby and the missionaries saw them were that Britain had consistently refused to take formal possession of New Zealand, leaving in place a legal power vacuum. It was open to any state willing to throw military might (or lots of bribes to the tribes) into the equation to try their luck in New Zealand. It was also not beyond the realms of possibility that if a French Baron brought a shipload of French settlers and colonised a 40,000 hectare block in the name of France, that it might be seen back in Paris as an opportunity handed them on a plate.

The French, of course, did indeed nurse such ambitions and were only narrowly beaten to the post by the Treaty of Waitangi declaration – the tiny 1840 settlement of Akaroa on Banks Peninsula a lasting testament to France's dashed hopes. While the name of "The New Zealand Company" looms large in our official histories, no one now recalls "The Nanto-Bordelaise Company" – the French equivalent, whose shareholders included King Louis-Philippe. The arrival of French Catholic Bishop Jean-Baptiste Pompallier in New Zealand in 1837 as the head of the Roman Catholic church in New Zealand was not entirely coincidental.

For their part, Busby and the missionaries felt they could force Britain's hand, by taking matters into their own. And indeed, that's exactly what they did. The decree set in train events that would eventually culminate at Waitangi.

The Declaration of Independence emboldened New South Wales "land sharks" into trying to do vast land deals with Maori tribes. They sensed colonisation was now only a matter of time, and wanted to scoop up as much land as they could at bargain basement prices, to on-sell to settlers.

One such shark was Sydney-based William Charles Wentworth, who signed a deed with six visiting Maori in New South Wales to buy the entire South Island of New Zealand for one hundred pounds sterling.

It would be wrong, however, to quantify the early land deals as evil Pakeha fleecing innocent Maori, which is pretty much the plotline of modern victim mythology as taught in New Zealand schools. Sure, there

---

168 Letter, Busby to de Thierry, 30 October 1835, see www.nzetc.org/tm/scholarly/tei-HydChee-t1-body-d10-d2.html

were some that were, but Maori were just as much into a bit of trading entertainment as the next person.

"Maori often played the game in quite the same spirit," explained Pember-Reeves in his history of New Zealand, "selling land which they did not own, or had no power to dispose of, again and again. In some cases diamond cut diamond. In others, both sides were playing a part, and neither cared for the land to pass. The land-shark wanted a claim with which to harass others; the Maori signed a worthless document on receipt of a few goods."

It was an easy way for a tribe to gain a few warm blankets and tin cups, without actually ever facing a real risk of losing their land. The real victims in most cases were the mug settlers who paid out vastly inflated sums for a bit of beachfront South Island land, only to later discover the deeds were as worthless as a plot of land on the Moon.

Baron Charles de Thierry, in fact, was the victim of exactly this kind of rort. Having paid a sum of a thousand pounds to Hongi Hika for 40,000 acres in the Hokianga, when he actually arrived in New Zealand in 1837 to claim his allotment he discovered Hongi Hika's tribe had resold the land to others, and were only prepared to give him 800 acres – less than one fortieth of what he'd paid for. Now, you can argue that a thousand pounds for 40,000 acres was a joke price anyway, but pretty much the same price purchased most of Banks Peninsula for the French. More to the point, Hongi Hika used de Thierry's money to buy 400 military muskets, giving him military superiority and conquest across the North Island. The value to Nga Puhi of that land trade in terms of power and wealth far exceeded the value to de Thierry. Nobody, after all, ever got seriously rich in the Hokianga.

Nonetheless, it was obvious to everyone that if land speculation wasn't quashed and a system of law and order brought in, it would only be a matter of time before a group of settlers who'd been misled by speculators would end up in violent clashes with Maori over land.

In addition to the Australian land-sharks, Busby's declaration document had well and truly put the cat among the pigeons back in London.

CHAPTER EIGHT

From Wakefield To Waitangi

Edward Gibbon Wakefield's name lives on in this country on street signs and in the name of a town. His influence on the New Zealand we have today is far greater. Born in the late 1790s and after a brief career as a diplomatic courier, he eloped at the age of 20 with a 17 year old heiress, and gained a £70,000 dowry in the process. Suddenly he was a wealthy man, but Wakefield wanted more. After wife Eliza died in childbirth, a now 31 year old Wakefield eloped with a 15 year old girl hoping to repeat the stunt. This time, however, her parents disapproved and had Wakefield arrested and charged with abduction and fraud. He cooled his heels in Newgate Prison for three years, emerging into the daylight in 1829 with a new vision for society.

Sick of the class structure of Britain, Wakefield wrote of how utopian societies could be created in new colonies like New Zealand. His vision was to buy land cheap and sell it high, reinvesting the profits from land sales into building infrastructure – roads, schools, hospitals, and the purchase of ship passenger tickets for more new migrants – everything a new colony needed.

While he'd been in jail others had tried and failed to get colonisation of New Zealand on the agenda, but Wakefield had a passion and was determined to see it through. His enemies were many, particularly the influential group of Christian MPs led by William Wilberforce who'd been crucial to getting slavery abolished. Wilberforce and his supporters felt Britain had treated the American Indians, and the African and Caribbean people, appallingly during previous colonisations. While professing to be a Christian country, he said, Britain had not acted with Christian principles toward their fellow human beings. They were

Edward Gibbon Wakefield, founder of New Zealand

determined that New Zealand would not become just another notch on the colonialists' belts.

Undeterred, Wakefield submitted his plans for the "New Zealand Association" to the British Prime Minister, Lord Melbourne, a favourite of the newly-crowned Queen Victoria. Melbourne kicked for touch, asking Colonial Secretary Lord Glenelg to look into the idea. Glenelg's deputy, evangelical Christian and supporter of the Church Missionary Society, Sir James Stephen, scorned the plan:

"It proposes the acquisition of a sovereignty in New Zealand which would infallibly issue in the conquest and extermination of the present inhabitants."[169]

While an 1836 parliamentary report had recommended a more formal role for Britain in New Zealand, it wasn't so keen on colonisation, for similar reasons to those later expressed by Stephen.

Britain, it said, should "devise a system of intercourse with uncivilised nations more consonant to justice and humanity, more in unison with the high character which Great Britain ought to maintain."[170]

Before nodding your head in absolute agreement with the undeniably noble aims being expressed, it's worth sparing a thought for the template Britain was wanting to adopt. Many of the small island states and African states ended up being administered in precisely that way, where tribal customs and structures were absolutely maintained and a British administrative structure was simply laid over the top. The image of retired colonels sipping gin and tonic in the sunset while the lot of the natives was pretty much ignored comes to mind.

New Zealand was approaching a fork in the road. Without widespread colonisation, Maori would indeed be left with control of their own resources, but without any major influx of British wealth and investment in their country. With colonisation, control of their country would be sacrificed to a large extent, but the tradeoff might be the much faster access to Pakeha technology and investment that came with it. The dilemma was similar to that facing entrepreneurs seeking capital to develop an invention: you can own 100% of something quite small, or 49% of something quite large but which you no longer control.

If anything, this is the defining moment for all the treaty debates that have followed: "if not this, then what?" You can argue that 70,000 to 100,000 Maori could make a go of it on their own as a nation, but tribal

---

169 C.O. 209/2
170 UK Parl. Pap. Reports, 1836, VII, 1-853

history across all cultures in the world shows tribalism is an unworkable form of national government. Comparatively recent genocides of millions in Africa and Asia last century were mostly ethnically or tribally based, and are simply replays on a larger scale of the Maori Musket Wars a century earlier.

Maori had arguably been in New Zealand for 600 years, and achieved a peak population of 100,000 in that time. The tribal customs of throwing the sick and the pregnant outside into the cold so as not to defile the sleeping huts, and refusing to feed them, had a huge impact on infant and adult mortality, as did the practice of killing baby girls at birth. The frequent tribal wars killed many men and women of child-bearing age, with a huge generational impact on Maori population growth.

The question readers honestly have to ask themselves, no matter which side of the debate they sit on, is whether tino rangatiratanga could genuinely have delivered a prosperous future for Maori, or whether New Zealand would have been just another sleepy (or alternatively war-wracked) Pacific Island state, only larger?

There are a range of possible answers to that question, and there will be some who argue that sovereignty and mana are more important issues than making a buck or having a vibrant economy. There are also good arguments that many Maori, particularly those in rural, semi-tribal communities where they do still have a strong sense of marae life, nonetheless still live subsistence lives. The answer to all these is 'Perhaps'. But in truth, you were just offered a construct of the issue that didn't contain *all* the relevant information: the problem facing Maori and Missionary alike in 1837 was the very real prospect that while London twiddled its thumbs debating the "noble savage" concept and whether Maori could rise above tribal infighting and utu, everyone back in New Zealand – Maori and settler alike – might end up speaking French as their native language.

The reason the French were keen on the South Island was because there was practically no one there. It would have been a piece of gateau for the French navy to have taken formal possession of the South Island and held it, thus gaining a springboard to colonisation of the North Island.

The Nanto-Bordelaise Company of Paris, counting the French king as an investor, was shoe-horning itself into New Zealand through the Banks Peninsula purchase that a private French citizen had negotiated. That same colonisation structure could just have easily been utilised to piggy-back in on Charles de Thierry's Hokianga purchase in the North Island.

As *History of the British Empire* puts the dilemma:

"The remoteness of the country [NZ] seemed to the British Government an unanswerable objection to colonisation until its hand was forced by Edward Gibbon Wakefield, by the French, and by its own sense of duty to protect the Maori from further exploitation by British subjects."

The Reverend Samuel Marsden, back in Sydney after a visit to the Hokianga, wrote to his mentor in the Church Missionary Society in London, the Reverend Dandeson Coates – an outspoken opponent of colonisation. While Coates certainly maintained that position in his London speeches, it must have been hard given what Marsden was telling him:

"A number of Europeans are settled along with the natives. Several Europeans keep public houses, and encourage every kind of crime. Here, drunkenness, adultery, murder, etc, are committed. There are no laws, Judges or Magistrates, so that Satan maintains his dominion without molestation.[171]

"Some civilised Government must take New Zealand under its protection," insisted Marsden, "or the most dreadful evils will be committed from runaway convicts and sailors and publicans. There are no laws here to punish crimes."

In sharp contrast, he noted, many of the Hokianga Maori were now followers of Jesus Christ. "I found many were enquiring after the Saviour, and a large number attended public worship. One principal chief who has embraced the Gospel and has been baptised, accompanied us all the way [on a 40 mile journey through the forest to Waimate]. He told me he was so unhappy at Hokianga that he could not get to converse with me [because of] the crowds that attended, that he had come to Waimate to speak with me. The schools and church are well attended, and the greatest order is observed amongst all classes."

Ironic, perhaps, that as Maori accelerated away from the stone age and into the modern era, that their secular European colleagues were on the reverse journey, in Marsden's eyes.

That same year, elaborating on the urgent need for civil government, Marsden wrote:

"You are aware there are no laws in New Zealand; there is no king. They feel the want of this, and they cannot make a king from their own chiefs, as every chief would think himself degraded if he should be put under the authority of a chief of their own."[172]

---

171 Letter, Marsden to D Coates, 27 March 1837, see http://www.nzetc.org/tm/scholarly/tei-McN01Hist-t1-b10-d77.html

172 Letter, Marsden to Jowett, 11 August 1837, see http://www.nzetc.org/tm/scholarly/tei-McN01Hist-t1-b10-d79.html Marsden's health was badly failing by this stage. His final letter to the Church Missionary Society, in April 1838, noted how he'd been a pastor to New South

In June 1837, the UK Parliament's House Select Committee on Aborigines in British Settlements delivered its report into colonisation options. Recommendations included that areas colonised should have their own colonial governments, but that responsibility for the welfare of aborigines should not fall into local government hands because of an inherent conflict of interest – a settler majority may force their advantage over an unprotected native population. Instead, the Committee proposed that native affairs should be directly controlled by Britain, through an appointed Governor.[173]

The Committee also took a dim view of signing treaties with native peoples, on the grounds that the two parties would be so far apart in terms of legal understanding that it would be a recipe for disaster, and treaties "are rather the preparatives and the apology for disputes than securities for peace...a ready pretext for complaint will be found in the ambiguity of language in which their agreements will be drawn up."

The Committee's solution however, was that "disengagement" model of colonial administration we looked at a moment ago – leave the Maori to their own devices with a minimal administration:

"The safety and welfare of an uncivilised race require that their relations with their more cultivated neighbours should be diminished rather than multiply."

To a large extent, that policy was adopted in Australia, where the lack of social integration on a daily basis created a "them and us" nation. By the time Australia realised its light-handed approach to aboriginals had left those people languishing too far back in the neolithic, its solution – stealing their children to bring them up with white families – swung too far the other way.

Again, had the Committee's policy actually been adopted for New Zealand, how would Maori society be today when compared with, say, Australia or the United States? The colonisation of New Zealand was never going to be simple, it was always going to involve a tradeoff. To adopt a cannibal analogy, they couldn't have their mana and eat it too.

Wales and later New Zealand since 1793 – a period of 45 years straight – "My eyes are very dim; it is with difficulty I can read or write...I have an intention to visit the missionaries in New Zealand if my strength will permit". It didn't. He died shortly afterwards. His role in creating the modern nation of New Zealand cannot be overstated. See his final letter at http://www.nzetc.org/tm/scholarly/tei-McN01Hist-t1-b10-d83.html
173 This, incidentally, is where New Zealand's dirty dealing over the Treaty arose – because in the decades after the Treaty was signed the colonial government took upon itself responsibility for native affairs and then cheated Maori when the government's interests conflicted with Maori interests.

The price of innovation and progress was integration, and integration meant compromise on all sides.

Edward Gibbon Wakefield's New Zealand Association meanwhile was fighting a bitter political battle for permission to colonise New Zealand. Lord Glenelg, head of the Colonial Office and – like Sir James Stephen – a supporter of the Church Mission Society, was coming under heavy fire in parliament for failing to protect the Maori as he was promising his system would:

"Not less than 2,000 British subjects have settled in New Zealand," thundered Wakefield supporter, MP Sir William Molesworth in one debate, "that as many as 200 of them are absconded convicts; that they are not subject to any law or authority; that they do exactly what pleases them; that they have pleased to commit crimes towards the natives at which humanity shudders; and that, in fact, the native race is rapidly disappearing before them.[174]

"What has the noble lord, who should have been most conversant with this evil and this danger, what has he done?" challenged Molesworth as he moved a vote of no confidence in Lord Glenelg as Colonial Secretary.

Glenelg, in fact, was already wilting. The previous Christmas just a few weeks earlier he'd written:

"The repression of practices of the most injurious tendency to the natives of New Zealand[175] can, as it would seem, be accomplished only by the establishment of some settled form of government within that territory.

"The only question therefore, is between a colonisation, desultory, without law, and fatal to the natives, and a colonisation organised and salutary."[176]

---

174 Sir William Molesworth, 6 March 1838, UK Hansard, 3rd ser., XLI, 476

175 One of those scandals was the "Girl Wars" at Kororareka in 1830, when a whaling ship captain shacked up with a Maori girl and carrying 50 Maori women on his ship incited intertribal warfare that left around 70 Maori dead or wounded, and bodies left "lying on the beach". To add insult to injury, the victorious tribe had chopped off the heads of the vanquished and sold them to European traders who were flogging the trophies off in Sydney. Maori took the view that seeing as a Pakeha had started the fight, Pakeha should pay the penalty for it, and wanted to know what British justice, in the form of Reverend Samuel Marsden, was going to do about it. Reporting to Governor Darling in Sydney, Marsden writes of his dilemma: "Your Excellency is aware there is no legal authority, civil, military or naval, to restrain the bad conduct of the masters and crews of those ships which put into the harbours of New Zealand, nor to notice their crimes, however great; and from the great quantity of arms, powder, and ammunition now in the possession of the natives there is much reason to apprehend that they will at some period redress their own wrongs by force of arms, if no remedy is provided to do them justice." Letter, Marsden to Darling, 2 August 1830, see www.nzetc.org/tm/scholarly/tei-McN01Hist-t1-b10-d66.html

176 Appendix No. 8 to Report of Select Committee on New Zealand, UK A. and P., 1840, VII, 447

By the end of 1838 and more parliamentary scraps between the Christians and the lions of empire, the lions had formed an investment organisation, the New Zealand Company, with which to raise funds for the colonisation. They purchased a ship, the *Tory*, and began scouting for land to purchase.

In the end, it was probably French pressure that finally put the wind in Britain's sails. Reports published in the French press indicated France was looking to establish a penal colony in New Zealand, much like Australia was to England. The missionaries knew the impact of that on

The Tory, Wellington Harbour

New Zealand would be horrific, and in the end they had to weigh up whether their continued opposition to British colonisation and its impact on Maori would be as bad as French colonisation by convicts.

On December 12, 1838, Lord Glenelg of the Colonial Office announced he was considering appointing a British Consul to administer British affairs in New Zealand. Lord Palmerston at the Foreign Office agreed to cover the costs of the position on 31 December 1838. Bureaucrats opposed to colonisation managed to slow things down in red tape.

Downing Street was groaning inwardly at the factional warfare over the fate of New Zealand. As William Pember-Reeves wrote in 1898:

"The word 'colony' was not in favour when William the Fourth came to the throne. It was associated with memories of defeat and humiliation in America, and with discontent and mutterings of rebellion in Canada. Australia was scarcely more than an expensive convict station. Against the West Indian planters the crusade of Wilberforce was in full progress, and the very name of 'plantation' had an evil savour. South Africa promised little but the plentiful race troubles, which indeed came. The timid apathy of the Colonial Office was no more than the reflex of the dead indifference of the nation. None but a man of genius could have breathed life into it. Fortunately the genius appeared."

That genius, he says, was Wakefield who, refusing to wait for official permission, simply loaded his pioneers onto the *Tory* and set sail for the antipodes in May 1839, in secret. When news of that leaked, French news media became outraged that Britain was on the verge of colonising New Zealand and whipped the French government into sending their own fleet down under. It was a drag race. Suddenly Downing Street was back in the picture with a vengeance.

That same month, May 1839, Britain's Secretary of State, the Marquess of Normanby, fired off a request for legal advice from the Attorney-General. Initially, only a partial declaration of sovereignty was being considered, so that all land purchased by non-Maori became British territory:

"It is proposed to obtain from the chiefs of New Zealand the cession in sovereignty to the British Crown of the territories which have been, or which may be, acquired by Her Majesty's subjects by proprietary titles, derived from the grants of the different chiefs. It is further desired, if possible, to add the sovereignty thus obtained to the Colony of New South Wales as a dependency, in the same manner as Norfolk Island, which is nearly equidistant from Port Jackson, and is now a dependency of the same colony."[177]

Whilst such a minimalist approach to sovereignty might have appealed to those who had never wanted colonisation in the first place, it was thoroughly impractical. One paddock here would be British, the paddock next to it Maori, and so on through the country like a patchwork quilt.

Two weeks later, James Stephen sent a letter to Treasury, noting that "certain parts of the Islands of New Zealand should be added to the colony of New South Wales as a dependency."[178] Stephen confirmed Captain William Hobson of the Royal Navy had been chosen as Consul, and would also now assume the title Lieutenant-Governor on a salary of £500 per annum.

"It will probably also be necessary to provide for the appointment of a Judge, of a Public Prosecutor, of a Colonial Secretary, of a Police establishment, of a Treasurer, and of the subordinate officers of revenue," Stephen added.

It was the bean-counters in Treasury, not the Attorney-General, who first raised questions about how precisely this new British territory was going

---

177   Letter, Normanby to Attorney-General, 30 May 1839, see www.nzetc.org/tm/scholarly/tei-McN01Hist-t1-b10-d121.html
178   Letter, James Stephen to Spearman, 13 June 1839, see http://www.nzetc.org/tm/scholarly/tei-McN01Hist-t1-b10-d122.html

to be annexed. They insisted that all this "should be strictly contingent upon the indispensable preliminary of the territorial cession having been obtained by amicable negociation with and free concurrence of the native chiefs."[179]

In August 1839, Captain Hobson received his marching orders.[180]

"Her Majesty's Government," wrote Secretary of State Normanby, "have watched these proceedings with attention and solicitude. We have not been insensible to the importance of New Zealand to the interests of

Governor William Hobson

Great Britain in Australia, nor unaware of the great natural resources by which that country is distinguished, or that its geographical position must, in seasons either of peace or war, enable it in the hands of civilised men to exercise a paramount influence in that quarter of the globe. There is probably no part of the earth in which colonization could be effected with a greater or surer prospect of national advantage."

Lord Normanby's praise was followed by an almighty 'but':

"On the other hand, the Ministers of the Crown have been restrained by still higher motives from engaging in such an enterprise. They have deferred to the advice of the Committee appointed by the House of Commons in the year 1836 to enquire into the state of the aborigines residing in the vicinity of our colonial settlements, and have concurred with that Committee in thinking that the increase of national wealth and power promised by the acquisition of New Zealand would be a most inadequate compensation for the injury which must be inflicted on this Kingdom itself by embarking in a measure essentially unjust, and but too certainly fraught with calamity to a numerous and inoffensive people, whose title to the soil and to the sovereignty of New Zealand is indisputable, and

---

179 Letter, Pennington to James Stephen, 22 June 1839, see http://www.nzetc.org/tm/scholarly/tei-McN01Hist-t1-b10-d128.html
180 Lord Normanby's instructions to Captain Hobson, 14 August 1839, see http://www.nzetc.org/tm/scholarly/tei-McN01Hist-t1-b10-d120.html

has been solemnly recognised by the British Government.

"We retain these opinions in unimpaired force, and though circumstances entirely beyond our control have at length compelled us to alter our course, I do not scruple to avow that we depart from it with extreme reluctance," remarked Normanby.

However, he added, Britain's hand had been forced, firstly by escaped convicts, and latterly by land-sharks:

"It further appears that extensive cessions of land have been obtained from the natives, and that several hundred persons have recently sailed from this country [in the *Tory*] to occupy and cultivate those lands. The spirit of adventure having been effectually roused, it can be no longer doubted that an extensive settlement of British subjects will be rapidly established in New Zealand, and that unless protected and restrained by necessary laws and institutions, they will repeat unchecked in that quarter of the globe the same process of war and spoliation under which uncivilised tribes have almost invariably disappeared.

"To mitigate, and, if possible, to avert these disasters, and to rescue the emigrants themselves from the evils of a lawless state of society, it has been resolved to adopt the most effective measures for establishing amongst them a settled form of civil government. To accomplish this design is the principal object of your mission.

"I have already stated that we acknowledge New Zealand as a sovereign and independent State, so far at least as it is possible to make that acknowledgment in favour of a people composed of numerous dispersed and petty tribes, who possess few political relations to each other, and are incompetent to act or even to deliberate in concert. But the admission of their rights, though inevitably qualified by this consideration, is binding on the faith of the British Crown.

"The Queen, in common with Her Majesty's immediate predecessor, disclaims for herself and her subjects every pretension to seize on the Islands of New Zealand, or to govern them as a part of the dominions of Great Britain, unless the free and intelligent consent of the natives, expressed according to their established usages, shall be first obtained. Believing, however, that their own welfare would, under the circumstances I have mentioned, be best promoted by the surrender to Her Majesty of a right now so precarious, and little more than nominal, and persuaded that the benefits of British protection and of laws administered by British Judges would far more than compensate for the sacrifice by the natives of a national independence which they are no longer able to maintain, Her

Majesty's Government have resolved to authorise you to treat with the aborigines of New Zealand for the recognition of Her Majesty's sovereign authority over the whole or any part of those islands which they may be willing to place under Her Majesty's dominion.

"I am not unaware of the difficulties by which such a treaty may be encountered. The motives by which it is recommended are of course open to suspicion. The natives may probably regard with distrust a proposal which may carry on the face of it the appearance of humiliation on their side and of a formidable encroachment on ours," stated Normanby to Hobson.

When it came to dealing with Maori on this issue, Normanby told Hobson to be open and frank:

"Especially, you will point out to them the dangers to which they may be exposed by the residence amongst them of settlers amenable to no laws or tribunals of their own, and the impossibility of Her Majesty extending to them any effectual protection, unless the Queen be acknowledged as the Sovereign of their country, or at least of those districts within or adjacent to which Her Majesty's subjects may acquire lands or habitations."

Now that last bit is an interesting point. As late as August 1839 Britain at the highest levels was still contemplating the possibility of only partial sovereignty in New Zealand, of a situation where in effect British rule presided in some parts, and Maori rule in another.

That certainly does not give rise to the modern idea of all New Zealanders being ruled over by Maori and the Crown in partnership, but it does allow for Maori self-governance of their own tribal lands. No one in the Foreign Office appeared to have figured out that partial sovereignty – the two paddock concept – was unworkable, even if it still looked good on paper.

To protect Maori from land-sharks, Normanby insisted that any deal had to include a guarantee that Maori would no longer sell their land directly to settlers, but only to the British Crown. Britain's idea was to follow the Wakefield concept: buy cheap, sell high, use the money as revenue for the infrastructure of the fledgling nation.

"You will, therefore, immediately on your arrival announce, by a Proclamation, addressed to all the Queen's subjects in New Zealand, that Her Majesty will not acknowledge as valid any title to land which either has been or shall hereafter be acquired in that country which is not either derived from or confirmed by a grant to be made in Her Majesty's name and on her behalf."

Although it sounded dire, Normanby told Hobson the intention wasn't to take back land that had been sold on fair terms, but merely to ratify fair trades and catch out sharks by virtue of Crown veto. As for the low prices to be paid to Maori tribes, there were good practical reasons, he explained:

"I thus assume that the price to be paid to the natives by the local Government will bear an exceedingly small proportion to the price for which the same lands will be resold by the Government to the settlers; nor is there any real injustice in this inequality. To the natives, or their chiefs, much of the land of the country is of no actual use, and in their hands it possesses scarcely any exchangeable value. Much of it must long remain useless, even in the hands of the British Government also, but its value in exchange will be first created, and then progressively increased by the introduction of capital and of settlers from this country. In the benefits of that increase the natives themselves will gradually participate.

"All dealings with the aborigines for their lands must be conducted on the same principles of sincerity, justice, and good faith as must govern your transactions with them for the recognition of Her Majesty's sovereignty in the islands. Nor is this all: they must not be permitted to enter into any contracts in which they might be ignorant and unintentional authors of injuries to themselves. You will not, for example, purchase from them any territory the retention of which by them would be essential or highly conducive to their own comfort, safety, or subsistence. The acquisition of land by the Crown for the future settlement of British subjects must be confined to such districts as the natives can alienate without distress or serious inconvenience to themselves."

On the subject of the social integration of Maori, Normanby seemed to contradict his earlier assertions as to partial sovereignty, by then anticipating British law in place over all, white and brown alike:

"The establishment of schools for the education of the aborigines in the elements of literature will be another object of your solicitude; and until they can be brought within the pale of civilised life, and trained to the adoption of its habits, they must be carefully defended in the observance of their own customs, so far as these are compatible with the universal maxims of humanity and morals. But the savage practices of human sacrifice and cannibalism must be promptly and decisively interdicted; such atrocities, under whatever plea of religion they may take place, are not to be tolerated in any part of the dominions of the British Crown."

This last point had Captain Hobson himself scratching his head. "May I request more explicit instruction on this important subject? Shall I be authorised, after the failure of every other means, to repress these diabolical acts by force: and what course am I to adopt to restrain the no less savage native wars?"[181]

Normanby's response the following day was swift, authorising "actual force" as a matter of last resort, "within any part of the Queen's dominions" for the purposes of stamping out cannibalism and human sacrifice. However, he added, it was more likely that growing Maori embarrassment at their practices would become more acute as Christian faith hit critical mass, and "the New Zealanders will probably yield a willing assent to your admonitions".[182]

There would be no military garrison, Normanby added, at least for the first while.

Hobson also had some questions on how to deal with the South Island, given that virtually no one lived there. Normanby shrugged: "If the country is really, as you suppose, uninhabited except by a very small number of persons in a savage state, incapable from their ignorance of entering intelligently into any treaties with the Crown, I agree with you that the ceremonial of making such arrangements with them would be a mere illusion and pretence, which ought to be avoided."

Judge it on the day, he told Hobson, and if you need to decree sovereignty by virtue of discovery, then so be it.

These, then, were the primary orders that Hobson sailed with from London, on his rendezvous with history at Waitangi.

---

181 Letter, Hobson to Under-Secretary of State, August 1839, see http://www.nzetc.org/tm/scholarly/tei-McN01Hist-t1-b10-d134.html
182 Letter, Normanby to Hobson, 15 August 1839, see http://www.nzetc.org/tm/scholarly/tei-McN01Hist-t1-b10-d135.html

CHAPTER NINE

The Littlewood Treaty

Hobson's ship berthed at Kororareka on January 29, 1840, the peak of the New Zealand summer. He issued his proclamation on land sales as ordered by Queen Victoria, then got down to the tricky business of drafting a treaty to put to Maori.

One of the big issues that's emerged in recent years is why the English version of the Treaty is so different from the Maori (signed) version of the Treaty. The sequence of events and a recent discovery may remove some of the mystery from this.

By February 1, Hobson and his secretary, James Freeman had knocked out a rough draft of a treaty text in English. British Resident James Busby, whose official reign had come to an end with Hobson's arrival, nonetheless found himself roped in to assist.

"When it became necessary to draw the Treaty, Captain Hobson was so unwell as to be unable to leave the ship. He sent the gentleman who was appointed Colonial Treasurer, and the Chief Clerk, with some notes, which they had put together as the basis of the Treaty, to ask my advice respecting them," Busby records.[183]

Busby found the rough draft, well, rough.

"I stated that I should not consider the propositions contained in those notes as calculated to accomplish the object, but offered to prepare the draft of a Treaty for Captain Hobson's consideration. To this they replied that that was precisely what Captain Hobson desired.

"The draft of the Treaty prepared by me was adopted by Captain Hobson without any other alteration than a transposition of certain sentences,

---

183   Appendix to Journals of the House of Representatives, 1861, E-02, page 67

which did not in any degree affect the sense," Busby wrote.

Busby may have been looking back on his participation through rose-coloured spectacles, because the Treaty draft of February 3 is the one in his handwriting that has become the official English text of the Treaty today. However, it must have been changed because – as stated earlier – its wording is quite different to the Maori version. What happened between February 3 and February 6?

We know, from historical records, that there was a final English version of the Treaty compiled on February 4, 1840, from which missionary Henry Williams and his son Edward were asked to translate a Maori version that could be presented to the chiefs on February 5 for consideration. But as historian Claudia Orange point out in her book, "The original draft, in English, on which Henry Williams based this Maori translation, has not been found."[184]

Lacking a final English draft, the New Zealand Government has been forced to go with a modified form of the draft Busby version of 3 February as the 'official' English text of the Treaty of Waitangi. It is this version that is found in the Treaty of Waitangi Act 1974, even though we know it was not the final version.

The mystery might have remained unsolved, but for a chance discovery in the bottom of a drawer in 1989. Ethel Littlewood of Pukekohe had recently passed away, and her children John Littlewood and Beryl Needham were working through her estate when Beryl found an old envelope tucked amidst papers in an old sideboard drawer.[185]

Opening the envelope, she found a hand-written version of the Treaty of Waitangi, signed by none other than "William Hobson, Consul & Lieut.-Governor" and dated 4 February, 1840.

The document was eventually sent to the National Archives in Wellington for analysis and, to cut a long story short, it has been forensically confirmed as a document written by James Busby, the man known to have written the final English draft from which the Maori translation of the Treaty was made. The *missing* English draft.

As you can see from the signatures in the photos, it certainly resembles Hobson's signature, but the point has never been finalised by scholars.

Some historians, while acknowledging Busby's authorship, have ques-

184   *The Treaty of Waitangi*, by Claudia Orange, 1987
185   The document was written on 1833 paper stock owned by James Clendon, named as one of those who helped work on the Treaty drafts. Clendon's solicitor was one Henry Littlewood, into whose possession the 4 February Treaty draft eventually ended up, forgotten in an old sideboard drawer passed down the family.

tioned whether the Littlewood Treaty is the missing English version, or just a later back-translation of the Maori version. They question why Busby would have bothered dating it, but the logical answer to that is to keep track of the different drafts floating around. It is unlikely to have been a later back-translation because, not long after the Treaty was signed, Governor Hobson suffered a massive stroke and his signature changed drastically. Critics who say it was just a keepsake English copy of the Maori text need to explain why, then, the Governor himself signed it, and by the same token, why anyone else signed it if were just a keepsake copy of the text. Then, if it were just a random exact copy, why is it in the handwriting of the man who actually wrote the final English treaty draft, James Busby? The challenges to the status of the Littlewood document may raise arguable points, but they breach the KISS principle - requiring the simplest explanation - at all levels.

Far more likely is that it was the February 4 draft, and Hobson probably signed it to show translators Henry and Edward Williams he was now happy with the text to be translated into Maori that night ready for discussion by the chiefs on February 5. It is known that Hobson and Busby were together for this final day of drafting, and that it was Hobson himself who handed the final draft to Henry Williams.

The key point about the Littlewood document, however, is that it is an almost exact match for the Maori text, making it a credible candidate as the 'official' English text, rather than the earlier draft currently carrying that title and used in legislation. Some critics have argued that it's irrelevant because the Maori version is the only one that was signed, however that overlooks the fact that the Government still uses the 'official' English version in law to justify some treaty actions.

You can read the full versions of the 'official' English text, the Littlewood text, the Maori text, and the English translation of the Maori text, in the Appendix at the back of this book.

However, the key differences are these. Article II of the 'official' English version states *"Her Majesty the Queen of England confirms and guarantees to the Chiefs and Tribes of New Zealand and to the respective families and individuals thereof"*, which appears to limit the benefits of the Treaty to Maori people only.

However, the Littlewood version says, *"The Queen of England confirms and guarantees to the chiefs and tribes and to all the people of New Zealand,"* implying the Treaty covers both Maori and the Pakeha settlers.

It is true, and you have seen it repeatedly in this book, that "New Zealanders" generally meant Maori in official documents in the years before Waitangi, but that was primarily in documents or reports to London written mostly by missionaries who saw themselves aloof, as mentors, for a people who they did not want colonised. They therefore did not include themselves as New Zealanders. By the time Waitangi rolled around, however, there were several thousand European residents of "New Zealand", and the vast majority of them were not missionaries.

The 'official' English text is primarily based on Busby's 3 February draft, so we can safely presume that by 4 February (the Littlewood text), he and Hobson had realised they needed to somehow sweep the existing Pakehas into the mix. There were, for example, Americans, Tahitians, French and other nationalities not normally subject to Queen Victoria's jurisdiction, living here as well.

The fact that Busby and Hobson intended the final Treaty to cover the tribes and "all the people of New Zealand" is obvious both from its addition, and that they had purposely altered the 3 February draft, and the reality that the Maori version, as signed, says:

"The Queen of England agrees to protect the chiefs, the subtribes and all the people of New Zealand."

Specifically, the all the people of New Zealand is written, "ki nga tangata katoa o Nu Tirani", which, as you can see, bears a subtle difference to a phrase later directed specifically at the Maori people in Article III: "...te Kuini o Ingarani nga tangata *maori* katoa o Nu Tirani." In other words, where Henry Williams specifically wanted to spell out "all the Maori people", he actually wrote that.

Proof of this intention to be inclusive is also found in the Treaty preamble. In the Littlewood version:

"...seeing that many of Her Majesty's subjects have already settled in the country and are constantly arriving: And that it is desirable for their protection as well as the protection of the natives to establish a government amongst them..."

In the Maori version:

"...and also because there are many of her subjects already living on this land and others yet to come. So the Queen desires to establish a government so that no evil will come to Maori and European living in a state of lawlessness."

In other words, the clear intent of the Treaty is to sweep all peoples up within it, and you would not have expected anything less from the British civil service.

The next difference centres on what was being promised to these people. The official English version (confining itself solely to Maori) says they were promised *"the full exclusive and undisturbed possession of their Lands and Estates Forests Fisheries and other properties which they may collectively or individually possess so long as it is their wish and desire to retain the same in their possession."*

The Littlewood version says the promise was *"the possession of their lands, dwellings and all their property,"* comments which could apply equally to Maori and Pakeha, thus making the document internally logically consistent so far. No reference either to forests or fisheries.

The Maori version (modern Kawharu translation) says the promise was *"the unqualified exercise of their chieftainship over their lands, villages and all their treasures,"* while the 1869 official Buick translation says it was *"the full chieftanship of their lands, their settlements and their property."*

Sharp readers will have noted how closely the Littlewood text mirrors the Maori version of the Treaty. Neither Littlewood nor the Maori versions carry the "forests and fisheries" protection that has been at the centre of Waitangi settlements over the past quarter-century.

For all these reasons, the Littlewood document is a more highly-evolved English language version which, given its date, supersedes the existing English language version in our archives, and which much more closely matches the intent of the Maori Treaty.[186]

If Darwin had stuck around just five years longer after his 1835 visit to Kororareka, he'd tell you, "Littlewood is the missing link". It's the version that comes between, and therefore explains, how the official English version became the Maori version.

The Littlewood Treaty has been somewhat politically sensitive, even within the news media. *NZ Herald* journalist Audrey Young wrote a

---

186   To read more on this, and weigh up the pros and cons of the debate around the authenticity of the Littlewood document, see Martin Doutre's "The Littlewood Treaty", available online: http://www.celticnz.org/TreatyBook/Chapter07.htm and also historian Dr Donald Loveridge's counter punch, http://www.victoria.ac.nz/stout-centre/research-units/towru/publications/Loveridge-Littlewood-1May2006.pdf

story on Winston Peters referencing the Littlewood Treaty, on 18 March 2004. The words "Littlewood Treaty" were contained in the first edition of the *Herald* that rolled off the press that morning, but wiped from the later editions that went to subscribers and for city distribution. Mysteriously, at midnight, a sub-editor had taken it upon themselves to censor copy from a senior parliamentary bureau journalist. The story was the same size, the photo of Winston was the same size, but any mention of Littlewood was gone.

Despite the heat surrounding it, the Littlewood document doesn't change one fundamental fact. In law, the only actual Treaty is the one that was signed in the native language of the inferior treaty participants. In other words, the Maori version is the only authentic Treaty.

Having sorted out the script, the gamesmanship at Waitangi, on the front lawn of James Busby's house, began. Ironically, the threat of France taking over New Zealand having provoked the Treaty, at this last moment it was France – with colonisation ships already on route to the South Island – that nearly managed to put a spanner in the works. The Roman Catholic Bishop of New Zealand, Frenchman Jean-Baptiste Pompallier, and his priests, had been working behind the scenes with Maori Catholics, allegedly urging chiefs not to sign the Treaty, telling them they'd end up as slaves in their own country.[187]

"This is nothing other than a crude attempt by England to take possession of New Zealand…I was quite sure that the request for signatures was only a pretext, the annexation was decided on," Pompallier, who flew the French flag at his residence, wrote.[188]

The speeches at Waitangi, transcribed at the time by William Colenso, reflect a lot of that seed-planting, and the very first Maori speaker, Te Kemara of Ngatikawa, was one of the chiefs Pompallier had whispered 'slavery' to:

"Health to thee, O Governor. This is mine to thee. I am not pleased toward thee. I will not consent to thy remaining here in this country. If thou stayest as Governor, then perhaps Te Kemara will be judged and condemned. Yes indeed, and more than that – even hanged by the neck. No, no, no, I shall never say yes to your staying.[189]

"Were we to be an equality, then perhaps Te Kemara would say yes.

---

187 The Maori- Pakeha relationship in New Zealand turned out to be very different from the way the French treated Polynesian peoples in the Pacific territories they settled.
188 Letter, Pompallier to Father Colin, head of the Marist Order, May 1840
189 *The Authentic and Genuine History of the Signing of the Treaty of Waitangi*, by William Colenso, 1890, see http://www.enzb.auckland.ac.nz/document?wid=123&page=0&action=null

But for the Governor to be up and Te Kemara to be down – Governor high up up up, and Te Kemara down low, small, a worm, a crawler. No no no, O Governor. This is mine to thee. O Governor, my land is gone, gone, all gone. The inheritances of my ancestors, fathers, relatives, all gone, stolen, gone with the missionaries. Yes, they have it all, all, all. That man there, the Busby, the Williams, they have my land. The land on which we are now standing this day is mine. This land even under my feet, return this to me. O Governor, return me my lands. Say to Williams. 'Return to Te Kemara his land'. Thou thou thou, thou baldheaded man, thou hast got my lands.

"O Governor, I do not wish you to stay. You English are not kind to us like other foreigners. You do not give us good things. I say, go back Governor; we do not want thee here in this country. And Te Kemara says to thee, go back, leave to Busby and to Williams to arrange and settle matters for us natives as heretofore."

Pompallier had also wound up Ngati Taweke's chief, Rewa:

"Go back; let the Governor return to his own country. Let my lands be returned to me which have been taken by the missionaries – by Davis and Clarke and by who and who beside. I have no lands now – only my name. Foreigners come, they know Mr. Rewa, but this is all I have left – a name.

"What do native men want of a Governor? We are not white or foreigners. This country is ours, but the land is gone. Nevertheless, we are the Governor – we the chiefs of this our fathers' land. I will not say 'Yes' to the Governor remaining. No no no, return. What! This land become like Port Jackson, and all the lands seen by the English. No no no, return. I, Rewa say to thee, O Governor go back. Send the man away. Do not sign the paper. If you do you will be reduced to the condition of slaves, and be compelled to break stones on the roads. Your land will be taken from you and your dignity as chiefs will be destroyed."

Ngatirehia chief Tareha – a large warrior with "a deep sepulchural voice" in William Colenso's words, told the gathering at Waitangi he was prepared to ditch everything Western and go back to grubbing for fern roots if it meant retaining his sovereignty:

"No Governor for me–for us Native men. We, we only are the chiefs, rulers. We will not be ruled over. What! Thou, a foreigner, up, and I down? Thou high, and I, Tareha, the great chief of the Ngapuhi tribes, low? No, no; never, never. I am jealous of thee; I am, and shall be, until thou and thy ship go away. Go back, go back; thou shalt not stay here. No, no; I will never say 'Yes.'

"Never mind; what of that–the lands of our fathers alienated? Dost thou think we are poor, indigent, poverty-stricken–that we really need thy foreign garments, thy food? Lo! note this." (Here he held up high a bundle of fern-roots he carried in his hand, displaying it.) "See, this is my food, the food of my ancestors, the food of the Native people. Pshaw, Governor! To think of tempting men–us Natives–with baits of clothing and of food! Yes, I say we are the chiefs. If all were to be alike, all equal in rank with thee–but thou, the Governor up high-up, up, as this tall paddle" (here he held up a common canoe-paddle), "and I down, under, beneath! No, no, no. I will never say, 'Yes, stay.' Go back, return; make haste away. Let me see you [all] go, thee and thy ship. Go, go; return, return."

As Lord Normanby had pointed out in his orders to Hobson, however, the Maori chiefs were in a precarious position with only nominal power. Despite all the muskets that had poured into the country and the possession of the tribes, they were useless without an ongoing supply of powder and shot, and any European power serious about invading New Zealand could simply choke off the gunpowder and then conquer with devastating consequences. It was precisely to avoid such carnage, and to prevent outbreaks of violence caused by lawless settlers, that the Colonial Office had agreed to claim New Zealand.

Tamati Waaka Nene, of the Ngati Hao branch of Ngapuhi, alluded to aspects of this as he rebuked the doubters, pointing out that regardless of Maori strength, the reality was that the world had arrived whether they liked it or not:

"I shall speak first to us, to ourselves, Natives" (addressing them). "What do you say? The Governor to return? What, then, shall we do? Say here to me, O ye chiefs of the tribes of the northern part of New Zealand! What we, how we?" (Meaning, how, in such a case, are we henceforward to act?) "Is not the land already gone? is it not covered, all covered, with men, with strangers, foreigners – even as the grass and herbage–over whom we have no power?

"We, the chiefs and Natives of this land, are down low; they are up high, exalted. What, what do you say? The Governor to go back? I am sick, I am dead, killed by you. Had you spoken thus in the old time, when the traders and grog-sellers came–had you turned them away, then you could well say to the Governor, 'Go back,' and it would have been correct, straight; and I would also have said with you, 'Go back;'–yes, we together as one; man, one voice. But now, as things are, no, no, no."

Turning to His Excellency, he resumed, "O Governor! sit. I, Tamati

Waaka, say to thee, sit. Do not thou go away from us; remain for us—a father, a judge, a peacemaker. Yes, it is good, it is straight. Sit thou here; dwell in our midst. Remain; do not go away. Do not thou listen to what [the chiefs of] Ngapuhi say. Stay thou, our friend, our father, our Governor."

He was backed up by Hone Heke:

"To raise up, or to bring down? Which? which? Who knows? Sit, Governor, sit. If thou shouldst return, we Natives are gone, utterly gone, nothinged, extinct. What, then, shall we do? Who are we? Remain, Governor, a father for us. If thou goest away, what then? We do not know. This, my friends," addressing the Natives around him, "is a good thing. It is even as the word of God" (the New Testament, lately printed in Maori at Paihia, and circulated among the Natives). "Thou to go away! No, no, no! For then the French people or the rum-sellers will have us Natives. Remain, remain; sit, sit here; you with the missionaries, all as one."

There were more speeches to and fro, before eventually Te Kemara leapt up again:

"Let us all be alike [in rank, in power]. Then, O Governor! remain. But, the Governor up! Te Kemara down, low, flat! No, no, no. Besides, where art thou to stay, to dwell? There is no place left for thee."

Here, wrote Colenso, "Te Kemara ran up to the Governor, and, crossing his wrists, imitating a man handcuffed, loudly vociferated, with fiery flashing eyes, 'Shall I be thus, thus? Say to me, Governor, speak. Like this, eh? like this? Come, come, speak, Governor. Like this, eh?' He then seized hold of the Governor's hand with both his and shook it most heartily, roaring out with additional grimace and gesture (in broken English), 'How d'ye do, eh, Governor? How d'ye do, eh, Mister Governor?' This he did over, and over, and over again, the Governor evidently taking it in good part, the whole assembly of whites and browns, chief and slave, Governor, missionaries, officers of the man-o'-war, and, indeed, "all hands," being convulsed with laughter.

"This incident ended this day's meeting."

As the proceedings closed on 5 February, William Colenso wrote of another incident he saw as "serio-comic" at the time:

"A truly laughable event (serio-comic, I might call it) happened as the Governor and his suite, with the captain and officers of the man-o'-war, were embarking. The anecdote is too good to be wholly lost. I was one of those who escorted the Governor to his boat, some distance off on the sandy beach below. His Excellency was talking with me, by the way, about the printing of the treaty and other kindred matters. To get to the boat we had to go down a short, easy, though rude pathway in the side of the hill (Waitangi House being situate on high ground).

"We had arrived near the boat, which the sailors were launching – it being low water – when a Native chief, an elderly man from the interior, who had only just arrived (a few others had also kept dropping in during the morning) – almost another Te Kemara – rushed down the decline, burst before us, laid his hands on the gunwale of the captain's launch to stop her (the sailors, half-amazed, looking at their chief), and, turning himself round, looked staringly and scrutinizingly into the Governor's face, and, having surveyed it, exclaimed in a shrill, loud, and mournful voice,

" 'Auee! he koroheke! Ekore e roa kua mate.'

"I felt 'wild' at him," writes Colenso. "The Governor, turning to me said, 'What does he say?' I endeavoured to parry the direct question by answering, 'Oh, nothing of importance. A stranger chief only just arrived from the interior, running hither to catch you, and bidding you his greeting.' But, as His Excellency's desire to know was keenly aroused, with that of Captain Nias and his officers by his side, and perhaps that of many of the whites present, including the sailors, who had ceased dragging down the boat, the Governor rejoined imploringly to me, 'Now pray do, Mr. Colenso, tell me the exact meaning of his words. I much wish to know it all.'

"So, being thus necessitated (for there were others present who knew enough of Maori), I said, 'He says, 'Alas! an old man. He will soon be dead!' His Excellency thanked me for it, but a cloud seemed to have fallen on all the strangers present, and the party embarked in silence for their ship."

Colenso didn't know it when he diarised it, but within three weeks Captain Hobson suffered a massive stroke, the effects of which crippled his governorship and eventually killed him two years later.

Early on the morning of 6 February as deliberations resumed, Wil-

liam Colenso pulled Governor Hobson aside and questioned whether Maori knew the full implications of the Treaty. While it is arguable as to the degree of understanding of the finer points, there seems no doubt that among those who spoke, in Maori, to their fellow chiefs, the big issue of sovereignty was well and truly understood.

It was only after the French Catholic Bishop and his priests had departed the Waitangi grounds, that some of the most strident opponents of the Treaty suddenly came up to sign the document.

"After some little time," reported observer William Colenso, "Te Kemara came towards the table and affixed his sign to the parchment, stating that the Roman Catholic bishop (who had left the meeting before any of the chiefs had signed) had told him 'not to write on the paper, for if he did he would be made a slave'."[190]

So too with some of the others:

"Rewa was now the only chief of note present who still refused to sign, but after some time, being persuaded by some of his Native friends as well as by the members of the Church of England Mission, he came forward arid signed the treaty, stating to the Governor that the Roman Catholic bishop had told him not to do so, and that he (the Roman Catholic bishop) had striven hard with him not to sign."

Having gathered signatures at Waitangi, the document or copies of it

190 *The Authentic and Genuine History of the Signing of the Treaty of Waitangi*, by William Colenso, 1890, see http://www.enzb.auckland.ac.nz/document?wid=123&page=0&action=null

were dispatched around the country, collecting in the end 512 signatures. It was only a chance remark from one of the Catholic contingent that tipped Hobson off to French plans to claim the South Island, prompting him to urgently dispatch a British ship and proclamation there as well.

It is clear, then, that the Treaty was signed at Waitangi and throughout the North Island, and most of the sparsely populated south. Just to make doubly sure, Hobson had taken possession of the South Island by virtue of discovery and occupation. But all of this still leaves a crucial question if you accept the ongoing public debate: what did Maori believe they were signing at Waitangi on 6 February 1840, and the dates that followed around the country?

CHAPTER TEN

The Tino Rangatiratanga Question

Entire forests have been harvested for the paper used to print the books and academic papers discussing this issue, but a large number of those documents have concentrated on the translation of the Treaty itself.

Historian Michael King, in his *Penguin History of New Zealand*, writes: "The word used for sovereignty – that which the chiefs were asked to give away to the Queen of England – was rendered as 'kawanatanga'. Kawanatanga was an abstraction from the word kawana, itself a transliteration of 'governor', and hence meant literally 'governorship'. In the Declaration of Independence of New Zealand, however, the word used for sovereignty had been 'mana', in the sense of 'authority over'. Future critics of the Treaty would thus be able to argue that the chiefs believed they were retaining sovereignty, 'mana', and giving away only the right to 'governorship' of the country as a whole."

There are several massive assumptions in Michael King's statement worth addressing. In Maori society at the time, mana was a relative term with a sliding scale. The mana of an ariki, or paramount chief, was far higher than the mana of an ordinary person. Yet both could enjoy the benefit of their own mana to varying degrees. Your mana might be dented by events, but it was not a commodity you could 'give' away, any more than you could give away your shadow. It did not exist in and of itself, it was merely a reflection of its owner. An ariki's shadow was longer and larger than a rangatira's, and Maori signing the Treaty knew a Queen's shadow was longer and larger again.

Michael King's claim that in the 1835 Declaration of Independence "the word used for sovereignty [was] mana" is also wrong. The precise phrase in the Declaration was "Ko te kingitanga ko te mana i te wenua"[191], and – as you might have guessed – 'kingitanga' was the sovereignty bit and 'mana' meant authority, in the sense of having the authority of kings over the land (wenua). Given Michael King's deserved status as a historian, it is hard to explain why he left out the "kingitanga" qualifier in his paragraph quoted above.

Kawanatanga was a somewhat abstract concept, as Maori had never seen a Governor in action in their islands, and did not really have anything of their own to compare it with. They were of course familiar with the Bible and Governor Pontius Pilate, but while Maori may have been less advanced they were not stupid – they knew they were not actually living in ancient Israel and that Hobson was not there to crucify them. Those who had travelled to Sydney and met the Governor there – and by 1840 a fair few Maori had crossed the ditch and come back – knew it was a position carrying high 'mana' in the sense of authority, similar to the role of ariki. Indeed, as you've already seen, one chief even asked whether New Zealand was to become a repeat of Port Jackson [Sydney], so he clearly understood.

Except Maori also knew something else. They already had ariki within each tribe, but they were ariki of equal status to each other. As you've read in this book, Maori had often lamented that they needed someone of even higher mana to rule over them and settle their disputes, because their existing political structure was incapable of that. They also repeatedly made the comment that the person with the highest mana had to come from outside the tribes completely, hence the ongoing pitches for the British to step in.

To turn around and now argue that Maori signing the Treaty of Waitangi did not understand they were surrendering their sovereignty to an entity of even higher mana defies belief, and history.

Yes, within their sliding scales of mana, the mana of ariki flowing down through rangatira to the ordinary peoples would continue unsullied – all sides recognised this in terms of daily life which is why Maori villages were pretty much left to run themselves – but when the Crown had to step in it was precisely because the Crown was seen as having the mana to do so, and that mana was high enough to outrank that of any one ariki. Maori were a patriarchal society who looked to their elders and

---

191   If you've been following the footnotes, you will recall Maori had no 'F' sound, and whenua was written as plain old wenua at the time of the Treaty.

betters – kaumatua and kuia – to rule. In turn, the elders and betters had specifically wanted someone else to keep themselves in check and prevent wars and utu attacks, hence the Treaty and the Code of Laws. The modern treaty industry within academia might just be failing to see the wood for the trees.

The Treaty may not have specifically used the word 'mana', probably with good reason, preferring instead to try and express how that 'mana' would be manifested – through governorship, 'kawanatanga' – but it was obvious to those at the time that the higher mana of the Crown was recognised. Without it, there could be no governorship by consent. Without it, the Governor could not be 'high' and the chiefs 'low'. That's why some tribes refused to sign.

There's another clue as well: Mana motuhake. The phrase means, "mana severed", and in its context the movement wants to cut off Crown mana. There would be nothing to sever, if none had been recognised. And therein lies the fallacy of the academic argument. The Mana Motuhake movement, by its very existence, proves sovereignty was ceded to the Crown.

Article Two of the Treaty in Maori talked of guaranteeing "tino rangatiratanga" – or chieftanship over their lands, villages and other properties. In modern times, tino rangatiratanga has been redefined as "sovereignty", and you can find it listed as meaning exactly that in the Maori Dictionary online. There is good reason to further examine that re-interpretation as well.

Rangatira were further down the pecking order than paramount chiefs. Generally they were leaders of hapu rather than iwi, equivalent to mayors rather than prime ministers. They administered village life on a daily basis, but they were not sovereign of themselves – the ariki outranked them. In the very first Maori dictionaries, rangatiras were "ladies and gentlemen", leaders of their own households. The redefinition of tino rangatiratanga to mean 'sovereignty' in the real sense of the word is a politically convenient modern linguistic trick.

For the reasons mentioned a few paragraphs ago, Maori had specifically sought an outside ruler with laws capable of bringing warring tribes to heel – the ultimate test of a ruler's sovereignty, one would suggest. To acknowledge that, and then to decree that ordinary chiefs were not beholden to Crown law would have defeated the purpose of the invitation to Britain in the first place. The chiefs couldn't unite behind a paramount leader of their own race because that would insult the mana of the rest of them. Whoever sat in judgement above the paramount chiefs had to have a higher mana than them, that's the simple logical endpoint.

Leading Maori lawyer and politician Sir Apirana Ngata made exactly the same point to Maori back in 1922:

"The Maori did not have any government when the European first came to these islands. There was no unified chiefly authority over man or land, or any one person to decide life or death, one who could be designated a King, a leader, or some other designation. No, there was none, the people were still divided, Waikato, Ngati Haua, Te Arawa, Ngapuhi and tribe after tribe. Within one tribe there were many divisions into sub-tribes each under their own chief. How could such an organisation, as a Government, be established under Maori custom? There was without doubt Maori chieftainship, but it was limited in its scope to its sub-tribe, and even to only a family group, The Maori did not have authority or a government which could make laws to govern the whole of the Maori Race."[192]

For Ngata, and many others, the suggestion that the Treaty immediately enshrined Maori with equal status as a lawmaking partner for the whole of New Zealand was laughable.

Tino rangatiratanga, or chiefly authority, Ngata defines as follows:

"Well, it has been said that the Maori did not have any Government, how can he cede something, he did not have? Let me explain again. The explanation is in the meaning of the words "Chiefly authority". It was this chiefly authority held by each chief who subscribed his mark to the Treaty of Waitangi that each chief ceded to the common weal and to Governor William Hobson, as an offering to Queen Victoria. The sum total of the authorities of the Maori Chiefs ceded to the Queen was the Government of the Maori people.

"Now what was the chiefly authority? What was the authority of the Maori chiefs at the time of the signing of the Treaty, to the people, to the land, and to the tribes under their separate authorities?

"Let us express in brief, the chiefs gave away to the common weal the kiwi cloak, the dog skin cloak, ornamental cloaks to hang in Museums for Europeans to view, and to expound the virtues of the Maori. 'These were the treasures of the Maori while they had authority': now the Maori looked on, sighed, recited and uttered 'Farewell to the abode of death, to England the abode of pleasure'. Having received these treasures the Queen gave red blankets in return. It is said these made up the greater part of the gifts laid by Governor Hobson, his officers and the missionaries before the Maori chiefs who signed the Treaty.

---

192   *The Treaty of Waitangi: An Explanation*, by Sir Apirana Ngata, 1922, see http://www.nzetc.org/tm/scholarly/tei-NgaTrea-t1-g1-t1.html

Tángi kúra; A bloody lamentation. Proper name.
Tángi wádu; The eighth (month) lamentation. Proper name.
Tángi wáre; The house cry. Proper name.
Tanii, *a.* Blind of one eye: name of a person.
Tániwa, *s.* A sea monster so called.
Tánu, *a.* Buried; as, " E méa tánu; A buried thing." *v.n.* " Tánu mía ki te óne óne; Bury it in the ground."
Táo, *s.* A long spear: proper name of a person.
Taó ke; A different spear: proper name of a person.
Táo kéte; A brother- or sister-in-law.
Taónga, *s.* Property procured by the spear, &c. Name of a person.

"During the time when the Maori chiefs had authority and there was no authority of British law, the word of the chief was law to his tribe. It was he who declared war, and he who sued for peace. Here are some of the words of that period; 'The fire burning yonder, go forth to put it out'. A great number of the people thus disappeared – loss of man, loss of land. The chief was separated from his daughter who was used as an offering to the invaders to bring about peace. It was the chiefs who bespoke the land and gave it away. They had the power even for life or death. These were the powers they surrendered to the Queen. This was the understanding of each tribe. The main purport was the transferring of the authority of the Maori chiefs for making laws for their respective tribes and sub-tribes under the Treaty of Waitangi to the Queen of England for ever."

It seems clear, then, that sovereignty was ceded and understood to have been ceded.

Then there are the other important phrases in the Maori version of the Treaty. Michael King raises the difficulty of working out the meaning of the phrase "ratou taonga katoa", saying "In the English version this supposedly corresponded to 'other properties' which Maori would be allowed to retain, but in fact the expression came to have far wider meaning: 'all their treasures'."[193]

It isn't actually that difficult to work this one out. The Maori version of the Treaty was scripted by missionary Henry Williams, who along with his brother William had learnt all his Maori language from the northern tribes of the Ngapuhi. By 1826 they had translated part of the Bible into Maori, no mean feat. It follows then, that his words would have plainly meant what they said to Ngapuhi ears. Helpfully, William Williams is also the editor of an 1844 dictionary of the Maori language,[194] and he translated 'taonga' as, "Property; treasure." Clearly, the Maori who taught

193 *Penguin History of New Zealand*, p160
194 *A Dictionary of the New Zealand Language*, by William Williams (1852 edition), available as a free e-book from http://books.google.co.nz/books?id=FaASAAAAIAAJ&printsec=frontcover&redir_esc=y#v=onepage&q&f=false

the Williams brothers knew of taonga as property, in the sense that they also regarded their property as treasure. The word treasure was qualified by the primary word of the definition, 'Property'.

Missionary Thomas Kendall's original dictionary of the Maori language, compiled in 1820 with the help of Hongi Hika, is even more explicit about how early Maori understood it:

"Taónga, *s.* Property procured by the spear".[195]

In this sense, taonga could mean captured wealth, like slaves or territory. The root word, 'tao' meant spear, which is why many modern declarations of what taonga meant to ancient Maori are hugely wide of the mark. You cannot 'capture' language by spearing it.

Maori lawyer and Cabinet Minister Sir Apirana Ngata added his weight to this in 1922:

"What is this authority, this sovereignty that is referred to in the second article? It is quite clear, the right of a Maori to his land, to his property, to his individual right to such possessions whereby he could declare, 'This is my land, there are the boundaries, descended from my ancestor so and so, or conquered by him, or as the first occupier, or so and so gave it to him, or it had been occupied by his descendants down to me. These properties are mine, this canoe, that taiaha (combination spear and club), that greenstone patu (club), that kumara (sweet potato) pit, that cultivation. These things are mine and do not belong to anyone else'."[196]

The one thing taonga cannot mean is mystical treasures never conceived of in 1840. The word was possessory in nature, and you cannot possess what does not yet exist.[197] Maori and Pakeha in 1840, for example, had no means of controlling – or even entering – airspace, so under no viable construction of the word 'taonga' can a tribe have possessed airspace, or for that matter radio waves, as would later be seriously claimed. The treasures that Maori had accumulated in 1840 could only be those things they held and which were dear to them then, like fishing spots, eel weirs, burial grounds and the like. If, as the Court of Appeal later upheld, their physical taonga (such as ownership of a riverbed) enabled money to be made from that taonga (power generation for example), then Maori could

---

195 See Kendall's *Vocabulary of New Zealand*. http://www.nzetc.org/tm/scholarly/tei-KenGramm-t1-body-d3-d15.html
196 *The Treaty of Waitangi: An Explanation*, by Sir Apirana Ngata, 1922, see http://www.nzetc.org/tm/scholarly/tei-NgaTrea-t1-g1-t1.html
197 Professor Margaret Mutu has stated Pakeha run risks when they try and define Maori concepts. The flip side of that is Maori academics can run risks when they try and re-define archaic Maori words with the vastly more nuanced English language, giving them a range of definition options the original Maori language never had.

make a claim for a slice of that income stream. They could not, however, lay direct claim to electricity as one of their treasures.

And yet, thanks to modern academics rewriting the definitions of ancient Maori words to suit new purposes, taonga is much warmer and fluffier than its original meaning:

"A taonga in Māori culture is a treasured thing, whether tangible or intangible. Tangible examples are all sorts of heirlooms and artefacts, land, fisheries, natural resources such as geothermal springs and access to natural resources, such as riparian water rights and access to the riparian zone of rivers or streams. Intangible examples may include language, spiritual beliefs and radio frequencies."[198]

Wikipedia then quotes the Waitangi Tribunal with further developments on what ancient Maori understand 'taonga' to mean:

"The First Chapter of volume 1 (of the full 2 volume report) considers the relationship between taonga works and intellectual property. The Tribunal provide a working definition of a 'taonga work' as being that:

> "A taonga work is a work, whether or not it has been fixed, that is in its entirety an expression of mātauranga Māori; it will relate to or invoke ancestral connections, and contain or reflect traditional narratives or stories. A taonga work will possess mauri and have living kaitiaki in accordance with tikanga Māori." (Vol 1, 1.7.3 p. 96)

"These working definitions involve concepts which are described by the Tribunal as being: Mauri is having a living essence or spirit. Kaitiaki can be spiritual guardians that exist in non-human form; kaitiaki obligations also exist in the human realm. The related concept is that 'Kaitiakitanga is the obligation, arising from the kin relationship, to nurture or care for a person or thing it has a spiritual aspect, encompassing not only an obligation to care for and nurture not only physical well-being but also mauri.' Kaitiaki obligations are described by the Tribunal as being that, 'those who have mana (or, to use treaty terminology, rangatiratanga) must exercise it in accordance with the values of kaitiakitanga – to act unselfishly, with right mind and heart, and with proper Mana and kaitiakitanga go together as right and responsibility, and that kaitiakitanga responsibility can be understood not only as a cultural principle but as a system of law'."[199]

---

198 Wikipedia definition of the word
199 *Investigate* magazine columnist and author Amy Brooke has made a substantial case for

Amazing, really, how a word that once simply meant "property procured by spear" is now an esoteric mystical word worthy of a Hindu guru and meaning whatever its 21st century translators want it to mean. The problem for ordinary New Zealanders, Maori or Pakeha, is that the Waitangi Tribunal has official dibs on interpreting the Treaty, regardless of what ancient dictionaries or documents tell us the words really meant.

Did the Maori expect every last inch of their lives to be controlled by British law? Probably not. Nor did Britain expect to intervene in their customary habits except to the extent alluded to by Lord Normanby in his instructions to Hobson: "*Until* they can be brought within the pale of civilised life, and trained to the adoption of its habits, they must be carefully defended in the observance of their own customs, so far as these are compatible with the universal maxims of humanity and morals." That paragraph, right there, is tino rangatiratanga in action – the governance of daily life retained by Maori *until* such time as they seek further access to British laws, and subject to exception for matters like cannibalism and human sacrifice.

It is submitted that no one in 1840 was really in the dark about what the Treaty meant. Overall sovereignty would transfer to Britain, day to day life would continue as normal for most Maori. Where there was intertribal conflict, or major crimes, British justice would intercede and adjudicate to the extent they were able. For routine matters, the rangatira – the 'mayors' – would sort it out within the hapu.

In practical terms, with no army and next to no police force, the British colonial administration was pretty much powerless for its first few years, so Maori justice continued to exist by default, tempered by missionaries

---

the abolition of the Waitangi Tribunal. "Even if we regard this body as set up in good faith in an attempt to accommodate genuine Maori grievances – which New Zealanders at large, with their renowned sense of fair play, have always wanted to see listened to, respected, and, where possible, compensated for – the tribunal has by no means been free from charges of bias, and even conflicts of interest in relation to some of its members. These are serious accusations, but apparently are never followed up. Its reliance, when verifying claims, has been on tribal-hired lawyers and well-paid, largely academic-only historians. This has been matched by its exclusion of other well-informed researchers and historians well able (on the basis of factual, historical evidence not allowed to be brought forward) to challenge self-serving claims which may seem impeccable – until more closely examined. Rigorous scrutiny has not been characteristic of the Waitangi Tribunal in operation, and its recommendations have been damaging. A good case can be made that it is well and truly time for it to be disbanded and for any grievances mounted by tribal chief executives to be examined, where they always should have been, in a genuine court of law subject to the kind of professional cross-examination absent from the tribunal's operation." See Brooke's full essay at "The Case for Abolishing The Waitangi Tribunal", *Investigate*, Dec 2010, http://www.investigatemagazine.co.nz/Investigate/?p=2627 . Her website www.100days.co.nz is also informative.

and the appointment of native assessors, or magistrates.

To be fair, there was confusion within colonial ranks. In 1842 after Hobson's death, upon reports of a tribe – who had not signed the Treaty – killing and eating members of a tribe who had – the Acting Governor Willoughby Shortland decided to impose the long arm of the law on the culprits. Chief Justice William Martin, Bishop Selwyn and Attorney-General Swainson tried to dissuade Shortland from his mission, primarily on the grounds of biting off more than they could chew, and secondly upon the novel legal argument that tribes who had not signed the Treaty were outside its jurisdiction. Historian and politician William Pember-Reeves would later describe this as "an opinion so palpably and daringly wrong that some have thought it a desperate device to save the country." Certainly, the Colonial Office in London gave the New Zealand administration a swift kicking when it heard about it, "Her Majesty's rule, said Lord Stanley, having once been proclaimed over all New Zealand, it did not lie with one of her officers to impugn the validity of her government."[200]

Since 1972, however, the Treaty of Waitangi has taken on a modern spin of its own that appears to bear no resemblance to the way the Maori who signed it saw it.

Lawyer and passionate treaty activist Annette Sykes summed up the views of many within Maoridom today when she wrote: "The ... tribes have reached a crossroads in their journey to protect their sovereignty and self-determination. In recent decades these highly articulate tribal nations have been leaders in a number of political, legal and economic strategies that promote the recognition of individual tribal entities as sovereigns enjoying government-to government relationships with the New Zealand Government. Their cries for self government having being made in forums from the Waitangi Tribunal through to the United Nations, and from the hallowed halls of political power in Wellington through to rank and file protests on the street."[201]

Like it or not, that's the perception being sold to Maori and Pakeha on a daily basis – that the tribes always kept their own supreme sovereignty, never relinquished it, and deserve to be treated as equals to the New Zealand government for the purposes of setting the laws of this country. This all hangs on the word "kawanatanga" allegedly not meaning sovereignty.

If, as Michael King wrote, Maori at Waitangi truly did not equate

200 *The Long White Cloud* by William Pember-Reeves, 1898, Chapter 11, p156
201 "The sovereignty debate, has it been silenced?", Annette Sykes, 1 January 2008, see http://unityaotearoa.blogspot.co.nz/2008/01/annette-sykes-sovereignty-debate-has-it.html

kawanatanga with sovereignty, then what are we to make of the comments of Ngapuhi's Rewa at Waitangi in 1840, quoted here directly from King's own book:

"What do we want of a governor? We are not whites nor foreigners. We are the governor – we the chiefs of this land of our ancestors!"[202]

You couldn't get a clearer example that Maori knew kawanatanga was interchangeable with sovereignty: "We are the sovereign – we the chiefs of this land of our ancestors".

King – perhaps because it would have shot his thesis down – did not quote the end of Rewa's speech, where he stated:

"Do not sign the paper. If you do you will be reduced to the condition of slaves, and be compelled to break stones on the roads. Your land will be taken from you and your dignity as chief will be destroyed."

It is hard to believe that academics and authors have been able to draw taxpayer funded salaries and study grants to argue that Maori had no awareness they were transferring sovereignty at Waitangi.

Remember Te Kemara's speech?:

"Were we to be an equality, then perhaps Te Kemara would say yes. But for the Governor to be up and Te Kemara to be down – Governor high, up, up, up, and Te Kemara down low, small, a worm, a crawler. No, no, no."

Another Ngapuhi leader, Kawiti, told those gathered at Waitangi:

"We Native men do not wish thee to stay. We do not want to be tied up and trodden down. We are free. Let the missionaries remain, but, as for thee, return to thine own country…I, even I, Kawiti, must not paddle this way or paddle that way because the Governor said 'No', because of the Governor, his soldiers and his guns."

How can anyone reconcile these paragraphs with the claim that Maori did not know the Treaty involved a transfer of sovereignty and control?

But a legalistic word-by-word approach to decoding the Treaty is not necessarily the last word, so to speak. There is another way to find out what Maori understood.

When courts have difficulty understanding the context (and therefore precise meaning) of an Act of Parliament, they sometimes go back to the parliamentary debates that accompanied the passing of the law in question, to get a feel for what legislators actually intended. In the same manner, concentrating on the precise wording of the Treaty of Waitangi only gets you so far.

---

202 *Penguin History of New Zealand*, p161

Kohimarama conference venue, 1860

To get a proper handle on it, we jump forward now 20 years, to a gathering of ariki – paramount chiefs – and rangatira, at Kohimarama in Auckland in July 1860. The purpose of this "runanga" – or tribal council – was to discuss how Maori had fared in the 20 years since Waitangi had been signed, and seek their views on current issues affecting them.

The proceedings, and thus the speech transcripts below, were published in *Te Karere*, the main Maori newspaper, that month.

To those who argue that Maori never intended to sign away sovereignty over New Zealand to the Crown, and never understood that to be the case, we produce chief Wikiriwhi Matehenoa of Ngati Porou on the East Cape, who told the up to 200 chiefs gathered (a much higher number than those who had gathered at Waitangi): "We are all under the sovereignty of the Queen, but there are also other authorities over us sanctioned by God and the Queen, namely, our Ministers."

The Maori translation is illustrative of what he understood. He used the words "te maru o te Kuini", where the word 'maru' means literally "power, authority" translated in 1860 at the conference as sovereignty.[203] Wikiriwhi further backs that up in his phrase "sanctioned by God and the Queen", rendered in Maori, "mana whakahaere o te Atua raua ko te Kuini". The word "raua" in this sense means "combined" and refers back to the "mana" of both God and Queen".

To flip Michael King's analysis back on itself, the chief did not use the phrase "te kawanatanga o te Kuini", if governorship was all they actually understood the Queen's sovereignty to be.

It is abundantly clear that Ngati Porou fully understood Queen Victoria's sovereignty over New Zealand. Te maru; the power, the authority.

The Ngati Raukawa chief Horomona Toremi, of Otaki, went so far as to explain that – post Waitangi – "You over there (the Pakehas) are the only Chiefs. The Pakeha took me out of the mire: the Pakeha washed me.

---

203 The 1844 *Maori Language Dictionary* by William Williams translates 'maru' primarily as power, and gave the example, "Na te maru i a ia koia matou i matuku ai," meaning, "In consequence of his power we were afraid".

This is my word. Let there be one Law for all this Island."[204]

Then there's Te Ahukaramu's position: "First, God: secondly, the Queen: thirdly, the Governor. Let there be one Queen for us. Make known to us all the laws, that we may all dwell under one law."[205]

The concept that the Queen set the law for all New Zealanders, Maori and Pakeha alike, was clearly understood, as was the Queen's position under God, and the Governor's ranking underneath the Queen. Beneath the top three, Maori and Pakeha citizens. "Kia kotahi te Kuini mo tatou" – one Queen over all of us.

Te Ahukaramu was even more explicit about the evolution of the Maori king movement, describing it as a usurpation of the Queen's sovereignty, and noting that the recently deceased first Maori king had recognised the authority of "the Queen, and the Government.

"If any of the tribes should set up a Maori King, then let them be separated from the Queen's 'mana'." In Maori, it reads, "me wehe ratou i runga i te mana o te Kuini".

A few paragraphs back we looked at why Maori had invited the British monarch to become sovereign over New Zealand, because they needed to unite behind someone with higher mana than any individual New Zealand chief.

As chief Wiremu Patene told the Kohimarama gathering, even the Maori King's mana was next to nothing against Victoria's:

"But remember, Governor, that (the Maori King) is child's play. The Queen's mana is with us. Let me repeat it, that work is child's play."

With the huge inroads that Christianity made in the 1830s, it's actually important to realise in this discussion that most of the Maori chiefs at Waitangi probably had a better and deeper understanding of the Bible than many people today. For Maori, the concept of submission to a higher authority was something many of them had now personally done, and that was part of the understanding they brought to Waitangi; they knew they were submitting.

"Let me make use of an illustration from the Scriptures," chief Hamuera of Ngaiterangi told the runanga. "Jesus Christ said he was above Satan. So the Governor says he is above both Pakeha and Maori – that he alone

---

204 In Maori: "Whakarongo mai e nga rangatira Pakeha. Na koutou i tu mai ai ahau inaianei. Ko koutou anake te rangatira. Kia ki atu au kahore kau he rangatira o tenei motu, kahore rawa, kahore rawa. Na te Pakeha ahau i huhuti mai i te paru, nana ahau i horoi. Ko taku kupu tenei, kia kotahi te Ture mo te motu katoa."

205 In Maori, the words were expressed: "Ko te Atua te tuatahi, ko te Kuini te tuarua, ko te Kawana te tuatoru. Kia kotahi te Kuini mo tatou. Whakamaramatia mai nga ture katoa kia noho ai tatou i roto i te ture kotahi."

Governor Thomas Gore Browne

is Chief. Now, when Satan said, I am the greatest, Christ trampled him under foot. So the Queen says, that she will be chief for all men. Therefore, I say, let her be the protector of all the people."

Others were even more strident, well and truly nailing their futures to the Pakeha ways, not the ancient Maori customs:

Te Ngahuruhuru (Ngati-whakaue): "The deceits do not belong to the Pakehas, but to the Maories alone. The Maori is wronging the Pakeha. I am an advocate for peace. Shew kindness to the Pakeha. Shew good feeling to this Governor. Look here, Maories! My word will not alter. I belong to the mana of the Queen, to the mana of the Governor. As to the setting up o a King – not that. Do not split up, and form a party for the Queen, and another for the Maori King: that would be wrong."

It is this July 1860 runanga, or tribal council, that provides vital clues about how both Crown and Maori saw their relationship post Waitangi. As a tribal council where chiefs were required to vote in favour or against, and where – like Parliament today – a Hansard was taken of each speech and given to the speaker to double check its accuracy before being published, it was also an important and binding ratification of the terms of the Treaty which were now clearly expressed, both in English and in Maori.

If there was any ambiguity arising out of the 1840 Treaty regarding the cession of sovereignty, there was no ambiguity this time, and any honest debate of the "treaty principles" cannot take place without consideration of the 1860 speeches.

The gathering had been opened by the Governor, Thomas Gore Brown, who told the assembled leaders, that the Treaty of Waitangi meant. His words are reprinted here, in their entirety, because essentially this document and this conference superseded Waitangi:

My Friends, – Chiefs of New Zealand,

1. I have invited you to meet me on the present occasion that we may have an opportunity of discussing various matters connected with the welfare and advancement of the two Races dwelling in New Zealand.

2. I take advantage of it also to repeat to you and, through you, to the whole Maori people, the assurances of goodwill on the part of our Gracious Sovereign which have been given by each succeeding Governor from Governor Hobson to myself.

3. On assuming the Sovereignty of New Zealand Her Majesty extended to her Maori subjects her Royal protection, engaging to defend New Zealand and the Maori people from all aggressions by any foreign power, and imparting to them all the rights and privileges of British subjects; and she confirmed and guaranteed to the Chiefs and Tribes of New Zealand, and to the respective families and individuals thereof, the full, exclusive and undisturbed possession of their lands and estates, forests, fisheries, and other properties which they may collectively or individually possess, so long as it is their wish to retain the same in their possession.

4. In return for these advantages the Chiefs who signed the Treaty of Waitangi ceded for themselves and their people to Her Majesty the Queen of England absolutely and without reservation all the rights and powers of Sovereignty which they collectively or individually possessed or might be supposed to exercise or possess.[206]

5. Her Majesty has instructed the Governors who preceded me, and she will instruct those who come after me, to maintain the stipulations of this Treaty inviolate, and to watch over the interests and promote the advancement of her subjects without distinction of Race.

6. Having renewed these assurances in the name of our Gracious Sovereign I now ask you to confer with me frankly and without reserve. If you have grievances, make them known to me, and if they are real, I will try to redress them. Her Majesty's wish is that all her subjects should be happy, prosperous, and contented. If, therefore, you can make any suggestions for the better protection

---

206   This is a key passage, so please note the Maori translation read to the chiefs in 1860: "...tino tukua rawatia atu ana e ratou ki Te Kuini o Ingarani nga tikanga me nga mana Kawanatanga katoa i a ratou katoa, i tenei i tenei ranei o ratou, me nga pera katoa e meinga kei a ratou". The word "tukua" means "cede" or "surrender" and "nga tikanga" the laws and lore, and "mana Kawanatanga katoa" means all sovereign authority.

of property, the punishment of offenders, the settlement of disputes or the preservation of peace, I shall gladly hear them and will give them the most favourable consideration.

7. The minds of both Races have lately been agitated by false reports or exaggerated statements; and, in order to restore confidence, it is necessary that each should know and thoroughly understand what the other wishes and intends.

8. There is also a subject to which I desire to invite your special attention, and in reference to which I wish to receive the expression of your views. For some time past certain persons belonging to the tribes dwelling to the south of Auckland have been endeavouring to mature a project, which, if carried into effect, could only bring evil upon the heads of all concerned in it. The framers of it are said to desire that the Maori tribes in New Zealand should combine together and throw off their allegiance to the sovereign whose protection they have enjoyed for more than twenty years, and that they should set up a Maori King and declare themselves to be an independent Nation. Such ideas could only be entertained by men completely ignorant of the evils they would bring upon the whole Native Race if carried into effect.

9. While the promoters of this scheme confined themselves to mere talking, I did not think it necessary to notice their proceedings, believing that, if allowed time to consider, they would abandon so futile and dangerous an undertaking. This expectation has not been fulfilled. At a recent meeting at Waikato some of the leading men proposed that Wiremu Kingi, who is in arms against the Queen's authority, should be supported by reinforcements from the tribes who acknowledge the Maori king, and armed parties from Waikato and Kawhia actually went to Taranaki for this purpose. These men also desire to assume an authority over other New Zealand tribes in their relations with the Government, and contemplate the forcible subjection of those tribes who refuse to recognise their authority.

10. Under these circumstances I wish to know your views and opinions distinctly, in order that I may give correct information to our Sovereign.

11. It is unnecessary for me to remind you that Her Majesty's engagements to Her Native subjects in New Zealand have been faithfully observed. No foreign enemy has visited your shores, Your

lands have remained in your possession, or have been bought by the Government at your own desire. Your people have availed themselves of their privileges as British subjects, seeking and obtaining in the Courts of Law that protection and redress which they afford to all Her Majesty's subjects. But it is right you should know and understand that in return for these advantages you must prove yourselves to be loyal and faithful subjects, and that the establishment of a Maori King would be an act of disobedience and defiance to Her Majesty which cannot be tolerated. It is necessary for the preservation of peace in every country that the inhabitants should acknowledge one Head.

12. I may frankly tell you that New Zealand is the only Colony where the aborigines have been treated with unvarying kindness. It is the only Colony where they have been invited to unite with the Colonists and to become one people under one law. In other colonies the people of the land have remained separate and distinct, from which many evil consequences have ensued. Quarrels have arisen; blood has been shed; and finally the aboriginal people of the country have been driven away or destroyed. Wise and good men in England considered that such treatment of aborigines was unjust and contrary to the principles of Christianity. They brought the subject before the British Parliament, and the Queen's Ministers advised a change of policy towards the aborigines of all English Colonies. New Zealand is the first country colonised on this new and humane system. It will be the wisdom of the Maori people to avail themselves of this generous policy, and thus save their race from evils which have befallen others less favoured. It is your adoption by Her Majesty as her subjects which makes it impossible that the Maori people should be unjustly dispossessed of their lands or property. Every Maori is a member of the British Nation; he is protected by the same law as his English fellow subject; and it is because you are regarded by the Queen as a part of her own especial people that you have heard from the lips of each successive Governor the same words of peace and goodwill. It is therefore the height of folly for the New Zealand tribes to allow themselves to be seduced into the commission of any act which, by violating their allegiance to the Queen, would render them liable to forfeit the rights and privileges which their position as British subjects confers upon them, and which must necessarily entail

upon them evils ending only in their ruin as a race.

13. It is a matter of solicitude to Her Majesty, as well as to many of your friends in England and in this country, that you should be preserved as a people. No unfriendly feeling should be allowed to grow up between the two Races. Your children will live in the country when you are gone, and when the Europeans are numerous. For their sakes I call upon you as fathers and as Chiefs of your Tribes, to take care that nothing be done which may engender animosities the consequences of which may injure your posterity. I feel that the difference of language forms a great barrier between the Europeans and the Maoris. Through not understanding each other there are frequent misapprehensions of what is said or intended: this is also one of the chief obstacles in the way of your participating in our English Councils, and in the consideration of laws for your guidance. To remedy this the various Missionary Bodies, assisted by the Government, have used every exertion to teach your children English, in order that they may speak the same language as the European inhabitants of the Colony.

14. I believe it is only needful that these matters should be well understood to ensure a continuance of peace and friendly feeling between the two Races of Her Majesty's subjects; and it is for this reason, and in a firm hope that mutual explanations will remove all doubt and distrust on both sides, that I have invited you to meet me now.

15. I shall not seek to prove, what you will all be ready to admit, that the treatment you have received from the Government, since its establishment in these Islands down to the present hour, has been invariably marked by kindness. I will not count the Hospitals founded for the benefit of your sick; the Schools provided for the education of your children; the encouragement and assistance given you to possess yourselves of vessels, to cultivate wheat, to build mills, and to adopt the civilized habits of your white brethren. I will not enumerate the proofs which have been given you that your interests and well-being have been cared for, lest you should think I am ungenerously recalling past favours. All will admit that not only have your ears listened to the words of kindness, but that your eyes have seen and your hands have handled its substantial manifestations.

16. I will not now detain you by alluding to other matters of great

importance, but will communicate with you from time to time and call your attention to them before you separate. Let me, however, remind you that though the Queen is able without any assistance from you to protect the Maoris from all foreign enemies, she cannot without their help protect the Maoris from themselves. It is therefore the duty of all who would regret to see their Race relapse into barbarism, and who desire to live in peace and prosperity, to take heed that the counsels of the foolish do not prevail, and that the whole country be not thrown into anarchy and confusion by the folly of a few misguided men.

Finally, – I must congratulate you on the vast progress in civilization which your people have made under the protection of the Queen. Cannibalism has been exchanged for Christianity; Slavery has been abolished; War has become more rare; Prisoners taken in war are not slain; European habits are gradually replacing those of your ancestors of which all Christians are necessarily ashamed. The old have reason to be thankful that their sunset is brighter than their dawn, and the young may be grateful that their life did not begin until the darkness of the heathen night had been dispelled by that light which is the glory of all civilized Nations.
Earnestly praying that God may grant His blessing on your deliberations and guide you in the right path, I leave you to the free discussion of the subjects I have indicated, and of any others you may think likely to promote the welfare of your Race.
(Signed) Thomas Gore Browne, Governor.

If you were looking for clarification on what the Treaty of Waitangi meant at the time, you've found it. Every main concept in the English version of the Treaty was re-stated in Maori, before a congress of Maori leaders – the biggest gathering of Maori leaders ever held to that point.

If there was ever a time to shout out "liar!", this was it. If there was ever a time for Maori to say, "that's not what we agreed to!", this was it. So what did the paramount chiefs say?

Sixty percent of those attending spoke in absolute explicit agreement with the way the Governor had described the Treaty and what it meant, and pledged their allegiance to Governor and Queen. A further 17% expressed similar sentiments, without making an outright declaration about it. Twenty one percent didn't state an opinion on the matter, but talked of other things. Two percent appeared to be leaning against the Governor.

The tribes, as they would say on *Survivor*, had spoken, and in doing so had ratified the Treaty of Waitangi as most people understand it:

Eruera Kahawai (Ngatiwakaue, Rotorua): "Listen, ye people! There is no one to find fault with the Governor's words. His words are altogether good."

Menehira Rakau, (Ngatihe, Maungatapu): "Let us inquire into the character of the Governor's address. I did not hear one wrong thing in the speech of the Governor."

Ririreku Te Perehu, (Ngatipikiao, Rotoiti and Maketu): "The Governor's address is right."

Henare Pukuatua, (Ngatiwakaue, Rotorua): "Listen my friends, the people of this runanga. I have no thought for Maori customs. All I think about now is what is good for me. I have been examining the Governor's address. I have not been able to find one wrong word in all these sayings of the Governor, or rather of the Queen. I have looked in vain for anything to find fault with. Therefore I now say, O Governor, your words are full of light. I shall be a child to the Queen. Christ shall be the Saviour of my soul, and my temporal guide shall be the Governor or the Law. Now, listen all of you. I shall follow the Governor's advice. This shall be my path forever and ever."

Tamihana Rauparaha, (Ngati Toa, Porirua): "The words we have heard this day are good."

Karaitiana Tuikau, (Ngati Te Matera, Hauraki): "The Governor's words are good."

"The words of the Governor are good. Let the Queen be above all," exclaimed Tohi, a Ngatiwhakaue chief.

The list could stretch on and on. Suffice to say not one chief accused the Crown of lying when it said it had taken absolute sovereignty over New Zealand when the Treaty was signed.

Constitutionally, their speeches and votes at the Kohimarama runanga amount to a full ratification of the English version of the Treaty, and it seems clear from the quotes above and on the preceding pages that the chiefs fully understood the concept of sovereignty.

However, this is also the reason the Littlewood Treaty document becomes irrelevant – it was superseded by Kohimarama.

For those who take issue, for example, with the "forests and fisheries" aspect of the Treaty, on the grounds that the words don't appear in the Maori version, here's the bad news: Governor Gore Browne read them into the record at Kohimarama, as you can see in his clauses listed earlier. This issue of attention to historical detail applies to goose and gander alike. The conference ratified sovereignty, but it also ratified forests and fisheries.

So let's pause for a moment and return to contemporary scholarship. In 1990, Professor Ranginui Walker wrote that rangatiratanga meant sovereignty and kawanatanga was merely a limited form of governorship:

"The chiefs are likely to have understood the second clause of the Treaty as a confirmation of their own sovereign rights in return for a limited concession of power in kawanatanga.

"The Treaty of Waitangi they signed confirmed their own sovereignty while ceding the right to establish a governor in New Zealand to the Crown. A governor is in effect a satrap…a holder of a provincial governorship; he was a subordinate ruler, or a colonial governor. In New Zealand's case he governed at the behest of the chiefs…in effect the chiefs were his sovereigns."

In this respect, Walker follows treaty historian Claudia Orange who says rangatiratanga would be a "better approximation to sovereignty than kawanatanga."[207]

And yet, you've seen what Maori – and some of the Kohimarama attendees had actually signed the Treaty personally – understood the Treaty to mean, and sovereignty to mean. Can the academic claims about the Treaty actually be reconciled with historical fact?

It's an important question. The meaning of the Treaty of Waitangi as it is currently pitched dominates public policy in this country, and it dominates the school curriculum. Our children are learning the academic version of the Treaty. There are many jobs you cannot be appointed to in the public sector unless you can demonstrate an acquaintance and allegiance to the modern interpretations of the Treaty.

None of this is written to belittle the wrongs that were done to Maori in breach of the Treaty. That's not what this is about. Those grievances in many cases are real and require settlement. But if we are going to be honest about our past, it cuts both ways. We cannot move forward unless we have a clear understanding of the foundations. If our opinions and beliefs about the Treaty in the 21st century are based on a misunderstanding about what 1840 Maori thought, then our opinions and beliefs are founded on a lie. What actually matters is what Maori at the time really did think they were signing. The only way to find that out is to listen to

---

207   *The Treaty of Waitangi*, by Claudia Orange, Allen & Unwin, 1987, p41

their voices, rather than engage in endless debates about the meaning of the words as we currently understand them.

Claudia Orange was one of the first scholars to revisit the Kohimarama documents, in a paper for the *New Zealand Journal of History* in 1980.

"In spite of a number of books or articles on various aspects of the Treaty of Waitangi," she wrote, there has been little attempt to assess the meaning of the treaty to the Maori people." Apart from two 1972 articles by Ruth Ross which looked at 1840 and its immediate aftermath, "beyond the 1840s...lies almost uncharted territory," commented Orange.[208]

When she examined Kohimarama, however, she didn't agree with the points made here. Although Orange's paper, for example, does agree that the conference ratified the Treaty of Waitangi, she argues Maori still did not understand it and had "only a vague and confused comprehension".

"Historians have passed over the Kohimarama conference with barely a mention," she wrote, "evaluating the gathering correctly as just one more government attempt to manipulate Maori affairs to secure the government's position. This, however, ignores its significance in Maori history."

Orange prefers to translate the word 'maru' – meaning power and authority – as 'shelter' and 'protection', which are two alternative nuances the word carries. She nonetheless concedes that Maori attending the conference also described the Queen's sovereignty as 'mana', as has been shown above. She quotes Paora Tuhaere's description of the Kohimarama gathering as "the real treaty upon which the sovereignty (mana) of the Queen will hang."

And look at Te Ahukaramu's comments: "First, God: secondly, the Queen: thirdly, the Governor. Let there be one Queen for us. Make known to us all the laws, that we may all dwell under one law."

We can have abstract arguments about subtle shades of the meaning of the various words for 'sovereign', or we can look at what Maori perceived it to be.

Claudia Orange talks of a Maori belief that the "shadow" of power passed to the Crown, while the "substance" continued to remain with the chiefs. Again, let's examine that for a moment.

What is the manifestation of your own sovereignty and power, if not to make your own laws and enforce them? That's what sovereigns through history have done, that's what Maori ariki did. That is the "substance" of sovereignty. So did the chiefs want a continuation of their own laws

---

208   http://www.nzjh.auckland.ac.nz/docs/1980/NZJH_14_1_05.pdf

and customs within their tribal districts, or was the grass greener on the other side?

One who echoed the views of many at Kohimarama was Whangarei chief, Wiremu Pohe of Ngapuhi: "We are bound with one girdle. It is not a Maori girdle but a golden one; therefore it will not part asunder. In other words, we are surrounded by a fence, constructed not with puriri and totara posts, but of iron. If a person attempts to leap over the rail of this fence we know what the result will be.

"Let us keep within this fence forever and ever. Now, there is a practice which causes us much trouble. We have 'tauas' [armed raiding parties] for curses. This is following up Maori custom. We have 'tauas' on account of the desecration of sacred places; this too is Maori custom. And on account of the violation of women we have 'tauas'. This is Maori custom. Now that we have entered this new order of things, and have been bound in this golden girdle of the Queen we should all consent to abandon all these customs."

For twenty or so years after Waitangi, tribal Maori pretty much had continued to enforce their own laws and customs, because the British colonial apparatus of state in New Zealand was weak and spread too thinly to administer British justice against Maori by force. It was either voluntary compliance, or it was nothing.

What we see at Kohimarama, constitutionally, however, is an evolution of consent. After 20 years of partial integration, the chiefs not only ratified Waitangi in full but expressly called for a complete adoption of Pakeha tikanga.

Let's hear the chiefs on how they perceived sovereignty operating. Was the Governor a ruler in name only, or one with the power to enforce the law, even to hold these same chiefs to account:

Hemi Metene Te Awaitaia: "I shall make the Governor's address the subject of my speech. I shall speak first of the 4th clause, namely, – 'In return for these advantages the chiefs who signed the Treaty of Waitangi ceded for themselves and their people to Her Majesty the Queen of England, absolutely and Without reservation, all the rights and powers of sovereignty which they collectively or individually possessed or might be supposed to exercise or possess.' That was the union of races at Waitangi. I was there at the time, and I listened to the love Of the Queen. I then heard about the advantages of the treaty.

"In my opinion *the greatest blessings are Christianity and the Laws.* While God spares my life I will give these my first concern. *When I commit a wrong, then let me be brought before the Magistrate and punished according to law.* [emphasis added] Those are the good things."

Winiata Pekamu Tohiteururangi: "The only thought that has occurred to me, is this – in former times I had but one lord (ariki), and now I shall have but one lord – only one. *I shall have but one rule – not two.* [emphasis added]"

Eruera Kahawai: "Listen! This is not an ordinary discussion. Do not speak rashly, because this is a most important subject. The Governor's request that we should speak frankly is a very proper one. The Governor perhaps thinks that we shall conceal our views. No, the Maories will fully express their opinions to him. The Governor probably expects that we who have now assembled to meet him should take a part to ourselves. Let it not be said that the opinions have changed afterwards. No, let there be no changing of opinion.

"Let me state here that should a Pakeha take the liberty of injuring or killing a Maori I shall not retaliate in the same way. I shall give him up to the hand of the Law. My hand shall not touch him; but I will leave it to the law to punish him. Though the wrong may be committed as far off as Rotorua, I shall bring the offender here to be tried.

"And in like manner, if a Maori should injure a Pakeha, I would hand him over to the Law. These are the sentiments of all the tribe. I mean the people of Rotorua. This speech is as much theirs as mine. Even though it should be Tukihaumene, (Tukihaumene interposed "or you rather,") or Tohi, or Taiapo, or Ngahuruhuru, who committed himself by injuring a Pakeha, I would give him up to be tried for it. There is an old man in the tribe named Tawangawanga who holds the relation of father to me. If even he committed himself, I would give him up. And if Awekotuku or Paora should do so, I would give them up, and the law should try them.

"We will bring our troubles for you to try. I mean our great troubles. As to the quarrels about women, we will arrange those ourselves, unless indeed, they are of a serious nature.

"When the law came the evils of the Maori customs became evident. I approve of the Governor's words. If they were wrong I should tell you so. Had he said that my lands should be taken away, I should disapprove of that; or that my sick friend should be put to death without cause, or that my provisions should be used without my having any payment, I should disapprove. But now when the Governor says that the Pakeha and Maori races should be united as of one flesh, who is able to disapprove? Who is the man? The Pakeha customs have been made manifest to us in the days that past, and we have accepted one half of them, inasmuch as we take our differences to the Magistrate's Court to be adjusted. The Governor's words now under discussion are good."

If a transfer of sovereignty means a submission to a new higher authority with the power to make life or death rulings (in the case of capital punishment for murder), then chief Eruera Kahawai knew exactly what he was saying.

Precisely because of decades of groundwork by the missionaries, the Mosaic law on which Western justice is based was well-known to Maori, even by the time they first signed at Waitangi. They understood the Crown's Code of Laws to be far superior to their own, and that's one of the advantages and "benefits" (as Claudia Orange would say) that they expected the Treaty to bring them.

The Arawa people, too, who had not signed at Waitangi, nonetheless realised the transfer of sovereignty was a good thing:

Tohi te Ururangi: "When war breaks out in any place, let the law inquire into it. Should evil spring up in my midst (i.e., among my people) let the law enquire into it. My entrance on the Queen's side is true and clear. When I saw my corpse [alluding to his relative Kera who was murdered by a pakeha]; I left it to law, and it was right. It was then that I became attached to the Law. That was my first consenting to the Queen through which I came to know good.

"Had I then followed Maori customs many lives would have perished. I left it to the Queen's law and I saw good. With my understanding I discovered the evil of my heart, and abandoned it. I now give my adherence to the Queen. I now give my adherence to the one law. Let there be only one law for the Arawa people, that our way may be clear. If evil should appear in any place, let the law dispose of it. People of the Arawa, let not your opinions follow diverse ways, but let our opinions now be one. Listen, all of you, I give my adherence now to the Governor."

On the very first day of the conference, in fact in the very first minutes, Auckland-based Ngatiwhatua chief Paora Tuhaere told the gathering why he had supported the Treaty:

"Hearken, all ye people, to my words! These were my words to the first Governor, to the second Governor, and to the third Governor: *I want the Laws of England* [emphasis added]. Hearken, ye people, two things commend themselves to my mind – the Governor and the Queen. For thereby do we, both Pakeha and Maori, reap good. This is my speech. *The best riches for us are the Laws of England*. In my opinion, the greatest of all evils is war."

Tuhaere goes on to explain why the laws were important to prevent utu, then closes his speech with a comment which we will come to in a moment. Before we do, first let's examine how treaty historian Claudia Orange reported Paora Tuhaere's speech:

"Other chiefs debated the extent to which the treaty applied. Paora Tuhaere, a Ngatiwhatua from Orakei, supposed that it had definite limitations. He dismissed the treaty impatiently as 'Ngapuhi's affair'," wrote Claudia Orange.

Given that Tuhaere had openly called for submission to the "Laws of England" as you've just seen, it might be hard for us to understand where he was seeing "definite limitations" as argued by Orange. But now let's read his further comments, and you can see what he says about "Ngapuhi's affair" and how he says it:

"I entertained the Pakeha a long time ago, and I found him good. Hence, I say, I shall always remember the Pakeha, and I shall always remember too, with affection, the Governor who was sent here to protect us. The benefits which we received from him are – Christianity and the Laws. Now, listen! My affections at the present time lie between these two blessings. Listen, again! My heart is satisfied. All that the Law keeps from us is – Guns, Powder, and Brandy.

"Another subject comes under my attention. It is the misunderstanding between the Pakeha and the Maori about land. The Pakeha has his mode of selling land, and the Maori has his mode. O people, hearken! The Pakeha came to New Zealand to protect the Maori. As to the talk about Waitangi (treaty), that is Ngapuhi's affair."

Did that seem "impatient" to you? Did you see "definite limitations" being set out about the Treaty?

How does Claudia Orange's interpretation of Paora Tuhaere sit with this comment from him: "This is my speech to you – a word respecting the Treaty of Waitangi, the covenant now spoken of. The union of the two races commenced with it. By it the sovereignty of these Islands was ceded to the Queen."

Far from suggesting the Treaty had "definite limitations", Tuhaere told the conference he was well aware in 1840 that signing the Treaty meant ceding real sovereignty. It wasn't a "limited" document but an all encompassing document. Tuhaere reminded the conference he hadn't signed the Treaty himself because he knew the hook inside it no matter how the missionaries dressed it up:

"Mr. Williams's bait was a blanket; the hook was the Queen's Sovereignty. When he came to a Chief he presented his hook and forthwith drew out a subject for the Queen."

It is impossible to use Tuhaere's speech as proof that the Treaty did not cede absolute sovereignty – he says the opposite. The irony was, from being an early critic, Tuhaere by 1860 had become pleased with the benefits of the Treaty, regardless of "Ngapuhi's affair".

Ngapuhi's Tamati Waaka Nene – one of the leaders who signed at Waitangi – made it clear what his tribe's "affair" was, and rejected the idea he did not understand sovereignty:

"My desire when Governor Hobson arrived here was to take him as our Governor, in order that we might have his protection. Who knows the mind of the Americans, or that of the French? Therefore, I say, let us have the English to protect us. Therefore, my friends, do I say, let this Governor be our Governor, and this Queen our Queen. Let; us accept this Governor, as a Governor for the whole of us. Let me tell you, ye assembled tribes, I have but one Governor. Let this Governor be a King to us. Listen again, ye people! When the Governor came here, he brought with him the Word of God by which we live; and it is through the teaching of that Word that we are able to meet together this day, under one roof. Therefore, I say, I know no Sovereign but the Queen, and I never shall know any other. I am walking by the side of the Pakeha."

Again, it is more evidence that the message of unity and law found in the Bible guided Maori understanding of the benefits of the Treaty. One Sovereign. One Law. One people together.

"Under the old [Maori] law we perished; under the present law we live," echoed Hemi Matini Te Nera, a Ngatimahanga chief from Waingaroa.

"Let me say a word about the Maori," said Manukau leader, Rihari. "In former times he was poor; since the arrival of the Pakeha, he has become rich. The Gospel too has reached this Island. My God in the olden time was Ouenuku. I have a very different God now. I am grateful to the Pakeha for the following benefits, namely – Christianity, the Laws, and Good-will. I must speak of these good things; for since the arrival of a Governor, good has remained in the land."

Rangi rose and said: "Waitaha is the place, and Waitaha the people. All I wish to see is justice, peace, and quietness. This will be our glory. Jesus Christ hath said – 'Let evil be overcome of good.' Another word. Let all things be conducted according to law, and under the Queen's rule. I shall sit under that rule."[209]

---

209 The relevant portion in Maori, note the Queen's rule, "whakakuinitanga": "Tenei hoki tetahi, Kia tika te whakahaere i runga i te ture, i runga ra i te whakakuinitanga, me noho au ki reira."

That doesn't sound like a chief retaining absolute sovereignty for himself. Were these chiefs, as modern academics argue, trying to retain supreme Maori justice and customs for themselves?

A perceptive speech from Ngatitoa's Tamihana Te Rauparaha, of Otaki, appears to answer this claim directly with a strong rejection of old Maori customs: "The customs of former days have been abandoned, and will, in future, be trampled under our feet. We are now following a new path, and a right one. It is this which causes the heart to rejoice. The fathers have disappeared. We are their children, who now meet to discuss questions; therefore, I say, let us not be inactive in this Council."

Te Rauparaha also clearly understood the nuances that came with Queen Victoria's sovereignty, and of the separatist Maori King movement, he told the gathering:

"I am grieved about this new thing. I mean this new name – the Maori King. Its tendency is to cause division and ill feeling between the Maories and the Europeans. Its tendency is to lower both Pakehas and Maories. I say let this movement be suppressed...and let the Pakehas and the Maories live together as brethren. Let the Queen be Queen for both England and New Zealand, It was not without good ground that the title of Queen of England and of New Zealand was assumed.

"I say, let our views be clear. Let it not be supposed the Pakehas wish to enslave (oppress) the Maories. It is not so. The Pakeha wishes to raise the Maori. I am therefore very much grieved on account of this movement. Our old Maori customs are at the bottom of it, and it has been set up to attract our younger brothers. What has changed our clothing, and caused the dog-skin mat to be laid aside? This new name will lead to our debasement; therefore, I say, let it be suppressed.

"Let this King be put down. We are becoming divided amongst ourselves by means of this King. It therefore appears to me we shall be of this opinion, Chiefs of the Conference, that we must support the Governor, and that we should avail ourselves of advantages offered to us and thus share in; the superiority of the Pakehas.

"Let us abandon Maori customs. Look at the superior condition of the Pakeha! This is not slavery. Let this title of King be put down. Even though the King's flag has been hoisted at our place Otaki it shall be cast down, it shall never be allowed to stand. It is calculated to produce ill-will and division, and if the Maori is separated from the Pakeha, he (the Maori) will find himself wrong. The Queen's shall be our only flag. We will hold our lands under the protection of the Queen."

Faced with a clear choice between tino rangatiratanga and the Queen's sovereignty, the son of the great Ngatitoa chief Te Rauparaha knew which side his sovereignty was buttered on.

Another making a clear sovereignty choice and showing he understood it was Ngatiwakaue's Henare Kepa, who also warned Maori about the dangers of being seduced by separatism: "I place myself now under the feet of (or submit to) the Queen and the Governor. Behold! The Pawharawhara (a parasite which bears a fine flower) is on fire. Do not climb that tree, lest you fall with it."

None of the speeches are being quoted here, by the way, to make a judgement call on whether their position was right or wrong – but only to establish that the chiefs had a much clearer understanding of sovereignty, law and land issues than modern interpretations of the Treaty debate suggest.

The Tarawera-based Tuhourangi's Matenga was another who spelt out in excruciating detail why he thought Pakeha sovereignty was better in practice:

"[The Governor's] good acts I have seen. He has explained the laws to us: they are understood by all the people. I say, therefore, nothing has been withheld: all the people are informed. Do you listen to what I have to say about my true oath?

"A man of our tribe was killed in the midst of the Ngatitematera. If it had been dealt with according to Maori Custom, no one could say what would have been done. But the law constrained me and it was settled according to law. According to your view the case was not one of murder but death by accident. I accepted this view, and so it was settled."

But Matenga also offers 21st century readers a piercing look at the tino rangatiratanga aspect of the Maori King movement. Again, he may be right or he may be wrong, but he was viewing it first hand at the time and his argument shows no sign of being "vague and confused" in regard to sovereignty:

"With respect to the King and the land. According to my idea this King is like a crying, fretful child. You brought your good things: they were eagerly sought after by the Maori, but he could not attain the standing of the Pakeha; he then parted with his lands to the pakeha in order to become possessed of money, because he and the Governor were friends – for Potatau was your loving friend. He understood the system of the Queen's Government; that it rested upon the principle of having one Chief. He perceived the means by which the Queen became great:

by her councils and by money. As soon as he had acquired this knowledge he separated himself from the shadow of the Governor, and set up a king for himself.

"If the Governor has a desire to bring this to nought, this is my opinion: stop all the channels of money and clothing throughout New Zealand, and prevent the Europeans, living in Native districts from giving money to any of the King's followers. In order that you may distinguish your people let them bear a mark on their forehead. If the King's men should come to sell wheat or pigs, do not buy them, lest that King become possessed of money. If you adopt this plan this King will not become great; it will not be long before the scheme dies away according to the words of Scripture "the works of man shall be brought to nought." This is all I have to suggest in reference to the King (movement)."

One of Matenga's colleagues recounted how the Queen's Law was crucial to Maori success and life expectancy:

"The good things which have come to us are for the welfare of our bodies," said Tuhourangi's Te Kihirini. "The goodness consists in the justice of the law. Now murder was a cause of contention and fighting in olden times. When the pa was captured, a hundred persons died for the sin of one man. At the present time the life of the murderer is the atonement for his guilt. I approve of this system; I approve of the laws of the Queen. My reason for liking the Europeans is that they bring us garments and mills."

But it wasn't just a more comfortable lifestyle that was causing Maori chiefs to repudiate their previous tikanga.

Wiremu Tipene, (Te Uriohau,) Kaipara: "I will speak about the Maori mana. The Ngapuhis have their mana, the Ngatimaru have their mana, the Ngatiwhatua, and the Ngatiwhakaue, have their mana, as their protection; but the mana to protect me is broken. The day of my salvation was the preaching of the Gospel. I will cleave to the Word of God as a parent for me. When the law of the Queen came as a protector for my body then all were warmly clad. The laws of God and of the Queen guard the gates of death. I beheld and thought this is a sign of salvation for all men threatened with death in this Island. I said, Christianity will guard the soul and the law of the Queen will improve our temporal condition: there will I take refuge.

"I will have nothing to do with the Maori mana. I will abide in the laws of God and of the Queen for ever and ever. These are the best laws I recognise; you, the Europeans, shall be parents to us the Maori people.

I will not acknowledge the Maori mana. The people of the Ngatiwhatua tribe intend to embrace and rest upon the law."

Arama Karaka, (Te Uriohau,) Kaipara: "We will speak that you may hear, for I was about so high (but a child) when I saw the practices which obtained under the Maori law, and perceived that they were bad. The old men said I must fly to the mountains for safety. I then said, 'Why should I fly, and what is the law by which I may know?' They then taught me thus, – 'War parties will attack us and destroy men's lives. These are the things which cause men to fly to the mountains.' I was also taught that men of inferior rank appropriated the produce of the soil to their own use; [and it was therefore OK that] they might be plundered, their houses burnt, and themselves speared. I am speaking about our laws down to the time our mana as a tribe was broken and I became small, while the other tribes maintained their mana.

"When the Gospel was preached in this Island, I asked my father, 'What is this?' He said, 'It is a Pakeha'.

'What does he say?'

'He preaches that we should believe on Christ, who was crucified that all men throughout the whole world might live…Then I embraced it (Christianity) and rested upon it. I said, This will put down all evil. I said, its laws are good laws, for they teach that all men should love one another and give up cannibalism.

"Afterwards Captain Symonds came and he said, 'There are soldiers coming to this Island'. I said, Come my ancestor, welcome my fathers.

"Afterwards came Governor Hobson. Then they told me of the laws of the Queen, and of the laws of England. Then I consented that you should be a parent for me, and that the Queen's mana should be my mana. I am under the mana of all men. You, O Governor, must be my protector. My laws must be given up; they are bad laws, cruel and dark. Your laws shall be my laws; let us be bound up that we may hold close together. This is what I have said down to this day. That which binds the Ngatiwhatua is the law of God and of the Queen. The laws of God are for the enlightenment of my heart, and those of the Queen are clothing for my body. The old men pass away, but I shall continue to speak the same language. You have heard what binds us; I refuse to acknowledge the Maori mana, or Maori government (chieftainship). I have seen its evils. It was the law of the Queen which showed me what is good for men – love and kindness."

Despite decades of exposure to the Bible, academics don't think Maori understood sovereignty, and in the footnotes to his English translation of the Maori Treaty text, Professor Hugh Kawharu maintains: "There could be no possibility of the Maori signatories having any understanding of government in the sense of "sovereignty" i.e. any understanding on the basis of experience or cultural precedent."[210]

Is Kawharu right: "No possibility"?

The Waitangi Tribunal has made rulings resulting in more than a billion dollars worth of settlements, based on arguments that the Crown (taxpayers both Maori and Pakeha), usurped the sovereignty of tino rangatiratanga without consent. After reading all of the above, you can reach your own decision on whether Maori understood the choices they were making when the signed the Treaty, and why those who had practiced traditional Maori tikanga were often the first to loudly and openly reject it.

Readers can now also judge for themselves whether Maori consented or not, to the abandonment of their tikanga.

Now, with a fuller understanding of what the Treaty of Waitangi meant to tribes at the time, we turn to the biggest issue of them all.

---

210 http://www.tiritiowaitangi.govt.nz/treaty/translation.pdf

CHAPTER ELEVEN

The Land Disputes

If there was one big gripe coming out of the Kohimarama Conference it was land, but possibly not in the way you think. As you should now all know, the Treaty guaranteed tribes "tino rangatiratanga" over such ancestral lands as they wished to retain.

The way the government did that was to leave tribal land in what's called aboriginal title, rather than freehold. That's because in the Maori system, most land was owned collectively by the iwi or hapu, not by individuals as in the British system. Until such time as an iwi or hapu got approval from their respective members to sell a portion of land to the Government where it was converted to fee simple estates, that land remained collectively owned and couldn't be sold to Pakeha.

That didn't stop some land slipping through, though: "Another grievance is the manner of negotiating land purchases. Notwithstanding there be only two or three consenting to the sale, their words are listened to, and the voice of the majority is not regarded," complained chief Wiremu Tamihana, a Ngatiawa from Wellington whose ancestral lands in Taranaki were under claim as we will see shortly. "However," he added, "the Laws are good, and the hospitals for the sick are good."

More frustratingly, though, Maori quickly realised they couldn't really sell their land to individual members of their tribes, either. Chiefs who saw their pakeha neighbours carving out a 40 acre block and making money from it, realised there was something to be said for the Crown property title system that turned land into a tradable commodity. But those same chiefs could not carve out their own individually-held 40 acre blocks and get a Crown title, without first selling the land to the Crown.

Again, faced with a choice between the traditional ownership model of tino rangatiratanga, and the settler model, many Maori were openly pitching for conversion to the European way, even though it would have meant tribes effectively cashing in their land holdings back then:

Matenga, Tuhourangi, Tarawera: "This is about the land. It is, in accordance with my opinion that it should be divided that each man should have a certain number of acres, that he may be able to sell his portion to the Europeans without creating confusion."

Wiremu Tamihana: "Let me state my grievance. It is this. Our lands are not secured to us by Crown Grant. Every man is not allowed to get a Crown Grant to his land."

This dilemma goes to the heart of the great divide. The missionaries following the 'noble savage' doctrine figured they were doing tribes a favour by advising the Crown to make it impossible for Maori to sell land privately. In this way, land sharks could not take advantage of Maori, and tribal resources would not be sold for a song. The problem was, with a tiny population, Maori had far more land than they had ever actually used. They'd never farmed cattle in pre-European times because they simply didn't have any, and they had no vast crops like wheat or barley until Pakeha arrived, so actual land use was at a minimum. If there was one way Maori could genuinely have got rich quick, it would have been through land sales.

Instead, they were forced to watch enviously from over the fence as settlers were able to snap up land, develop it and on-sell it at a profit. Fee simple estate,1. Tino rangatiratanga, Zip. It wasn't that the Maori system of ownership was wrong, it was just that it was different, and nowhere near as flexible for the new economy being created.

One could argue that a more equitable solution might have been to turn all land in New Zealand into fee-simple estate with Crown title, and then allocate Maori their share of that land for them to do with as they pleased, but that would have undercut the Church Missionary Society's strong issue with making tribes vulnerable to land sharks. In some respects, however, it's a remarkably similar debate to the one being held today over foreign investment in New Zealand farmland: if a farmer is offered ten million for a farm that he would only receive five million for on the local market, should he have the right to sell it for that higher price? Many New Zealanders argue 'no, the land is a strategic asset'. If each member of every tribe had been allocated land with Crown title, some might have become rich from the proceeds, and others would undoubtedly have been ripped off. There were no easy answers.

The lack of Crown title and defined boundaries, however, created extra woes. Under the tino rangatiratanga system of land occupation, tribes were still highly vulnerable after Waitangi to intertribal warfare over disputed land. By the very definition of tino rangatiratanga in the Treaty, the Crown had promised not to interfere in their general administration of their lands, and was pretty much powerless to interfere even when it wanted to.

It didn't take long after the Treaty was signed for troublesome examples of land squabbles to come to light, and it was something the Colonial Administration, on orders from England, took very seriously. There were several reasons for this.

Firstly, the Brits took their treaty obligations to heart, and continued to do so through the colonial era. A letter from the Secretary of State's office in the UK to the Governor records: "I need hardly tell you that it is the full intention and earnest desire of Her Majesty's Government (as it has been of their predecessors), that the Treaty of Waitangi shall be faithfully observed, both in its letter and its spirit,"[211] a comment from which you can trace the 20th century Court of Appeal rulings about "the spirit of the Treaty" continuing to be observed.

Secondly, the Governor wanted to find a way to prevent ongoing land wars between tribes, and thirdly the government wanted to fine tune a process for purchasing land from the tribes.

One of those with plenty of experience was Chief Protector of the Aborigines, George Clarke, who'd been appointed as part of Governor Hobson's administration from early 1840. His brief summary of how land was seen by Maori is worth repeating, but so first is the Waitangi Tribunal's commentary on Clarke's expertise and integrity:

"George Clarke was appointed the first protector on 6 April 1840. A missionary who had been in the country since 1824, Clarke was fluent in Maori, knowledgeable of tribal custom and well qualified to take on the position. Initially, as Normanby's instructions made clear, he was expected to be the official who bought land from Maori while promoting their amelioration. This dual role was an inherently contradictory one. The requirement to maximise profits from the resale of land created serious difficulties for the protector. It was impossible for him to offer Maori a good price, although he could ensure that sales were otherwise fairly conducted and that sellers did not part with land that they needed. There

211   Letter from Chichester Fortescue, Downing Street, to Governor Gore Browne, 27 August 1860

was a danger that it would undermine the protector's more important tasks if he continued to be an entrepreneur in land dealings, albeit for the Crown. Clarke requested to be relieved of this duty in 1842 and this was accepted."[212]

Clarke's credentials thus established, his comments from an 1844 report to Governor FitzRoy are as follows:

"If...the natives emigrated at different periods, we have at once a clue to the origin of titles. Each migration landed, subdued, and laid claim to a certain district now claimed by their posterity. Each party would most probably acknowledge a leader, either nominated or assuming such character by virtue of superior prowess, who would actually be considered as the first Chief of the iwi, or tribe...

"His children and those who attached themselves to them formed separate hapus: who, although a part of the original family, would form a separate and distinct community: uniting, however, in times of war to repel the common enemy, but claiming and exercising independent interests in the soil in times of peace.

"Bravery in war, and consequent power and rank as a Chief, will not determine the individual to be a great landowner. A man may be a great general and a small landowner; hence numberless mistakes have arisen among Europeans, who thought themselves especially safe in purchasing land from a powerful chief.[213]

"The Chiefs of every tribe or hapu, as well as the head of every family belonging to the tribe or hapu, have *distinct* claims and titles to land within their respective districts. At the same time it must be remembered that they have a *joint* interest in many of the lands.

"The particular [individual] claims of the Chiefs, hapu, or families are to lands either subdued or brought into cultivation, or upon which they have exercised some acts of ownership: as lands where they have been accustomed to procure flax, or erect weirs for eels, or where they have built a substantial house. In such cases they claim a particular property: none but the person so claiming can give title to the land, nor can he be dispossessed thereof. He may forfeit his right by killing, adultery or migration to a different tribe and district.

---

212 Waitangi Tribunal, "Ngai Tahu Report 1991", Paragraph 5.5.2
213 Which is one of the reasons the Crown didn't rely on chiefly authority as sufficient proof in itself for sale of land.

"In this way families hold and cultivate their ground, enlarging their individual cultivations from time to time, thus establishing an indisputable title to such lands as their special and particular property.

"In other respects, their title is more general: the hapu and families claiming in common with the principal Chiefs what may be termed their waste lands. But even here they must be able to substantiate some sort of title, such as having been the first discoverers, kindled ovens, built canoes, or exercised some other act of ownership which gives them the preference over such lands. The families have in common with the Chiefs the right of keeping pigs, gathering flax, snaring pigeons, catching rats, ducks, digging fern root etc.[214] Every individual of the tribe having these privileges in common, but still acknowledging the right of some particular family or individual member of a family to dispose of such property: that is, as president, head of family, or Chief of the tribe or hapu to make the first proposal of alienation; yet they could not consider the purchase valid without the consent of the majority of the principal men of the tribe.[215]

"Lands that are thus possessed in common, involving the interests of so many claimants, are exceedingly difficult to purchase, and may be reckoned as among the most fruitful sources of their quarrels and disturbances. It frequently happens that two natives, equally interested in the same lands, disagree on the question of its disposal. Numberless animosities originate from this source.

"To obtain a specific title to lands held in common, there must be some additional circumstances to support the pretension: first discovery of trees, shooting pigeons, constructing eel weirs, digging fern root, making a road, receiving a wound, losing a friend, recovering from sickness – all or any of these acts give an undeniable right to special property in land heretofore considered common.

"Conquest, unless followed by possession, gives no title. Were the Ngapuhis to claim the right of selling or exercising the sovereignty over the districts of the Thames, Kaipara, or Waikato in

---

214 For those who question the kind of evidence the Waitangi Tribunal accepts, this confirmation from 1844 of what the Colonial Government was prepared to accept is proof that the evidentiary process was acceptable to the Crown right from the get-go

215 In other words, whilst a principal person would act as chief negotiator over a land transaction with pakeha, that person, regardless of status, still had to get tribal approval to sell tribal "waste lands" owned in common.

virtue of their former conquests, their pretensions would be treated as contemptible and absurd: and so distinctly is this principle recognised, that I have no doubt that any attempt to support and maintain the validity of titles derived from conquest only, would be met by a most determined resistance even if attempted by Her Majesty's Government.

"I have known slaves tenaciously maintaining their territorial rights while in a state of captivity, but I never knew a master to claim by virtue of his slave, or attempt to advance any pretensions founded on the capture of a landed proprietor. I have had large offers of land for sale by natives still in captivity, and have been warmly reproved by these men for doubting the validity of their title.

"Great changes have taken place in the internal regulation and division of districts, and lands have completely changed owners, but in every case possession has followed immediately on conquest. The claim to Taranaki preferred by the Waikatos is good so far as they have taken possession, but they did not wholly succeed in driving the Natives out of that district, who maintained their independence by resorting to different pahs on the coast. I should therefore consider the principal right to land in the Taranaki district still vested in the original inhabitants." – Chief Protector of Aborigines, George Clarke

Another with experience in Maori tribal ownership was the Bishop of New Zealand, George Selwyn:

"There is reason to think that an independent right to alienate [sell forever] land, without the consent of the tribe, is unknown in New Zealand. On the other hand, in the ample territory which each tribe at first possessed, there was probably much freedom of choice in the particular spot which each member might wish to cultivate. This spot became his own by right of occupation, and in the absence of all forms of conveyance descended to all his children and grandchildren, sons-in-law and daughters-in-law, till the right which was at first personal became complicated by a multitude of claims.[216]

"In the neighbourhood of fortified places these plots of ground, from the necessity of the case, were as minute as cottage gardens near a populous town, and it may be taken for granted as a general rule that in such cases

---

216 Bishop Selwyn's Memorandum to the Governor, May 1860

every acre of land will contain ten or twenty plots (each between 200m^2 and 400m^2 in today's metrics), and for every plot there will be ten or twenty claimants, as I have repeatedly found. In such cases also, for the sake of mutual protection, the right of the tribe to control the alienation of land to foreigners would be most rigidly enforced."

Much like the Crafar farms debate today, Maori had always known that selling their land to members of rival tribes could bring trouble right to their doorstep, which is why the tribe collectively had a say. The European issue was seen slightly differently. Many tribes begged, "send us Europeans to live amongst us", by virtue of the fact the Europeans were outside of tribal rivalries, or that they spent money locally, or that having Europeans on your doorstep lessened the chance of a rival tribe beating you up and raising the Governor's wrath.

There are many examples of land disputes we could look at, worthy of an entire set of encyclopedias, but for the sake of shedding light in *The Great Divide*, one will suffice: it all came to a head in Taranaki.

In 1996, the Waitangi Tribunal released what it described as its biggest decision, the compensation for the so-called Taranaki land wars. In its ruling, the Tribunal determined that the Ngatiawa people had been "expropriated" from their ancestral land by the evils of Pakeha colonisation.

"One form of expropriation was that, at various times, absentees (ie, Taranaki Maori who were then living away) were excluded from having interests. We believe that those exclusions were not justified. Another form of expropriation, before the wars, were Crown purchases while customary rights and the process for alienation had not been agreed. In our view, for those reasons alone, in terms of the Treaty, those purchases should be vitiated."[217]

It is these two foundational declarations of fact by the Waitangi Tribunal that this book now investigates. Who were these "Taranaki Maori who were then living away" and therefore "excluded from having interests"? Likewise, what were these illegal "Crown purchases while customary rights and the process for alienation had not been agreed"?

In its opening chapter, the Tribunal report plays down any Maori guilt in the Taranaki affair, stating "There is *small* evidence [emphasis added] of Maori belligerence in this case, but, none the less, there was a firm expectation that Maori authority would be respected and reasonable dialogue maintained."[218]

---

217 Waitangi Tribunal, "The Taranaki Report: Kaupapa Tuatahi", Overview, p3
218 Waitangi Tribunal, "The Taranaki Report: Kaupapa Tuatahi", Chap. 2, p3

At the genesis of the Taranaki dispute is a chief named Wiremu Kingi Te Rangitake, of the Ngatiawa people (as they were then called, now known as Te Atiawa[219] by the Waitangi Tribunal today). When armed conflict broke out, Kingi was what the Tribunal called an "adherent" to the Kingitanga movement; "the movement under the Maori King[220], where the relationship between the separate authorities of the colonisers and Maori was exemplified in the symbolic depiction of 'the [Maori] King on his piece; the Queen on her piece, God over both; and Love binding them to each other'.

"The symbols were seen by the Governor as a challenge to the Queen's authority, but it is difficult to comprehend that that was ever intended,"[221] declared the Waitangi Tribunal. Readers will shortly be able to make their minds up as to the "intention" of the King movement.

To understand the politics of the Waitangi Tribunal, one can fairly swiftly see that it adheres to the same modern 'Maori supreme sovereignty' argument that we've already seen was not the way chiefs in 1840 and 1860 saw it. Nonetheless, *because the Tribunal is the only body officially permitted to interpret the Treaty of Waitangi and advise the government on its meaning*[222], you'd better read the Tribunal's starting position for yourself:

"On the colonisation of inhabited countries, sovereignty, in the sense of absolute power, cannot be vested in only one of the parties.

"In terms of the Treaty of Waitangi, in our view, from the day it was proclaimed, sovereignty was constrained in New Zealand by the need to respect Maori authority (or 'tino rangatiratanga', to use the Treaty's term).

"State responsibility, not absolute power, is the more necessary prerequisite to governance in this context... at least it can be said that both Government authority and Maori authority were recognised in the Maori text of the Treaty of Waitangi."[223]

As readers are already aware, the Kohimarama runanga debate and decisions superseded the Treaty of Waitangi in a constitutional law sense, so the very fact that the Waitangi Tribunal has the sole right to determine what the Treaty of Waitangi meant is itself questionable. The Kohima-

---

219 Because I am quoting extensively from official documents of the period, for the sake of consistency I have left tribal names as they appear in the documents, not as they may appear now.
220 The King movement today is a respected, apolitical manifestation of Maori dignity. Criticisms of it in this book relate to its early history and are not a reflection against the tremendous mana the Maori King enjoys from Maori and Pakeha alike today.
221 Ibid, p3
222 "The exclusive right to determine the meaning of the Treaty rests with the Waitangi Tribunal, a commission of inquiry created in 1975 to investigate alleged breaches of the Treaty by the Crown." See http://www.nzhistory.net.nz/politics/treaty/the-treaty-in-brief
223 Waitangi Tribunal, "The Taranaki Report: Kaupapa Tuatahi", Chap. 2, p4

rama conference chiefs made it patently obvious that absolute sovereignty rested with the Queen, so this modern whitewashing of history that's taken place is in stark contrast with the speeches in *The Great Divide.* That's why this book is important – because it cuts out the middleman to bring you authentic Maori and Pakeha voices from the past without the filters imposed by the Tribunal.

One of the first things to tackle, just to clear it away, is whether the Maori King movement was an authentic expression of Tino Rangatiratanga, as claimed by the Waitangi Tribunal which has declared it was not "a challenge to the Queen's authority", or whether it did, in fact, become a full-scale rebellion.

Chief Wiremu Nera Te Awaitaia, a Ngatimahanga chief of the Waikato confederation second only to the first Maori king, Potatau Te Wherowhero, is on record as warning the Government, "the war is not a struggle of the Maori with the Pakeha; it is not a war with the Missionary; it is not a war with the Magistrate; *it is a war of the King with the Queen*". [emphasis in the original][224]

In other words, a battle for the position of absolute sovereign. This in itself is a clear recognition Maori knew the Queen had supreme mana over New Zealand, and that some Maori wished to take that back.

Reverend J A Wilson, an Anglican missionary to the Waikato, reported on this and another conversation with a Waikato chief, "Te Wetini, the leader of the Ngatihaua, who fell on the sixth of this month at Taranaki, and who was really a manly and patriotic native. This chief admitted freely and openly that the war was not merely a contention for the land at New Plymouth, but for the chieftanship (rangatiratanga) of New Zealand.

"He said that 'wherever the King's flag went, they (the war party) would follow: that if the Governor sent troops to *any* part of this island they would meet them'."

Wiremu Kingi, the Taranaki chief who'd taken up arms, had initially resisted the Maori King movement but suddenly saw common purpose if he could get the Waikato king movement to back his rebellion:

"The pakeha wants our land, but this war is about your Maori King," he told a gathering of the king movement in the Waikato. "Do not listen to the pakeha, but bring your flag to Waitara. Go back and clear them out: send them all back to England."[225]

---

224 Wiremu Nera, Appendix E9 of The Governor's Despatch to Downing Street, 4 December 1860, quoted in Appendix to the Journals of the House of Representatives, 1861, E-01, page 24
225 Wiremu Kingi, Appendix D1 of The Governor's Despatch to Downing Street, 4 December

Readers can therefore make their own minds up as to the integrity of the Waitangi Tribunal's statement about the supposed benevolent intent of the Kingitanga movement.

The land dispute over Taranaki intimately involved the Waikato tribes from where the king movement later grew.

In a report to Downing Street explaining why New Zealand was now in a state of limited civil war, Governor Gore Browne set out the background to the dispute:

"In order rightly to understand the position which the Governors of New Zealand have uniformly assumed in reference to the title of the Ngatiawa at Taranaki, it is necessary to remember that they were a conquered, broken, and scattered tribe, and that the fairest and most fertile country in New Zealand, their ancient inheritance, was a deserted wilderness at the time of the European colonisation.

"About 30 years ago [1830], the great chief Te Rauparaha persuaded a large force of the Ngatiawa, Ngatiraukawa, and other tribes, to assist him in his wars with the original inhabitants of both shores of Cook's Strait.

"The Waikato natives, taking advantage of their [Ngatiawa's] absence, suddenly invaded the Taranaki district and took Pukerangiora, a large pah on the Waitara river...capturing or destroying nearly 2000 of the inhabitants.

"They then attacked Ngamotu, near the present site of New Plymouth, but without success, and returned to their own country. They never repeated their attack, though they frequently threatened to do so: and the remnant of the Ngatiawa tribe, finding themselves too weak to oppose effectually any renewed invasion from Waikato while their principal warriors were absent with Rauparaha, migrated with their women and children and rejoined their relatives at Otaki, Port Nicholson, Queen Charlotte Sound and other places, where they took possession of and cultivated the soil, and where their title was afterwards admitted by reason of such occupation,[226] against Rauparaha and others who claimed the land by right of conquest."

From a European perspective, wrote Governor Gore Browne, it was clear that some ten years before settlers arrived in the district, "the Ngatiawa tribe had either voluntarily migrated on conquering expeditions to other lands, or had left in dread of the Waikatos, or had been driven by force out of their ancient territory and had completely abandoned it.

1860, quoted in Appendix to the Journals of the House of Representatives, 1861, E-01, page 24
226   See footnote 33 (Rangitane). This Ngatiawa migration and conquest in the late 1820s displaced the Rangitane tribe from the northern South Island.

"When the first white men went there, there were only 60 people living in the whole district north of the Sugar Loaf Islands, and for a long time subsequent to 1840 they had not much more than 100 acres in cultivation.

"In the expressive language of two of their chiefs, in a letter to the people of Taranaki: 'All was quite deserted; the land, the sea the streams and lakes, the forests, the rocks were deserted; the food, the property, the work were deserted; the dead and the sick were deserted; the landmarks were deserted'."[227]

The Governor explained to England that New Zealand officials had needed to deal with some harsh realities as a result of signing the Treaty of Waitangi. One of those was that "desolating wars" had left some tribes "in full possession of their tribal territories" – like Ngapuhi, Waikato and Ngatimaniapoto – while other tribes had been "so broken and scattered by conquest" from bigger tribes that virtually none of their ancestral territories remained in their ownership. Ngatiawa, claimed the Governor, was a prime example of a vanquished and scattered tribe who had lived by the sword of conquest and, while they were away, lost to the sword of conquest in their own homeland.

These, then, are the people the Waitangi Tribunal mischievously referred to in its official findings as "absentees (ie, Taranaki Maori who were then living away) [who] were excluded from having interests." The Tribunal made it sound like the Taranaki tribe had nipped out to the shops and been burgled. The truth is something far different. Likewise, as will become obvious, their interests were not "excluded".

In December 1841, New Zealand's first Governor, William Hobson, had written to the Secretary of State in Britain detailing how the Crown had purchased the Taranaki homelands from the conquerors, Waikato and Ngati Maniapoto. Their hand had been forced somewhat by Wakefield's New Zealand Company which, in 1839, had snapped up large portions of land through payments made to several remnant Ngatiawa hapu in the area. Because the land was conquered by Waikato, the Waikato tribes accused the New Zealand Company of paying the slaves, when they should have been paying their masters.

"Te Wherowhero claims the country as his by right of conquest, and insists on it that the remnants of the Ngatiawa [the sixty or so left in the district] are slaves; that they only live at Taranaki by sufferance, and that

---

227 Letter from Chiefs Ihaia and Tiraurau, Appendix D4 of The Governor's Despatch to Downing Street, 4 December 1860, quoted in Appendix to the Journals of the House of Representatives, 1861, E-01, page 8

Te Werowero or Potatau

they [Ngatiawa] had no right whatsoever to sell the land without his [the Waikato paramount chief's] consent.²²⁸

"In illustration of his argument," remarked Governor Hobson, Te Wherowhero "placed a heavy ruler on some light papers, saying, 'Now, so long as I choose to keep this weight here, the papers remain quiet, but if I remove it, the wind immediately blows them away. So it is with the people of Taranaki', alluding to his power to drive them off."

It is true that Waikato were a mighty confederation of tribes. The Ngatiawa warriors who had shifted to the Kapiti coast, Wellington and the Marlborough Sounds and taken those southern lands by conquest did not feel confident to try their luck against Waikato to get their own ancient northern heartlands back.²²⁹

So, to give certainty, Hobson purchased Taranaki from the conquerors *as well*, just to make doubly sure. The Deed of Sale from the Waikato/ Maniapoto tribes to the Crown was dated January 1842. Waikato had claimed ownership of the lands by conquest, and through that right sold the Taranaki to the Governor. Ngati Maniapoto received the cash in the deal, and reached a separate side agreement with Hobson in April that year that allowed them to continue occupying some of what was now European Crown land, "distinctly warning them at the same time that they were not to interfere with the European settlement at New Plymouth."²³⁰

So far, so good. Empty land, conquered whilst Ngatiawa war parties were off conquering someone else, and onsold to the Crown.

The Crown then sold 60,000 acres to the New Zealand Company for

228 Governor Hobson's Letter to Secy. Of State, December 1841, as quoted at Appendix B1 of The Governor's Despatch to Downing Street, 4 December 1860, quoted in Appendix to the Journals of the House of Representatives, 1861, E-01, page 10
229 The Kohimarama conference heard, and it was not challenged by the assembled chiefs, that Waikato had sold the Taranaki district in "open daylight" to the Crown. Native Secretary Donald McLean later testified, "Any occupation of the land [before the sale] was entirely out of the question, but those Natives who were released from [Waikato] slavery from time to time were permitted by Waikato to occupy, but those who had fled to the South were not allowed to return, and they were distinctly warned that if a return were attempted it would be the cause for fresh war against Ngatiawa."
230 Governor Gore Brown's dispatch to Downing Street, 4 December 1860, page 10

the purposes of settlement of the Taranaki district, a decision ratified by the then Commissioner of Lands, William Spain, in the face of protests from "absentee" Ngatiawa based in the Wellington region.

The Government had been encouraged in their actions by Waikato and Ngati Maniapoto chiefs, who told Protector of Aborigines Thomas Forsaith, "Go and tell the Ngatiawas that the Waikato Chiefs remind them that the land is theirs [Waikato's], and advise them to settle their dispute with the Europeans or the Waikatos will settle it for them."[231]

The Colonial administration would have done well to heed the words of one of their own advisors: "It is from purchasing lands, the right to which is thus contested by two hostile parties, either of whom will gladly avail himself of an opportunity to sell independently of the other, that Europeans have unwarily fallen into so many difficulties," wrote Edward Shortland in a report to the Chief Protector of Aborigines.[232]

As predicted, the clamour from Ngatiawa exiles grew stronger, especially when Land Commissioner Spain issued a judgement in favour of the 60,000 acre purchase in June, 1844. That same week, on June 8, 1844, one of the Ngatiawa chiefs, Wiremu Kingi, wrote to the Governor complaining the voices of his tribe had not been heard.

"The Europeans are wrong in striving for this land, which was never sold by its owners, the men of Ngatiawa...This also is the determination of our people. Waitara shall not be given up; the men to whom it belongs will hold it for themselves. There was not a single man of the Ngatiawa

Wiremu Kingi

231 Report of Protector of Aborigines, Forsaith, quoted at Appendix B13 of The Governor's Despatch to Downing Street, 4 December 1860, quoted in Appendix to the Journals of the House of Representatives, 1861, E-01, page 11
232 Shortland's letter quoted at Parliamentary Papers, 29 July 1844. Contained in appendices of The Governor's Despatch to Downing Street, 4 December 1860, quoted in Appendix to the Journals of the House of Representatives, 1861, "Opinions on Native Tenure", page 12, see http://www.nzetc.org/tm/scholarly/tei-TurEpit-t1-g1-t6-g1-t10-body1-d13.html

tribe who received the payment of Col. Wakefield [of the New Zealand Company]. These are the only men who took the payment – the men of Ngamotu and Puketapu, and they had no right in Waitara."

As a matter of record, the "men of Ngamotu and Puketapu" were, in fact, Ngatiawa, so Kingi's claim that no Ngatiawa had been paid was not, strictly, true.

"There is no manner of doubt that these were hapus, or families, of the Ngatiawa ranking equally with the Manukorihi branch to which Kingi himself belongs," stated Governor Gore Browne.[233] Additionally, the Ngamotu and Puketapu hapu were the occupiers of Taranaki under Maori custom, whereas Waikanae-based Wiremu Kingi was not.

The problem was that two sets of Maori had been paid for the land by 1842. The first being the few Ngatiawa still living in the area, and the second being the Waikato iwi who claimed ownership by conquest. But this third set of people, the Ngatiawa hapu groups that had fled to Wellington and the top of the South Island, now wanted a slice of the action back in Taranaki. To make matters even more interesting, the Ngatiawa had been given official title to the lands they had conquered in the south. In essence, they already had that cake but wanted to have the one they had not yet returned to as well.

"It appears to me," wrote Land Commissioner William Spain in 1844, "that the Ngatiawa, who left this district after the fight, and sought for and obtained another location, where they lived and cultivated the soil, and from fear of their enemies did not return, cannot now show any equitable claim to the land they thus abandoned."[234]

It was only after the land had already been purchased by the New Zealand Company and the Crown, wrote Spain, and the settlement of New Plymouth had been built, that the Ngatiawa exiles felt safe enough to begin returning to the lands they had once called home – now owned by Europeans.[235]

The Government's problem was that the Ngatiawa population in Taranaki

233   The Governor's Despatch to Downing Street, 4 December 1860, quoted in Appendix to the Journals of the House of Representatives, 1861, page 12
234   Commissioner Spain's report on the Taranaki purchase, 12 June 1844
235   There is a certain historical irony at this point. In 1844, Moturoa, an exiled Ngatiawa chief then resident in Wellington, appeared back in the 'naki to lay claim to a portion of land at Omata. "The resident natives stated that he had no right to come and assert his claim to land from which he had been so long absent, having possessed himself of other lands in Cook's Strait, which he had sold to the Europeans, without considering his relatives, who were left behind to keep possession of and defend lands which he had forsaken." Report of Donald McLean, Protector of Aborigines, 17 December 1844.

shot from 60 when the land was originally purchased, to more than 250 by 1844, thanks to returning slaves freed by the Waikato tribes. Suddenly, 190 extra Maori were back, saying the land that had been sold was theirs.

A compromise position floated by the Government was, "Let a definite sum be fixed as a fair and equitable price" for a reduced land purchase of 7,150 acres, "from which deduct the amount of payment any of the present claimants may have received from the [New Zealand] Company; the unpaid resident Natives [recent arrivals] receiving their proportionate shares, and the residue lodged in trust for the absentees, who should have notice that unless their claims were preferred and substantiated within a given period (say, twelve months) they would be considered forfeited. Such award should be final and absolute."[236]

It wouldn't be the first time a government in this country thought it was inking a "final and absolute" settlement with iwi, but at stake was possibly the future of New Plymouth as a settlement. As it turned out, the fallback position in the end was only 3,500 acres.

Governor Robert FitzRoy, the former captain of Darwin's voyaging vessel *The Beagle*, made a personal visit to Taranaki to address 200 Maori and 80 Pakeha, and announced he was setting aside the 60,000 acre purchase agreement.

"My heart was very dark when I heard that you were in trouble about your lands. Some portions were rightly purchased, and some wrongly. It was not that the Pakehas wished to act dishonestly, it was through mistake. The men who owned the land did not consent to sell their portions," said the Governor, "I will seek some plan, some way of settling the matter.[237]

"But remember you, not one of the Rangatiras of the Queen of England will consent to a man acting dishonestly, and if he consented that the land of a Maori should be taken, the payment for which had not been completed, that would be a theft. If I consented to take for nothing your lands, I should be like a thief. I did not come to New Zealand to steal."

Governor FitzRoy told Maori and settler alike that while the plan was being worked out, he would not tolerate any "Pakehas being expelled... I will not agree to your molesting the Pakehas, nor will I agree to the Pakehas molesting you." If peace could not be maintained, he warned, "I will bring soldiers, that quiet may be kept."

FitzRoy then made a major statement, casting aside the Maori conquest doctrine as he reversed the sale of the 60,000 acres.

236 Report of Protector Forsaith to the Chief Protector, 23 November 1844
237 Speech at Taranaki by Governor Robert FitzRoy, 3 August 1844

"In my opinion, it is not just if a man carried off by a war party as a slave, when he returns from slavery finds his place gone, or his house or anything else. No, if we were at war with any other nation, and I was taken as a slave and afterwards liberated; if when I returned to my place I should find that my place had been sold, what would my thoughts be, would I consent? Not at all."

When some Maori questioned the level of payment being offered for their land, FitzRoy was blunt, pointing out that the Crown was seeking to purchase unsettled, uncultivated tribal 'waste lands' and charging a higher price to settlers in order to pay for infrastructure:

"What is it that makes land valuable? It is labour...If you were to work constantly on the land when sold, then you might expect a large payment. It is different when Europeans deal with Europeans, then the payment is great, but you must not suppose that it is all for the land; in addition to the price of the land it is for bringing out labourers, and tools, and seeds, and cattle, in ships; for making roads, and bridges, and surveys, and many other things. The payment for the land only is very small.[238]

"If you had anything to do with these works which makes land useful, you might ask a high price; but as I have said before, you have nothing to do but sell it, and therefore cannot expect a large payment."[239]

FitzRoy wasn't reversing the land purchase because he disagreed with its legal foundations, but merely the integrity of the process. The official papers show he was more concerned about quelling the angry voices from those newcomers who claimed they'd never been asked, never had the chance to either consent or refuse the land sale.

His solution was simple. He told the 200 Maori gathered that every one of them who believed they had a land claim in the disputed territory should "go to their teachers, or to the Protector of the district who lives among them, and state the names of their places, and the Protector will write down the names of the owners and their estate, whether belonging to man, or woman, or child. And if such owner agrees to sell his place on reasonable terms it will be purchased and he will receive payment...do not encroach on any other person's possession, but let every man point out his own. Do you ask why we are thus to take down the names of

---

238 Governor FitzRoy's Visit, Official Report, published in *Te Karere*, September 1844
239 To be fair to iwi, while the Governor's arguments were reasonable, in principle the income being raised from land sales was falling rapidly and being outstripped by the costs of building infrastructure, so the scheme was not actually working. One could argue that if Maori had been allowed to reach their own prices for their land, they would have had more money to spend on infrastructure themselves, such as towns for their people.

your places? It is to prevent future mistakes."

Initially, Wiremu Kingi indicated he was happy with this process, writing to his local aboriginal protector and to the New Zealand Company's Colonel Wakefield:

"Friends, Mr Kemp, Major Richmond and Colonel Wakefield. We are going to our place, Waitara. We are thinking of selling our place, Waikanae. We wish to sell this place."[240]

Kingi knew, however, that the Ngatitoa tribe were planning to lay claim to Waikanae if he left,

Governor Robert FitzRoy

so he was really offering to sell a can of worms. The Crown saw through it, and refused to purchase Waikanae, nor would the Governor consent to the Ngatiawa exiles returning to Waitara lest it provoke a war with the Waikato tribes.

Governor FitzRoy, meanwhile, was just discovering he'd been fired by Downing Street. The British Government was stunned at the Taranaki land decision reversal, and more particularly stunned that they had not been fully briefed on it. The problem was it had been a busy time for FitzRoy who, in 1844, had also had to deal with the chopping down of the flagpole at Kororareka in July during the brief Ngapuhi rebellion, and the still-lingering aftermath of the Wairau massacre in which 22 settlers had been killed after trying to force an illegal land settlement on justifiably angry South Island iwi led by Te Rauparaha.

As Ian Wards writes in his biography of FitzRoy, the Governor actually played with a straight bat when it came to Maori land issues:

"FitzRoy confirmed settler antagonism by treating land claims as if there were Maori legal rights, and Crown grants for land in Wellington and Nelson, on a much lesser scale than demanded by the company, were issued only on the payment of more money. FitzRoy's actions, judicious and firm, sparked off attempts by the New Zealand Company officials

---

240 Letter from Kingi to Kemp, 2 September 1845

to have him replaced. Settlers could not perceive that FitzRoy was acting in their best long-term interests."[241]

FitzRoy was recalled as Governor by the British Parliament in mid 1845[242], but the news did not reach New Zealand until September by gossip, with the official marching orders arriving on 1 October. Governor George Grey stepped up to the plate on 18 November, 1845.

Perhaps as a recognition that they'd left the New Zealand Governors dangling with no resources for too long, the British doubled the Governor's salary and vastly increased the colony's budget.

Grey found himself picking up the pieces in Taranaki, and discovered FitzRoy's reversal of the land sales had caused new problems: some of the Ngatiawa occupants who had originally happily sold the land and who, Grey wrote, "had been amply paid for the land they had disposed of, informed me that they intended to stand by my predecessor's arrangement and to repudiate the first transaction, and that they could neither permit the Europeans to occupy the land they had sold them, nor would they even do so upon receiving a further payment; but they insisted upon the Europeans confining themselves to the block of 3500 acres."[243]

Since the Europeans had arrived, making the region safer, noted Grey, "various individuals of the Ngatiawa tribe (which is a very numerous tribe), anxious to share in the expected payment, have been locating themselves temporarily at Taranaki, and every separate family of the tribe has been sending up some persons to look after their interests.

"These individuals have been quarrelling amongst themselves regarding their respective claims…indeed, the inability of the natives to adjust their respective claims now makes them unwilling to allow the land to be sold at all, and they constantly assert that those natives who wish to sell land have no right to dispose of it."

Grey's proposed solution to the impasse, reached after negotiations with Ngatiawa chiefs at the start of March, 1847, was to seize control of Taranaki, marking off "the most ample reserves" for present and future Maori, and to then send survey teams and investigators into the remaining territory now to be held by the Crown, so that a "Commissioner and…a

---

241 "Robert FitzRoy" by Ian Wards, *Encyclopedia of New Zealand*, see http://www.teara.govt.nz/en/biographies/1f12/1
242 The final straws had been FitzRoy's decision to issue "paper money", banknotes, as a form of currency in New Zealand, without approval from London, and his vacillating response to Hone Heke's ongoing aggression in the north, which killed hundreds of Maori and Pakeha and left Heke boasting that the 'mana' of the Pakeha had been destroyed.
243 Governor Grey's Dispatch to Secretary of State, 2 March 1847

Court should then be appointed to inquire into the Native titles to the whole, or portions," of the district that had been seized. "Those Natives who established valid claims to any parts of it should receive the corresponding portions of the payment to which they would become entitled," wrote Grey.

"Those natives who refuse to assent to this arrangement must distinctly understand that the Government do not admit that they are the true owners of the land they have recently thought proper to occupy."

Governor George Grey

In other words, Grey's administration was prepared to argue it had received proper title to the land in the original purchase, and that offering money to returning Ngatiawa was a take-it-or-leave-it deal in the tradition of speak-softly-but-carry-big-stick. This then, had the potential to become a mighty mess.

"Very few of the Natives seemed disposed to assent to this arrangement," noted an apparently surprised Governor, "but they distinctly understood that it was my intention to enforce it."

Perhaps even more surprisingly however, within 24 hours the Governor had added a postscript to his letter to London after further discussions with Ngatiawa, saying "The whole of the Ngatiawa tribe with the exception of one family of it, the Puketapu, have assented to the arrangement detailed in this dispatch, and that several European settlers have already been put in possession of their lands. I have now every hope that the Puketapu family will shortly follow the example of the rest of the tribe."

Grey's orders were codified in instructions to Donald McLean in early 1847. Within weeks, he received intelligence that Ngatiawa were building nine large waka at the Petone foreshore near Wellington, capable of carrying 540 people, and the Governor suspected they were destined for a migration to Waitara. He ordered the canoes to be disabled until the powderkeg "land question at Taranaki is settled."[244]

---

244   Letter from Grey to Lt. Col. McCleverty, 27 April 1847

Grey sat down with one of the exiled Ngatiawa chiefs, Wiremu Kingi, and offered him a deal: "Relinquish all pretensions to any lands on the south bank" of the Waitara river, he told him, and we will let you return to Taranaki, and buy Waikanae from you.[245]

"Upon all pretensions being at once relinquished to all lands to the south of the Waitara, the Government will, without further inquiry into such pretensions to these lands, admit that from the prompt settlement they are making of this question they are entitled to such compensation as may be agreed on between themselves and the officers of the Government.

"The Government will then also recognise and permit them to immediately dispose of their claims at Waikanae and Totaranui for such compensation as may be agreed on…the Government will survey regular village sites on the North Bank of the Waitara for native villages, at such points as they may select, and will endeavour to see that the amount of compensation paid to the natives shall be so expended as to secure their permanent advancement in civilisation and prosperity."

Given that virtually all of Wiremu Kingi's land-holdings were on the northern side of the Waitara river anyway, it seemed like a winning deal and indeed he agreed to it.

At the 1860 Kohimarama conference, Donald McLean reminded some of the chiefs that they'd been with himself and Wiremu Kingi at Waikanae in 1848 when Kingi told them, "Let me return [to Waitara]…when I get there, one side of the river shall be yours and the North side mine."

"That was his word," McLean told the Kohimarama gathering, "which is retained in the memories of myself and others here present who heard what passed between us."

No chief at Kohimarama who'd witnessed the exchange called McLean a liar on this.

When the Puketapu family agreed to sell what's now known as 'the Bell Block' of land, Wiremu Kingi did not prevent it from happening. Instead, he told McLean in Whanganui,[246] "I am willing that it be sold, but I have a claim on it. Let the payment be kept back until I arrive there [in Waitara]."

McLean agreed, but was surprised when later officiating at the Bell Block sale and payment function, attended by "all the people of Puketapu

245 Memorandum to Taranaki Land Claimants, Decisions of Gov. Grey, quoted in Session Papers, Gen. Assembly, 1860, E. No. 4
246 Yes, the town was referred to as Whanganui in official European documents at this time, but most likely pronounced Wanganui

and other places", to see that although Wiremu Kingi was there as well, he had no claim lodged and no share of the payment.

As Governor Grey had noted, many Maori hapu decided to sell their land holdings under his proposal. As the appointed official to investigate, Donald McLean "travelled over the district in company with some natives, King's [Wiremu's] own brother being one of the party, and they pointed out to me the respective claims of the different hapus or subdivisions of the Waitara tribes.

"Wiremu King was expected to come back from Kapiti. His own claims and those of his immediate followers were represented by the best possible evidence (that of his own brother) to be almost exclusively on the north bank of the Waitara River."[247]

Maori customary land wrangles were about to intervene, however. Kingi felt he had dibs on land belonging to a rival exiled chief, Ropoama from Queen Charlotte Sound. Ropoama's ancestral lands were on the south bank of the river, and according to McLean "Kingi designed to possess himself of a portion of the land at Waitara belonging to Ropoama."

Things seemed to be moving ahead quite rapidly. A number of large land holdings, like the 1,500 acre Bell Block and the Grey Block, had joined the 1844 FitzRoy Block of 3,500 acres and passed into Pakeha ownership via direct negotiation with hapu members. The Bell Block is a perfect example of some of the intertribal pressures, however. The land was sold with the blessing of Chief Rawiri Waiaua and a large segment of the Puketapu hapu, but not without challenge. It was sold, says McLean, "in the teeth of the most determined opposition from the Chief Katatore and others of the same family."

In the end, Katatore arranged for Rawiri Waiaua's murder and a roadside memorial still marks the spot of that today,[248] but Katatore himself met a murderous end only four years later in an ambush witnessed by settlers:

"Upon the evening in question I had occasion to visit the house of my neighbour Mr R Street," wrote a correspondent to the *Taranaki Herald* newspaper. "I observed as I entered six armed natives lying in ambush in the rear of his workshop. Tamati Tiraurau was seated in the house, he rose and passed out upon my entering.[249]

"The natives were repeatedly asked to withdraw, but refused, having

247 Evidence of Donald McLean, given on oath at the House of Representatives, 14 August, 1860
248 http://www.waymarking.com/waymarks/WM949D_Puketapu_Feud_Memorial_Cross_Bell_Block_New_Plymouth
249 Letter published in the *Taranaki Herald* from E W Hollis, 15 January 1858

taken up their quarters there during the greater part of the day.

"About 7pm, five Maories rode up and halted in the crossroads. They were Katatore, Tamihana, Rawiri Karira, Meihana and a youth called Wiremu. I shouted out to them to 'make haste' as there were natives lying in wait to shoot them.

"There was a moment's pause, and then the fellows ran to the hedge and fired a volley at those in the road. The fire was not effective, on perceiving which the assailants rushed into the road.

"One of them presented a gun at Rawiri's breast, and fired. He was badly wounded, rolled from his horse, struggled with his enemy a short time, and was seized by the hair by Tamati and tomahawked in an awful manner.

"It was a sickening sight to see the poor fellow imploring mercy, the blood streaming down his face in torrents, and the ruthless savage protracting his agony by a pause between the blows; twice di he succeed in getting from him, but weakened by loss of blood and much incapacitated by drink as well, he fell an easy victim.

"Katatore dismounted, but finding himself so closely beset, and seeing his relative mortally wounded, he fled up the road leading to the bush, protected as he went by Tamihana. He was shot down about 800 yards of this line and his head fearfully beaten with a gun, which was broken in the attack. He was also tomahawked.

"The whole affair was a deeply laid plot. Men may call it what they please, but to an Englishman, and an eyewitness, it was an atrocious murder and nothing else. The death of Katatore may be considered an act of retributive justice. Be it also remembered it took place within a few paces of our doors and under the eye of our wives and children."

Given that Chief Katatore was mostly loathed by the Pakeha settlers, you can get a feel for how bad the event must have seemed to evoke that kind of response from a settler.

In order to make sure they got it right, however, Governor Grey's men did not simply sign purchase agreements on the dotted line, preferring instead to take their time, wait for rival claimants to appear. They didn't want a repeat of the 1844 debacle. In regard to the Waitara block, it was exactly the same process.

European land purchases in Taranaki had jumped from 3,500 acres in 1844 to more than 32,000 acres by 1853, and as McLean later testified, "the whole of the purchases previously made at Taranaki had been effected on the same principle as the present one of Te Teira, namely, that of acquiring the land from the different clans and subdivisions of clans which came in from time to time to offer it."[250]

So what went so badly wrong with the Waitara purchase? Why did that single land transaction – just like all the others for two decades before it in structure, but at the same time utterly unlike them in outcome – become a defining moment in New Zealand history that's perpetuated a new mythology about the Treaty of Waitangi?

Why was the Waitangi Tribunal allowed to lie about the Waitara dispute and allow its findings to become case precedent and fodder for our school curriculum – thus further perpetuating the lie?

The answer is simple.

---

250 Donald McLean, evidence at the Bar of the House of Representatives, 1860

CHAPTER TWELVE

Waitangi's Fairytale Godfathers

If the phrase "Once upon a time…" wasn't effectively a Walt Disney trademark, you'd find it as the opening words of Waitangi Tribunal reports.

In this case, the mythology is found ensconced in this extract from the first chapter of the Tribunal's 1996 report on Taranaki:

"We see the claims as standing on two major foundations, land deprivation and disempowerment, with the latter being the main. By 'disempowerment', we mean the denigration and destruction of Maori autonomy or self-government. Extensive land loss and debilitating land reform would likely have been contained had Maori autonomy and authority been respected, as the Treaty required."

In plain English, the Waitangi Tribunal saw the Taranaki claim as an ideal stalking horse to hang the Maori sovereignty argument on. As you will see in this chapter, the argument goes that despite being granted the same rights as all British citizens, Maori were supposed to remain exclusively loyal to Maori tribal structure, that New Zealand should have been governed by two hierarchies, two "treaty partners", Maori and the Crown, where ordinary citizens were subjects of either the Queen or Maori leaders.

The British believed they had granted Maori the right to participate in European society, but the Waitangi Tribunal position is that tino rangatiratanga applied and Maori only had rights to participate in wider society insofar as their tribes and chiefs permitted them to. The Tribunal calls this "Maori autonomy" and says this rule by chiefs "is pivotal to the Treaty and to the partnership concept it entails".

In its 1996 report, the Tribunal zeroed in on what it alternatively called "tenure reform" or "land reform", and categorised everything done under it as "confiscation" by the Pakeha, and a breach of the Treaty.

What exactly is this "tenure reform"? It was the decision by the Governors to allow Maori hapu and individuals to sell their personal land-holdings to the Crown, as you saw in the last chapter, and the process that followed of giving such Maori "Crown title" to their land, allowing them to buy and sell as they wished. Readers will recall we touched on this briefly at the start of Chapter 11, when chiefs at the Kohimarama conference were voicing their preferences:

Matenga, Tuhourangi, Tarawera: "This is about the land. It is, in accordance with my opinion that it should be divided that each man should have a certain number of acres, that he may be able to sell his portion to the Europeans without creating confusion."

Wiremu Tamihana, Ngatiawa: "Let me state my grievance. It is this. Our lands are not secured to us by Crown Grant. Every man is not allowed to get a Crown Grant to his land... We are desirous that our pieces (of land) should be surveyed, and that each individual should receive a Crown Grant for his particular portion, so that when a desire springs up in an individual to part with his portion, he can do so, and the evil consequence will rest with himself. The evil is this, he will be without land. Now we know that the Governor is indeed a friend to the Maori, because he has consented that our lands shall be surveyed; for this reason I say let the plan be quickly carried out. Mr. McLean, you have heard the desire expressed by myself and Riwai that our lands should be surveyed. You agreed with us. Make haste and send some workmen on some future day."

Hukiki (Ngatiraukawa, Otaki): "Listen, people of the Ngatiraukawa, Ngatitoa, and Ngatiawa tribes. This is the word which we have been in search of in years that are past. The Governor has now revealed that word to us, about surveying our land, but when will it be put into effect? This has been shown us; three years have we waited for it; but when will the lands be surveyed? Pigs have been marked, cattle and horses have been branded.

"My name is Hukiki, the brand on my cattle is HU, but the land has not been branded (referring to Crown Title Grants). According to my opinion the land should be marked. Because the Chiefs are grasping at great quantities of land, leaving none for the poorer people. The Governor has now offered it to us. Now therefore I say we have indeed become children of the Governor. Because I have a great deal of land, therefore I have said let the land be given to the Governor and Mr. McLean; this land shall pass into the hands: of the Queen. I have declared these words in order that all the tribes may hear that this land has been surrendered to the Queen. The offer of Ohau has reached England."

Paora Tuhaere, (Ngatiwhatua,) Orakei: "I rise to speak to what Tamihana has said about the land. I agree to his speech. It is a thought which I have in my heart that i should give my lands to the Governor, and that the Governor should send a proper person to survey them, and I will cut the boundaries when surveyed. Let a notice be published in the newspaper that the Europeans, and also the Maories, may see. Let it be published for three or four months, and when it is seen that there is nothing wrong in the notice (no protest or objection), then let the Governor give a document for that land, which will enable me to sell it to the European, If it should be seen that, the map (or notice) describing the land is wrong (if the claim is disputed), then let a Committee settle it (by arbitration)...I refer to the Crown Grant; that is one of the things I very much wish to see given to the Maories, that is if the Governor should be willing to give us those documents; If the Governor grants this, then only will I say there is but one law.

"Now, Mr. McLean, mine is a land-selling tribe. I have been selling land for the last twenty years, but you will not remember any year in which a dispute arose. No piece of land has been paid for twice over. We are not in that practice. Our plan is this: when a block of land is offered for sale, we hold a committee, and when all who are interested in that land have consented to the sale, it is then sold to you, but when a person having no claim interferes with our land then a dispute arises, and ultimately it is adjusted. This is another matter. The Governor proposes subdividing the land. It is right that the land should be apportioned amongst the owners thereof."

Parakaia te Pouepa, Ngatiraukawa, Otaki: "I say to this Conference, I will wait. If the Queen's system come to nought, then I am wrong; but if the system of the Maori come to nought through the means of the gospel and the Queen's authority, then they (my opponents) will be found in the wrong in time to come."

According to the Waitangi Tribunal, those speeches never happened or, if they did, the speakers were joking and didn't really mean it. Under the Cultural Revolution that passes for some of academia today, leading Maori chiefs never called for an overhaul of the system that gave them individual Crown titles for their land. If they had done so, that would be "consent". We know they did not do so, because the only Government agency with the right to legally interpret the Treaty of Waitangi says Maori never consented.

Here's what the Waitangi Tribunal says happened:

"The confiscation of tribal interests by imposed tenure reform was probably the most destructive and demoralising of the forms of expropriation. All land that remained was individualised, even reserves and lands returned. No land was thus passed back in the condition in which it was taken; it came back like a gift with an incendiary device. This land reform, so clearly contrary to the Treaty when done without consent, made alienations more likely, undermined or destroyed the social order, jeopardised Maori authority and leadership, and expropriated the endowments to which hapu, as distinct from individuals, were entitled.

"The subsequent fragmentation of title and ownership was the inevitable consequence, making Maori land the illusory asset that it is for Maori today, and bequeathing to generations of Maori farmers frustration for their labours and divisions within their families.

"The purchase of individual interests began as soon as individual interests were created. The practice continued even when the extent of Maori landlessness was plain, so that little Maori land now remains."

The Waitangi Tribunal calls it a blatant breach of Article 2 of the Treaty, but if you read the Treaty carefully, Article 2 provides that:

"...the Chiefs of the Confederation and all the Chiefs will sell land to the Queen at a price agreed to *by the person owning it* [emphasis added] and by the person buying it (the latter being) appointed by the Queen as her purchase agent."[251]

Doesn't the Treaty of Waitangi, in the Maori version, actually prove that "individual interests" in land could be sold and bought? What else could be envisaged by the singular use of the word person, instead of iwi? Could it be that the Waitangi Tribunal has reached wrong decisions because it hasn't properly read the Treaty?

In journalism, it's called 'never let the facts get in the way of a good story'.

The 'facts' as the Waitangi Tribunal evidently sees them are that before the Treaty, Maori lived in a Smurf-like forest glade where everything ran like clockwork and everybody was happy with their lot in life, eating fernroots and being forced to sleep outside in the cold if they were sick, and that colonial administrators cheated Maori of their tino rangitiratanga

---

251   Treaty of Waitangi, official Maori version as translated by Professor Hugh Kawharu

by changing the rules on land without consent from the tribes. The 'facts' as they really are, inconveniently show that Maori chiefs were begging for the Pakeha land sales system as a step towards "one law for all".

And as for today's nostalgic memories for the Smurf-era? Try listening to what one Maori chief at the time said about that:

Parakaia Te Pouepa (Ngatiraukawa, Otaki) "Let the Maories lament over their bygone customs. If our proceedings be right, what have we to do with Maori Law? Let them go on lamenting."

Let's not simply rely on Article 2 of the Treaty to prove the point about Maori land sale practices. The Waitangi Tribunal makes it seem like a colonial conspiracy, but in fact the colonial bureaucrats had gone to great lengths to try and figure out how Maori ordinarily regarded land and land use.

The Crown had always maintained that because it recognised communal ownership of ancestral lands, it was also prepared to recognise the ability of hapu family groups to sell the plots that they had personally lived on and controlled. The government would not, however recognise that a chief had personal sovereignty rights over a tribe or hapu's land, precisely in the same fashion that it refused to allow any other tribal member to individually sell tribal land. If it was communally owned, argued officials, then it was communally owned, and the smallest units they would deal with were hapu or extended whanau speaking solely for land under their direct control.

There was, argued Governor Gore Brown in his 1860 briefing to London, no history of chiefs or, for that matter even tribes, selling land as a commodity in pre European times (a system known officially as 'alienation', or cutting off parcels of land, in perpetuity).

Having said that, the Government was also mindful that the paramount chiefs of large, unconquered tribes deserved to be consulted about land sales within their districts. As Governor Gore Browne told Downing Street: "No Government for instance would have thought of making a purchase at Ngapuhi, or at Waikato, in the teeth of the veto of great Chiefs such as Tamati Waaka Nene and Potatau te Wherowhero."

In other words, where there was evidence of an unbroken line of chiefly authority in a district, those chiefs would be consulted, but where only the remnants of a tribe remained, the official land purchasers would deal direct with the families and hapu groups who still lived there, in the absence of strong authority. This, of course, was the dismal situation that greeted them in Taranaki.

In 1837 the then British Resident, James Busby, had written to the Governor of New South Wales describing the ranking of chiefs. His description also has a bearing on the tino rangatiratanga debate:

"To those unacquainted with the status of a Native Chief, it may appear improbable that he would give up his own proper rank and authority. But in truth, the New Zealand Chief has neither rank nor authority but what every person above the rank of slave, and indeed the most of them, may despise or resist with impunity."[252]

This reflected some of the commentaries by the early missionaries like Marsden whose voices were heard earlier in this book. A chief had power over his immediate household, and of course his slaves, but he could not order other citizens of his tribe to do his bidding, unlike the way that English nobles in the Middle Ages could enforce loyalty.

New Zealand's first Chief Justice, Sir William Martin, who upheld the Treaty of Waitangi as inviolate, was nonetheless able to rule: "There is no paramount or controlling power, either in the tribe or the subtribe, to restrain or to direct the exercise of" the sale or purchase of land. "Each family or free man may use and appropriate [take] land without leave of any," said the Chief Justice.

Archdeacon Octavius Hadfield – who later became a staunch advocate for Wiremu Kingi's anti landsales position – in 1845 had taken the view that under existing Maori custom, "The Chief of the tribe, since he has no absolute right over the territory of the various hapu, nor over the lands of individual freemen of his own hapu, cannot sell any lands but his own, or those belonging to the tribe, which are undoubtedly waste lands."[253]

The flip side to that, of course, is that if a chief had no sovereign right to sell land he did not personally own, then he also had no right to personally veto the sale of land he did not personally own.

The issue confronting Governor Gore Browne and the settlers and Maori of Waitara in 1859 was essentially that – whether a chief had real power under tino rangatiratanga to veto the sale or purchase of land that belonged to other members of his tribe who wished to sell. As British citizens with the same rights to buy and sell as all other citizens, this tino rangatiratanga veto was imposing a restriction on the rights of Maori New Zealanders that appeared to be illegal under the Treaty.

---

252 Letter from Busby to NSW Governor, 1837, quoted as Appendix E11 of The Governor's Despatch to Downing Street, 4 December 1860, quoted in Appendix to the Journals of the House of Representatives, 1861, E-01, page 8
253 Appendix A9 in Appendix to the Journals of the House of Representatives, 1861, "Opinions on Native Tenure", page 12

As we move into the endgame phase of this historically vital crisis moment in New Zealand history and constitutional development, let's return again to the scene of the crime, Waitara and the events surrounding it.

~

With the murders of rival Puketapu chiefs Rawiri Waiaua and Katatore in the 1850s over the Bell Block sale, there was growing disunity within Maoridom about land sales. To be fair, territorial disputes had always been close to tribal hearts in pre-European times, so this kind of dispute was not new. Something else was, however.

The signing of the Treaty of Waitangi had shown Maori it was possible to have one sovereign, and it had shown Maori could themselves act in unity on occasion. Additionally, the influx of European settlers, laws and social interaction had given Maori a much stronger concept of what a culture acting in unison could achieve.

Up until Waitangi, New Zealand had not been a 'Maori' nation as such, but a collection of dozens of separate Maori nations altering between war and peace with each other periodically. A close European analogy might be the highland clans of Scotland, or the principalities that were later united into modern Germany.

The current 21st century belief that the Treaty created a governing "partnership" between Maori and the Crown is, like so much else in this debate, mostly neo-romantic fantasy. It was a Treaty between the Crown and the nation of Ngapuhi; the Crown and the nation of Ngatiwhatua; the Crown and the nation of Ngai Tahu, and so on down the list. Each of those Maori nations had their own laws, tikanga and other practices. There was, when the Treaty was signed, no pan-Maori overlord who could present himself as "the Treaty partner".

In the two decades since Waitangi, however, Maori culture shifted drastically as village communities became interconnected with a modifying influence: Pakeha culture. No matter where you went in New Zealand, Pakeha technology, laws, economic development, education and culture became the glue of conformity for the tribes. Suddenly Maoridom had a common focus, a common reference point.

The mana of Pakeha culture was plain to see for Maori back then, and readers have seen Maori appreciation of that in some of the Kohimarama speeches in this book. But for some Maori it raised obvious questions.

Were they being cultur-
ally swamped by the
newcomers with their
beguiling ways? What
would happen to Maori
in their own homeland
if they simply assimi-
lated as brown Pakehas?
What would happen to
their mana as chiefs if
their young people were
allowed to integrate fully into Pakeha society? What would happen to
the old ways if they sold most of their lands?

The Pa of the Wherowhero , Waikato district.

These are all valid questions, and we are still having those debates
today around immigration and foreign investment. The Kohimarama
conference shows most chiefs were in favour of unity of the races under
one sovereign, but a minority of Maori were not, and they became the
Kingitanga movement, and the focus of the so-called Maori renaissance
of the 20th century. Their followers, however, are the ones now in charge
of the Waitangi debate, the cultural gatekeepers. They are the ones who
can make the majority voices from the past fall silent – their words left
out of the popular history books and not quoted in universities – so the
only voices now heard are those who were once a minority. They have
re-defined Waitangi in their own utopian image.

In the mid 1850s, the first roots of what became the Kingitanga movement were spreading. Realising that Maori land was being purchased by
the Crown in a game of death-by-a-thousand cuts, some of the Ngatiawa
and their immediate neighbouring tribes made a decision after 1853 not
to sell any further land at all to Pakeha.

Given that the Treaty had promised Maori undisturbed possession of such
lands as they wished to retain, there was nothing illegal about this. The tribes
had a right to self organise and unite in common purpose if it suited them.

The problem was, not all Maori agreed, not by a long shot. Just as within
any society today there are a range of opinions from one extreme to another,
so too it was with Maori society in the 1850s. Where modern scholarship has
perhaps fallen victim to political correctness has been its assumption that
Maori shared the same view of the Treaty, the same view of tino rangatiratanga, the same view of land, the same view of sovereignty, of village life
– this is the 'homogenous Smurf' construction of pre-modern Maoridom.

For those tribes, and members of tribes, who wished to lock up their land and sell no more – they were entirely within their rights. But the big legal question became, did they have the right to impose their land sale moratorium on other tribes, or on members of their own tribes who disagreed?

"These opponents [to land sales] pushed their views, and sought to make it *te tikanga o te iwi* (the law of the tribe) that no individual or family should alienate land without the consent of the whole tribe. To make the law popular and binding, they determined on a more general meeting, and to invite all the tribes along the coast to join them in this measure.[254]

"This was the origin of the notorious Taranaki land league, which evidently contains the elements of the present King movement, which has proved so fruitful a source of dissension among the tribes of that district, caused so much bloodshed, and brought about the present collision between Wi Kingi and His Excellency the Governor.

"The land thus given over to the King is not to be alienated without his consent. This might be all fair if the party stopped here. But they resolve that no land shall be sold within their territory, even though the owner may not have joined the league. Any man, therefore attempting to sell a block of land would subject himself to summary proceedings at war; and any attempt to take possession of the purchased block by the Government would be resisted by force of arms, as in the case of the land at Waitara."

In tino rangatiratanga terms, this is where the rubber hit the road.

With the growing influx of European settlers to the colony, Governor Gore Browne in 1859 moved his chess pieces to try and break the stalemate.

"I held a meeting of the Ngatiawa chiefs at [Taranaki] in March, 1859, and made a public declaration of my intentions for the future," he reported to Downing Street. "I then laid down the principle that while on the one hand I would buy no land the title to which was in dispute by its rightful owners, I would not permit either Chiefs or people to forbid the sale of land by such members of the Ngatiawa tribe as were willing to cede their own land to Her Majesty."

Donald McLean was at that meeting, and later told a gathering of the Waikato tribes at Ngaruawahia exactly what had gone down.

"The Governor went to Waitara, and land was offered. One got up and said, 'I desire to sell my piece', and another got up and said, 'I wish to sell mine, I do not want to sell what is another's, but my own'."

---

254 Comments of Rev. Morgan to Parliament, "An Epitome of Official Documents Relatives to Native Affairs and Land Purchases in the North Island of New Zealand" edited by H Turton, 1883. See http://www.nzetc.org/tm/scholarly/tei-TurEpit-t1-g1-t6-g1-t12-g1-t1-body1-d8.html

McLean says he told the men making the offer that their holdings were too small to purchase. "Then Teira [Chief Te Teira Manuka] said to Wi Kingi, 'Listen, I am about to offer mine: Governor, here is mine'. But the Governor did not speak.

"Teira said again, 'Give me your word, Governor, McLean, will not you and the Governor consent to mine?'

"Wi Kingi sat there all the time and heard," McLean told the Waikato iwi. "When Teira had urged it once, twice, thrice, four times, the Governor said, 'If it be an undisputed claim, I accept it'.

"Then Teira laid down his parawai (mat), but Wi Kingi did not take it away, he only called out and said, 'Waitara shall not go', and went away."

Now this last paragraph is incredibly important. In Maori custom, the laying down of a parawai at the feet of another to seal the deal on a transfer was well recognised. Wiremu Kingi's response under Maori protocol should have been to withdraw the mat as a sign of dispute, but he did not. His fellow chiefs at the time understood the implications of that:

"When Teira sold his land and laid down the parawai as a pledge, William King did not come to take up the challenge but went away," remarked Ngatiraukawa chief Hukiki.

One of the chiefs at the Ngaruawahia gathering told the crowd he had personally investigated the parawai issue.

"I accompanied Wi Tako on his return from the Waikato. I wanted to have an explanation about the parawai," explained Chief Kapereira.[255]

"We saw Ihaia and Teira. Teira asked, 'for what purpose have you come?' We replied, 'To enquire about the mat and to take the truth back to Waikato'. He said, 'the piece is small. The greater portion of Waitara is King's, mine is in the centre'.

"I went to King and said, 'I have come to enquire about the mat'. He replied, 'The report is correct. I looked on in silence'. I said, 'That was your error, you ought to have taken it away'.

"'I did not,' he [Kingi] replied. 'I simply threw a word at the Governor and said to him, I will not give you my land. I did not take up the mat, but I spoke my word. The pakeha wants our land, but this war is about your Maori king. Don't listen to the pakeha, but bring your flag to Waitara. Go back and clear them out, send them all back to England'."

Kingi went further than claiming a veto over Waitara, where he lived. He then told the Governor he would veto any land sales in the entire

255 Speeches of Chiefs at Ngaruawahia, May 1860, as quoted at Appendix D of Governor Gore Browne's dispatch to Secretary of State, London

territory from New Plymouth to Mokau.

In its shakedown of the Waitara case, the Waitangi Tribunal made no reference to the tikanga process outlined above or the revelations at Ngaruawahia, and instead in 1996 made a finding that Chief Teira had exceeded his rangitaratanga by making a new law. The Tribunal argued that he was acting alone, without approval:

"In this way, the 'rangatiratanga' guaranteed by the Treaty was very much in issue, because the question was one not of ownership but of the customary process for managing land and its disposal. We have no doubt of the appropriate custom law principle. Any disposition that could introduce outsiders to the community, as in this case,[256] affected everyone, and accordingly a community decision, as expressed through the rangatira, was required. If there were two rangatira, no disposition could be made if they did not agree.

"Consequently, Te Teira was acting contrary to custom law principle in selling a part when not all were agreed. We suspect he was using the novelty of a sale to make a new law and to claim at the same time that he held more mana than Kingi, in that Kingi could not stop him. Kingi, on the other hand, was asserting the customary value, in our opinion, and was acting strictly in accordance with Maori law.

"For his part, the Governor was also creating a new law. He presumed to deal with individuals, when, by English law and the doctrine of aboriginal title, he was obliged to follow Maori law when buying land, which required that he deal with the collective interests through their representatives...

"A Maori rejoinder was impossible to constrain. In our view, it is a truism that conflict, even war, is inevitable when the freedom of a people is denied. Denied in this case was the freedom of hapu to make their own decisions, form their own policy, manage their lands and affairs in their own manner, and form pan-tribal associations. More particularly denied at the time was the right of rangatira to control recalcitrant individuals in alienating community land."

Just in case you didn't pick it up, the Tribunal says the illegal actions of the Governor in purchasing land illegally sold by Te Teira were a sufficient breach of the Treaty to justify Maori taking up arms in the Land Wars that followed.

The problem is, the Waitangi Tribunal appears to be wrong in fact and law. The clue to the mistake is the phrase, "Denied in this case was the

---

256   In fact, these sales did not "introduce outsiders to the community", as the Europeans were not coming to live in the Maori pa and claim mixed ownership rights over all the tribal land.

freedom of hapu to make their own decisions, form their own policy, manage their lands..." The Tribunal was technically right in its analysis of the core problem, but utterly wrong in its choice of prime suspect. Teira's hapu wanted the right to sell their own patch of land, it was that simple.

For a century, misguided Royal Commissions of Inquiry, aided by misguided historians and feeding into a thoroughly misguided Waitangi Tribunal, have painted Chief Teira as a villain and Chief Kingi as a hero. Their rulings and opinions have fleshed out into law an arguably false construction of the Treaty of Waitangi, because the Waitara case went to the absolute heart of the sovereignty debate.

Yes, these are big accusations to make, but the evidence appears to back it up. For a start, you've already seen that Article 2 of the Maori (signed) version of the Treaty allows for land owned by one Maori "person" to be sold, so the sale of land by even one person could hardly be "new law" as claimed by the Waitangi Tribunal. In this case though, it was far more than one person:

"You have said that one man sold the land, but there were seventy persons consenting to the sale!" protested Native Secretary Donald McLean to a meeting of 4,000 Maori gathered at Turangawaewae.

Seventy people? That sounds like a pretty large hapu. But hang on, didn't the Waitangi Tribunal uphold the right of hapu to sell their own lands? Chief Teira's hapu were clearly behind him. In fact, two and a half of the four resident Ngatiawa hapu apparently backed Teira over Waitangi Tribunal favourite Kingi.

"The Archdeacon's remarks[257] would lead to the inference that a block of six hundred acres at the Waitara has been ceded to the Government by one individual," wrote Donald McLean to Governor Gore Browne, "while he ought to be aware that the cession was the act, in the first instance, of two important hapus or sections – representing the Ngatitauhou and the Ngatihinga tribes, as well as a branch of the Puketapu, whose claims were intermixed with those of the two former tribes and rested exclusively on the southern extremity of the block in question, and moreover that subsequently it was confirmed and ratified by a large number of absentee proprietors residing in Queen Charlotte's Sound and elsewhere."

---

257   Archdeacon Hadfield later admitted on oath that his strident defence of Kingi's rights was based on hearsay information. One of his strenuous assertions, for example, was that Te Teira was going against the wishes of his own father who instead had "cooperated with William King in opposing his own son up to the very commencement of hostilities." You could almost hear Governor Gore Browne rolling uncontrollably with laughter on the floor as he held up the actual Deed of Sale, signed by Teira's father, Tamati Raru. Game, set, match against the disinformation, the Governor told London. See Appendix to Journals of the House, 1861, Session I, E-01, page 21

Further proof that Teira's sale was not unique is found, however, in Native Affairs Minister Chris Richmond's report on precedents. Richmond pointed out virtually all of the Maori land sales since the Treaty fell into two categories: those represented by paramount chiefs of entire iwi, and those made by "sub tribes (hapu), or of families or other comparatively small groups of individuals."[258]

In virtually all of the second class of sales, said Richmond, "the land sold has been territory actually divided amongst and appropriated by the different hapu or families of the tribe...All the purchases made to the north of Auckland, whether by Government or individual Europeans, belong to it. So do the purchases made of Ngatikahungungu in the Hawkes Bay district and the Wairarapa valley, of hapu of the Waikato tribe in the neighbourhood of Whaingaroa or Raglan, and of the Ngatiawa at Port Nicholson and Taranaki.

"In sales of vacant territory, the principal Chiefs have themselves been the vendors. In sales of occupied territory, an absolute and unquestioned right of alienation has always gone along with the right of occupancy, which is generally exclusive in certain hapu or families, and not [held in] common to the whole tribe."[259]

Richmond then delivered a key piece of advice: "No seignorial [Lord of the Manor] or tribal right of controlling sales by the Native owners *has ever been excercised or in anywise asserted since the commencement of land purchases in New Zealand.*"[260]

In other words, the Teira sale should have been just another day at the office, had it not been for the perfect storm about to break over sovereignty.

Despite being offered 600 acres by Teira and his hapu, the Governor still did not move immediately. He gave explicit orders to his officials to make certain that any land within the Pekapeka block subject to a disputed claim should be left out. Wiremu Kingi was invited to state the nature of his claim to the land but refused to do so. It was, however, obvious to officials that Kingi's pa, located on part of the block would have to be left out of the purchase. A 60 acre block was quarantined to safeguard Kingi's unspecific interests.

---

258 Appendix to Journals, 1861, E-01, page 26, supplementary to Governor's Despatch
259 Proof of this is found in the papers of Native Office interpreter J White, who listed numerous land sales signed off elsewhere in the country by hapu leaders just like Teira and not the paramount chiefs. See Appendix to Journals, 1861, E-01, page 54
260 Richmond did add a caveat to this. With chiefs still enjoying strong political power, the distinction between the niceties of property law and the practicalities of annoying an influential chief meant discretion should sometimes be the better part of valour. In this case, however, it would have made little difference. See Appendix to Journals, E-01, page 26

Kingi had, of course, only been allowed to return to Waitara on the basis of relinquishing "all pretensions" to a claim on the south bank of the Waitara River, and had agreed to that with Governor Grey 11 years prior. Nonetheless, the Governor was prepared to be convinced otherwise.

"I will not give the land to you," Kingi told the Governor.[261] "Some of the Maoris still desire to sell land, which causes the approach of death," he warned.

On April 25 that same year, Kingi wrote again. "All I have to say to you, O Governor, is that none of this land wil be given to you, never, never, never, not till I die."[262]

In trying to get to the bottom of whether Kingi had a legitimate personal interest in the south bank land, Donald McLean visited the other branch of the Ngatiawa tribe living in Queen Charlotte Sound and spoke to their chief, Ropoama Te One.[263]

"I mentioned that a portion of the Waitara had been offered. I recited the boundaries and asked, 'Does that land belong to Wiremu Kingi?'. The reply was, 'No. If it was on the other side of Waitara, his claim would be just, but this side belongs to us. Let us have the payment'."[264]

The Queen Charlotte Ngatiawa swung in behind Teira's proposed sale.[265]

Despite Kingi's protestations, then, a substantial minority of Ngatiawa had made arrangements to sell their land interests against his wishes. As British citizens, the minority Maori claimed this right to sell their own land as an exercise of their own personal tino rangatiratanga. You could even call it a vote of no confidence in their tribal leadership, if you wanted to frame it in democratic terms. But did they have a right to do that? When the Treaty guaranteed tino rangatiratanga, it explicitly provided it to all Maori people, not just the chiefs.

At stake was a considerable sum of money. Instead of receiving only a shilling and sixpence per acre maximum, Teira and his followers – in the tradition of true Maori entrepreneurship – had extracted a price of a pound per acre for the 600 acres, plus a £250 bonus on top of that.

261   Letter from Wiremu Kingi Te Rangitake to Governor Gore Browne, 11 February 1859
262   Letter from Kingi to Gore Browne, 25 April 1859
263   As a piece of historical trivia, the Te One whanau's name lives on in the name of Petone, near Wellington.
264   Appendix to Journals of the House, 1861, E-01, page 60
265   Ropoama Te One later drew a map of Waitara's south bank, showing Wiremu Kingi's small holdings, then his own and those controlled by Teira, which were much larger. Te One was a first cousin of Teira's, adding weight to the fact that Teira's hapu were largely behind the land sale. See genealogical details at http://www.wcl.govt.nz/maori/wellington/tupunaindex1_4.html

COPY OF SKETCH MADE BY ROPOAMA TE ONE, ON THE BEACH, AT PARIWHAKAOHO, MASSACRE BAY, ON THE 7TH. MAY, 1861, SHEWING THE PORTIONS OF THE DISPUTED LAND AT WAITARA, WHICH BELONGED TO HIMSELF TE TEIRA, AND WIREMU KINGI RANGITAKEI, RESPECTIVELY

COLLINGWOOD, 20TH. JUNE, 1861.   Sd. JAMES MACKAY JUNR., ASST. NATIVE SECY.

PINK—SHEWS THE LANDS BELONGING TO WIREMU KINGI RANGITAKEI.

GREEN—SHEWS THE LANDS BELONGING TO ROPOAMA TE ONE.

YELLOW—SHEWS THE LANDS BELONGING TO TEIRA.

"Eight months elapsed between the first offer and the final acceptance of the land, during which period every opportunity was given to adverse claimants to prefer and establish their right," records missionary Thomas Buddle. "On the 29th November, 1859, the District Commissioner called a public meeting of both Natives and Europeans to witness the payment of the first instalment of the purchase money; King and his people were present. A document was read setting forth the boundaries of the block, and also a declaration on the behalf of the Governor, that if any man could prove his claim to any piece of land within the boundary described, such claim would be respected, and the claimant might hold or sell as he thought fit. No such claim was put forward.[266]

"The question was put to King by the Commissioner, 'Does the land belong to Teira and party?' He answered 'Yes, but I will not let them sell it'."[267]

Kingi was then asked: "Why will you oppose their selling what is their own?"

"Because I do not wish for the land to be disturbed," he replied.

Of course, this put the fledgling colony on a collision course because it suddenly put the vague issue of absolute sovereignty sharply into focus: one law for all, or two peoples with two laws? Pakeha law or Maori tikanga? Were individual Maori being forced to swap their freedoms as British citizens, to once again became 'subjects' of the local chief?

It was a collision seven years in the making, however, as Taranaki tribes developed their policy of forbidding land sales from 1853 onward. The rise of the Maori King movement, although with a figurehead Waikato king, was driven by more separatist tribes from the central North Island, who had quickly picked up on the Taranaki policy.

"There is on their [the King movement's] part a determination to establish and uphold in all Maori districts an independent sovereignty over all Maories and Europeans resident therein, to the utter exclusion of any interference on the part of the Government," wrote missionary Reverend Morgan to Parliament.

"The vital question with the Maori Kingites now, is whether the King or the Queen shall possess the mana of New Zealand. Hence the frequent expressions of the Waikatos now in arms, 'We are going to fight for New Zealand. We sent the King's flag to Taranaki, and it is our duty to follow the King's flag. We are fighting for the mana of our island'."

Morgan, who'd been the Waikato missionary for twenty years, drew attention to the real issue: the King movement wasn't entering the fight because it cared about the intricacies of the Waitara sale, but because having planted its flag there Waitara was now King territory, not the Crown's.

"The Maori-King movement is the strength of the Taranaki war. … This entirely depends on the issue of the present war, which, on the part

---

266   The exact words were: "If any other person can prove that he owns any part of the land within the boundaries above described, his claim will be respected, and he will be allowed to retain or sell the same as he may think proper."
267   This is a key point. Kingi admitted publicly that Teira and his family owned the land as described, but continued to assert that he could prevent the sale regardless. See "The Maori King Movement in New Zealand" by Rev. Thomas Buddle, 1860, http://www.nzetc.org/tm/scholarly/tei-BudMaor-t1-body-d4.html#n27

of the Waikato, is a struggle for the mana of the Maori King, and not for the small piece of land sold by Te Teira at the Waitara. They only considered that small block of land as it refers to the mana of the King all lands on which his flag has been planted."[268]

In an effort to swing Maori sympathy the Crown's way, former British Resident James Busby wrote a letter to iwi everywhere, asking if tribes really wanted a return to the "might is right" doctrine they used to live by:

"Two ulcers have broken out – one at Taranaki, one at Waikato. Teira has sold his land to the Queen: Wiremu Kingi says 'The land shall not go to the Queen; the land is Teira's, let Teira keep his land; I will not suffer it to be sold, because though the land is Teira's the power is mine; I am Waitara, let Teira live under my shadow'.

"Friends, this is a great mistake of Wiremu Kingi's. In former times, before the Queen's shadow covered the land, when a strong man armed kept his palace, his goods were in peace; but when a stronger than he came he was overcome, and his goods taken from him. This was Maori custom. In those days Wiremu Kingi, being stronger, could overcome Teira; but when the Queen promised to every Maori that he should be as one of her own people, the law came.

"The law is the strength of the weak man, and the law says, 'Every man's land is his own, to sell to the Queen or keep; no one shall take it from him because he is weak; no one shall prevent his selling it if he wishes to sell it'.

"If the Governor allowed Wiremu Kingi to overcome Teira, he would make the Queen false to the promise she made to every Maori man when she entered into the Treaty," declared Busby.

The son of the great chief Te Rauparaha made exactly the same point, scoffing at the idea that Maori rules regarding land were set in stone:

"We know very well that according to our customs, might is right," Tamihana Te Rauparaha told the chiefs gathered at Kohimarama. "Our Maori plan is seizure. Let us enquire into these matters. Kapiti, for instance, was taken. The chieftainship of that belongs to me. According to Maori custom, when a man prevails in a struggle he claims it (the land). Now let us approve of the course pursued by Te Teira. He sold (the land) under the light of day. He gave a parawai as a covering for this land. William King did not take it away so as to repudiate Te Teira's claim to

---

268 *An Epitome of Official Documents Relatives to Native Affairs and Land Purchases in the North Island of New Zealand* edited by H Turton, 1883. See http://www.nzetc.org/tm/scholarly/tei-TurEpit-t1-g1-t6-g1-t12-g1-t1-body1-d8.html

the land. Should I come forward and offer land for sale, perhaps some relative of mine would say you have no land. In that case, if I had strength I would carry my purpose. We, the Maories, have no fixed rules."[269]

Again, given that a chief with the mana of a Te Rauparaha was saying this and backing up Te Teira's right to sell, how could the Waitangi Tribunal make the claim that "Te Teira was acting contrary to custom law principle"? Interviewing their typewriters appears to be the only explanation. Under ancient custom, Wiremu Kingi had the chance to withdraw Te Teira's parawai, but chose not to. How could the Waitangi Tribunal make a ruling that due process was not followed?

It is worth listening further to the voice from 1860 of Ngatitoa's Tamihana Te Rauparaha, who had close ties to Wiremu Kingi Te Rangitake [his full name]:

"I have now something to say in condemnation of the conduct of my son, Te Rangitake. I refer to his taking Te Teira's land and thereby causing the present war... It was the returned slaves from Waikato who instructed him in evil. That land belonged to Te Teira. He inherited it from his ancestors...when he got back to Waitara, to the land of his ancestors, then he spoke with authority as to the possessions of his forefathers. Therefore I say that Te Teira's conduct is straightforward, but William King's is wrong. William King tries to maintain his land-holding influence (mana-pupuri-whenua), the "mana" of New Zealand, but perhaps one reason is jealousy of the pakeha."

For Te Rauparaha, there was a sense in his speech that Wiremu Kingi was just being provocative and should get over himself. Kingi had barely escaped his former homelands with his life after receiving an early tip-off about the Waikato invasion all those years ago. He in turn had conquered fresh territory at Wellington and been given the financial benefit of that, but now having taken 500 of his exiled tribe back to Waitara Kingi apparently felt he could push people around. Te Rauparaha told the delegates that if every Maori wanted to go back to lands they once occupied and cause a fuss, conflict was bound to follow:

"The case is similar to ours," he said. "The lands of our ancestors are at Kawhia and Maungatautari. There are probably boundary lines, but I don't know them; perhaps the old men remember them. It was a deserted land. It was not left as the pakehas leave their lands, the title deeds being in the possession of their children.

---

269 All Kohimarama conference speeches cited in this book are available online at http://www.nzetc.org/tm/scholarly/tei-BIM504Kohi-t1-g1-t1-body1-d2.html

"I have land at Rotorua by virtue of my mother, but perhaps her relations who occupy it would not admit my claim. Nevertheless it is true that the land is mine. Now, if I should ask the old men to point out the boundaries (of this land) they would probably say that they had forgotten them."

You won't learn it from the Waitangi Tribunal, or any of the bestselling Waitangi books of recent years, but a large number of chiefs agreed with Te Rauparaha:

"In my opinion Teira's piece of land is his own, and he has a right to sell it to the Governor. I condemn William King," stated Hohepa Tamaihengia of Ngatitoa.

A Ngatiwhatua chief urged the Governor to give Taranaki Maori a damn good thrashing:

"I have one word to say about Taranaki. Should a child cry or be troublesome, the parent's rod will be applied, and not till he has ceased his naughtiness will the punishment cease," said Ihikiera Te Tinana, a Kaipara leader.

As an example, perhaps, of majority Maori feeling about the Taranaki War, *Te Karere* reported that South Island iwi were raising money for the besieged Pakeha settler families in Taranaki:

"On the 26th of June last, Hohepa, Nopera, and all the other chiefs of the Ngatitoa tribe, wrote a letter to the Ngaituahuriri, of Canterbury, to recommend them to abide by the 'clear laws of our mother, Queen Victoria, who is the nourisher of both the whites and the Maories.' On receipt of this letter, the natives of Canterbury met at Rapaki to consider the contents, thereof; and they all came to the resolution to be like the Ngatitoa, and 'cleave to the laws of the Queen by which they have become men.'

"Afterwards they gave a token of their good feeling towards the whites 'who are living on the land covered with darkness, that is Taranaki'. They heard that many of them are in distress, their property having been destroyed by the spoiler – and that their friends the white people of Canterbury were collecting money to assist the aged, the women, and the children: and they thought they would do the same. Accordingly, at Kaiapoi they collected £10 14s., at Rapaki £1 14s. 6d., at Port Levy £4 7s.; and other villages are doing the same thing but have not yet reported the amount."[270]

At the Ngaruawahia gathering, chiefs had almost come to blows over

---

270   *Te Karere*, 31 July, 1860

Wiremu Kingi's actions and the way he had dragged the King movement into it. In one respect, it was a match made in heaven. The Kingitanga people had figured out that if British sovereignty was represented by a flag, then the Maori king should have a flag too. And everywhere that flag was planted was supposed to come under the authority of the King movement which, like Kingi, was opposed to further land sales.

However, a number of chiefs who saw merit in the Maori unity of the King movement were nonetheless smart enough to smell a rat in the Waitara dispute that had led to war.

After hearing that Kingi had not withdrawn the parawai to dispute Teira's sale, some of the chiefs – including the brother of the ailing King Potatau – demanded answers from Kingi's representatives:

Tamati Ngapora: "Rangitake, give me that piece of land that has caused the war. Give me that piece that has been purchased and paid for by the Governor."

Patene (Ngatimaniapoto, representing Kingi): "I shall not give it up."

Tamati Ngapora: "Give it to me!"

Patene: "I am under some mistake".

According to the tribal missionary, the Reverend Thomas Buddle who was tasked with keeping the record, Patene then planted a stick in the ground to represent Potatau and Waitara, and said, "This is Potatau, my mana stands there. After my mana rested on the land, the scrofulous [look it up in the dictionary, I had to! – Ed.] man arose, offered it for sale and the Governor accepted the offer."

The reference to King Potatau's mana was a reference to the King movement flag. What Patene was trying to assert is that the flag had arrived in Waitara, and "after" that Teira had then offered the land for sale. If what Patene said had been true, it would have been a direct challenge to the King movement's mana and justification for them entering the war – which indeed they did. However, Chief Kapereira had already visited Waitara to question Kingi about the Parawai, where Kingi then asked Kapereira for the flag to be brought to Waitara. Clearly, the Governor had accepted Teira's offer of the land long before the King's flag was raised there.[271]

Tamati: "That is Potatau, is it? And this land has been handed over to Potatau has it? Then it is mine. I represent Potatau here, and I give this land to the Governor."

---

271 The offer had been made and accepted in early March 1859 at a public meeting. The deposit on the land purchase, of £100, was paid in November 1859. The King movement flag arrived in early 1860.

Patene: "For what reason do you give that land to the Governor?"

Tamati: "That peace may be restored and our trouble cease."

But Tamati wasn't the only one laying into the Maniapoto chief backing Wiremu Kingi. Ngatiwhatua's Paora Tuhaere ridiculed the novel idea that Maori could somehow put their "mana on a piece of land":

"I perceive that you are very eager to pick out the errors of the Governer, but I have not discovered his error. You say that you have not seen wrong on the part of Te Rangitake (Wiremu Kingi). I have seen his wrong-doing. Letters have reached you that convict him of wrong, yet you say you have not seen it. I repeat, I have seen it, and I believe there is not a chief in Waikato that is not convinced that Te Rangitake is wrong. I have seen Wi Tako's letter addressed to you all, and that letter set my mind at rest on the subject. You have all seen the letter, and its statements should settle the question. [272]

"You speak of 'mana'. What is the mana? Where is the mana? There is no such thing as putting mana on the land...you have set up a king without authority, and this is the source of all our present troubles."

Maoridom was split. Most, going with their Biblical sense of ethics, sided with the Governor. A few, mostly interior tribes, sided with Kingi-tanga and Wiremu Kingi's attempt to force a war.

At Kohimarama just a couple of months later, there were allegations that Taranaki's rebellion had actually been long planned. This aspect of deceit appears to have been conveniently overlooked by the Waitangi Tribunal, but the evidence is there for all to read, in the proceedings of the Kohimarama runanga, thanks to testimony from a fellow chief who witnessed the events and told the conference Ngatiawa tried to persuade him to join their conspiracy:

Horomona Toremi. (Ngatiraukawa), Otaki: "It is now seven years since Matene and I returned from Mr. Smith's, at Rotorua: our object was to unite the tribes under the Queen's Government I am now referring to Taiporohenui. Letters were written by Taranaki and Ngatiruanui to us, namely: to me, to Matene, to Tamihana, to Hukiki, and to Hori te Anaua – indeed to all of us – requesting us to go to Taiporohenui: we assembled: I suppose there were 500 men. The incantation by which the Pakehas were to fail was repeated: it was Ngahuru (Tamati Wiremu) who chanted it: it was as follows: – 'Kati na ano he utu mou, ko te rarangi

272 In 1860, the idea of putting "mana on the land", as the Kingitanga movement was doing, was clearly a new one, and not traditional. Speech at Ngaruawahia, May 1860, reported by the Rev Thomas Buddle

maunga e tu ki Taua-tawhiti: utaina atu Tapa-ngorengore ki Hauraki e rima ka ao te rangi, e waru ka ao te ra.' This is the incantation by which the Pakeha was to fail. By this I knew that Taranaki had matured a plot.

"We entered the house. Paratene te Kopara arose, with a tomahawk having a twisted handle – the axe head turned one way and the handle another. It was not fixed in the usual manner. The handle was carved. Showing us the axe he said – 'Listen Ngatitoa, Ngatiraukawa, Wanganui, and all the other tribes! This is Okurukuru.' He then laid the axe before Hori Te Anaua. It was then brought to us. Matene rose up and said 'What is Okurukuru?' He answered, 'It is land we have sold to the pakeha: we wish to take possession of it again.' Matene said, 'Was that land paid for?' They replied 'Yes'. Matene said, 'It is wrong; leave that for our Pakeha kinsmen. But, as to land not yet sold, retain that.' I then rose (and said) 'Friends, it is wrong. Return to the places not yet sold. Take your axe back,' and the axe was thrown into the open space I then concluded that Taranaki was going wrong."[273]

Interestingly, the same chief also accused Ngatiawa's Wellington leadership of selling Taranaki to the New Zealand company back in 1839, when the *Tory* first landed there with Wakefield on board.

"Port Nicholson had been sold by Ngatiawa. They then sold Taranaki. The boundary was at Mokau: it was Mr. Spain who fixed it at Parininihi and Te Taniwha. I therefore concluded that Ngatiawa had sold their lands to the Pakeha. Potatau saw this and sold the very same land: the boundary of the land sold by Potatau extended as far as Piraunui. What is the use of preferring a claim to lands already sold, and taking forcible possession again?" questioned the chief, Horomona Toremi.

One who made the same allegation at Kohimarama was Native Secretary Donald McLean:

"Before reading the Governor's message, I will state to you a por-

---

273   That some tribes practiced multiple sales of the same piece of land was widely known, even within Maoridom, and frowned upon by the majority. Ngatiwhatua chief Paora Tuhaere had reminded McLean of this: "Now, Mr. McLean, mine is a land-selling tribe. I have been selling land for the last twenty years, but you will not remember any year in which a dispute arose. No piece of land has been paid for twice over. We are not in that practice." Given the integrity and leadership shown by Ngatiwhatua, one can only weep at how shabbily treated the tribe was over Bastion Point, where land seized under the Public Works Act for the defence of Auckland in 1886 was not returned to Maori but instead gifted by the Government to the city council. Bastion Point was being surveyed by its Maori owners with a view to turning it into prime waterfront real estate for settlers – an income stream for the tribe. The £3,000 paid by the Government as compensation for its seizure barely covered the survey costs, and certainly did not reflect the value of the land that would have been realised had the tribe continued to develop it.

Sir Donald McLean

tion of what has come under my own knowledge in connexion with this place (Taranaki). I will not go back to the invasion of the Ngapuhi, but will commence with the first sale to Colonel Wakefield at Aropaoa, in 1839, by the Atiawa residing on the opposite shores of the country, better known to you as Kapiti. Their names are in the deed transferring the land. Here are the names of Te Awe, of William King, of Rauponga, Ngarewa, Manurau, Mare and others of the Ngatiawa. I will not detain you by reading all the names. These are the principal chiefs who transferred the land. The name of William King Te Rangitake is the first of the signatures to the deed. The whole district was alienated at that time. No portion of it was excepted, for the Ngatiawa looked upon it as territory which they had left, abandoned and forsaken for ever; to which they had bidden a final farewell, and which had passed into the hands of the Waikatos. At that time they did not expect ever to return to it. This was the reason why the Atiawas wished to sell it to the Pakehas: hence the sale to Colonel Wakefield. The arrangement was made by William King himself, and the payment was received."

In other words, the Wellington exiles, in 1839 and in the knowledge that Waikato tribes now owned their ancestral Taranaki lands, figured they could flick the lands off to the wide-eyed Pakeha Wakefield, and leave him to sort out whatever problems arose with the Waikato iwi.

Armed with his deed of purchase for the entire Taranaki, signed by one Wiremu Kingi, Wakefield sailed north and then paid the remnant Ngatiawa living there a further sum of money. Once the Waikato iwi found out, the rest is history.

Just how many times had the land been sold? McLean again from the Kohimarama speech:

"On Colonel Wakefield's return to Wellington the chiefs of the Ngatiawa residing there deputed Tuarau, and another of their Chiefs to go to the people who were living at Ngamotu (Taranaki) to inform them of the sale of the land. Tuarau accordingly went, and on arriving assembled the people and told them what had taken place. They expressed their satisfaction: they were delighted at the prospect of Pakehas coming to live among them as friends. Now would they come forth to life and the light of heaven, secure from Waikato. The assent of Awatea, Eruera Te Puke, of Ngahirahira, Karoro, Poharama, Te Whiti, Tangutu and others, 79 in number, was given. These were all the people living upon the land at that time whose names appear on this Deed of Sale. This was the second purchase. This sale included Taranaki and Waitara. This territory was purchased, and the payment was given to the men who were at that time residing upon the land. It was then surveyed, and afterwards Europeans came to settle upon it."

In the end, of course, the whole thing had turned to custard. The land purchase was really about mana on both sides. The mana of the Crown to purchase land from any British citizen, and the mana of tribal authority to restrict British citizens within their circle of control from exercising personal property rights.

On February 22nd, 1860, the Governor had proclaimed martial law in the province of Taranaki, which gave powers to evactuate Pakeha settlers or enlist men for militia corps. The plan had been to commence a survey of the 600 acre block to work out which land belonged to whom, and confirm title to the undisputed portions.

The Government knew Kingi's hapu was occupying a portion of the land, and had already agreed to set aside any disputed territory once they'd had a chance to land survey it. Knowing there was now strong opposition, however, the Governor realised his survey team would need protection.

Wiremu Kingi decided to tweak British noses by constructing a new fortified pa, literally overnight, across one of the main roads the survey needed to travel to access the site, and managed to provoke British troops to open fire. This, of course, made the Government the 'aggressor' and Kingi the 'defender' in the war that followed, and in terms of Maori protocol enabled him to call in reinforcements from neighbouring tribes.

Historians have largely cast Kingi in the same light, a defender, and not entirely without cause. The evidence reviewed here, however, would tend to suggest self-defence was more or less a convenient and effective cover for the wider issue at stake – a clash of sovereignty. While the

Waitangi Tribunal is officially in denial on this, saying "it is difficult to comprehend that that was ever intended,"[274] the statements of Maori chiefs like Te Wetini Taiporutu make it painfully obvious the King movement in 1860 was a rebel movement: "The war is not merely a contention for the land at New Plymouth, but for the Chieftanship of New Zealand."[275]

War broke out on 17 March 1860 – two months before the May meeting of King movement supporters at Ngaruawahia and the subsequent July conference at Kohimarama.

At the end of 12 months, during which British troops had been unable to deliver a decisive blow to well armed Maori, both sides called an uneasy truce in Taranaki, although battles continued against the King movement in the Waikato.

Looking for a way out of the mess he inherited (some would argue he was part of the cause as well by the way he had moved to force the issue back in 1848), Governor Grey annulled the purchase of the Waitara Pekapeka block from Teira, on the grounds that title had not been properly established. Partly this was because the land survey team had been prevented from carrying out the boundary surveys – which is what finally precipitated the war – but partly also Grey came to the decision after receipt of what he believed was "new" information – that Kingi and his supporters had actually been living on the land in question.

The reality of Kingi's pa complex being built on Teira's family land on the south bank – and in fact being excluded from the purchase – had been well canvassed by the previous Governor, but his replacement appeared

unaware, particularly as Kingi was telling Grey he'd taken up arms to defend his home and paddocks.

The questions Grey wanted answers to from his officials were whether or not:

"That William King and more than two hundred of his people had valuable houses and other buildings, and cultivations upon the land agreed to be bought by the Government from Taylor [Teira]; and that they had been in occupation of these for about 12 years.

"That many of them asserted a claim to some portions of this land.

"That the Government nevertheless agreed to

---

274 Ibid, p3
275 Appendix of the Journals of the House, 1861, Session I, E-01, page 24

purchase it from Te Teira, and publicly notified to the natives as follows: 'Te Teira's title has been carefully investigated and found to be good. It is not disputed by anyone. The Governor cannot, therefore, allow Wiremu Kingi to interfere with Te Teira in the sale of his own land. Payment for

the land has been received by Te Teira. It now belongs to the Queen'."

Surely, exclaimed Governor Grey, even if Teira's title did prove to be good, wasn't it the dumbest idea in the world to bring a colony to war over an insignificant 600 acre patch of land by forcing its purchase and acquiring "against their will and consent the houses of more than 200 of [the Queen's] subjects, which they had occupied in peace and happiness for years, and who were not even accused of any crime against Her Majesty or Her laws, but some of whom had on the contrary risked their lives in rendering Her services in former wars?

"This is the question upon which the Governor has now to decide."

In this, Grey had a good point. Because of war breaking out, Te Teira had only ever received the £100 deposit on the land, not the rest of the payment. By the time Governor Grey decided he was backing out of the Pekapeka deal in April 1863, the military campaign had spent something in the region of a million pounds, and caused more than 400 dead or wounded on both sides.

Grey, naturally, threw his hands in the air declaring the whole thing a waste of time, money and lives. Although he would blame it on faulty title by virtue of the fact that Kingi's pa was on the land, and declare that Kingi and his followers had been wronged for acting in defence of their own property, again, that was more of a convenience to hang the backdown upon. It had never been the intention of the surveyors and the previous administration to take any land being occupied or subject to dispute.[276]

The real cause of the war, however, was sovereignty, and it was probably unavoidable. Historians can criticise the Governors for pushing land

---

276 "So carefully indeed did the Government adhere to this rule," testified McLean on oath at Parliament, "that in defining the boundaries of the block negotiated for, several portions of land, supposed to belong to the selling party, were excluded from the purchase to avoid the possibility of compromising in any degree the conflicting interests of rival claimants." Appendix to Journals of the House, 1861, E-01, page 62

purchases over what seemed like trivial issues, but the comments James Busby made were correct: The Crown had promised Maori all the rights of British subjects, but if it allowed chiefs to veto the ability of ordinary Maori to buy and sell, then the Crown would not be delivering on its promise of equality under the law. If such a system had survived until the present day, Maori New Zealanders might have found it difficult to buy and sell their own land, without the tribe asserting ownership over your own personal property, 'for the good of the tribe'.

If Waitara had not been the catalyst between an emerging sense of Maori nationalism and the Crown, something else would have been. Historically, the factual record shows Taranaki was "sold" by exiled Ngatiawa at Wellington in 1839, and "sold" again by the 60 Ngatiawa who still lived in the captured district in early 1840, then "sold" by the Waikato iwi, who owned the land via the Maori tikanga of conquest. Then further parts within those same boundaries were later "sold" again as exiles felt safe to return.

The record as we've seen shows a Ngatiraukawa chief who witnessed what he said was Taranaki deceit on land sales told of a meeting where Ngatiawa were plotting: "It is land we have sold to the pakeha: we wish to take possession of it again." Matene said, "Was that land paid for?" They replied, "Yes".[277]

Often, the pakeha were not innocent of stirring either. Up until 1840 the Europeans who had lived in New Zealand had done so effectively at the invitation and tolerance of the Maori owners of the country. After 1840, immigrants plucked from the streets of London, the vast bulk of whom who'd never seen a Maori in their lives before arriving here and who at best saw Maori as irrelevant to their own desires and needs, settled in New Zealand by the thousands.

"Why should Maori get special treatment?" was often the refrain, especially when settlers were looking enviously at vast tracts of land occupied by very few people. Some spoke openly in public meetings of forcing Maori to sell up and move out,[278] adding to the emergence of fears within Maoridom that perhaps their rights would not be protected after all.

277 Testimony of chief Horomona Toremi, (Ngatiraukawa), Otaki, recounted earlier
278 Governor Gore-Browne noted in one public dispatch, "That the Europeans covet the lands of the Natives, and were determined to enter in and possess them" and that this determination became daily more "apparent, and that neither law nor equity will prevent the occupation of Native lands by Europeans when the latter are strong enough to defy both the Native owners and the Government." Quoted at Appendix to Journals of the House, 1863, Session I, E-02, page 1

Governor Grey picked up on those Maori concerns in a letter to the Secretary of State:

"A great part of the Native race may be stated to be at the present moment in arms, in a state of chronic discontent, watching our proceedings in reference to this Waitara question. Large numbers of them have renounced the Queen's authority and many of them declare openly they have been so wronged they will never return under it.[279]

"Other most influential men state they will not aid the Government in any war that may arise out of this Waitara question. A great majority of them declare that if a war arises from this cause, they will rise and make a simultaneous attack upon the several European settlements in the Northern Island."

Then the Governor raises an interesting point, the one about perception becoming reality, especially among those more distant from the events in question:

"The reasons they urge for such proceedings are:

"That they did not take up arms to prohibit the alienation of territory to the Crown or to maintain any seignorial rights [the right of chiefs/lords of the manor to veto sales], but that the people of Waitara, without having been guilty of any crime, were driven at the point of sword from villages, houses and homes which they had occupied for years.

"That a great crime has been committed against them. That through all future generations it will be told that their lands have been forcibly and unlawfully taken from them by officers appointed by the Queen of England…

"For all these reasons they argue that they have no hope of obtaining justice; that their eventual extermination is determined on; that all that is left to them is to die like men, after a long and desperate struggle, and that the sooner they can bring that on, before our preparations are further matured and our numbers increased, the greater is their chance of success."

The facts behind the Waitara dispute you have now seen, and they are a little bit more complex than Maori had evidently been told. After all, Wiremu Kingi himself had told a Waikato chief, Kapereira, the dispute was not really about the land, but about enforcing the Maori King's mana against the British Crown – a clear challenge to sovereignty. Kingi had also admitted, at a public forum, that Teira owned the land in question.

It no longer mattered what the facts were, however, only what the silent

---

279 "Papers Relative to the Waitara", Dispatch from George Grey to Duke of Newcastle, 24 April 1863, quoted at Appendix to Journals of the House, 1863, Session I, E-02, page 1

and somewhat disconnected majority in other parts of the country [or, for that matter, 150 years into the future] "believed" the facts were. If exaggerated stories about Kingi and his hapu being evicted at swordpoint helped sell the news to Maori elsewhere, then it was little different from the "Weapons of Mass Destruction" claim that justified a war in the Middle East. In war, you use whatever PR you can lay your hands on and you can't blame Ngatiawa for doing so.

For all of Grey's handwringing, however, it came to nought and he soon re-entered the war with a previously unseen vicious streak. Despite deciding to walk away from the Waitara purchase on April 24, and formalising it by way of a proclamation two weeks later, the Governor still had not got around to publishing his decision when fate intervened. During the war, the Tataraimaka Block – purchased from Taranaki Maori years earlier, was retaken by Maori warriors who swore not to leave until Waitara was given back to them.

British troops had recaptured the Tataraimaka Block on April 4, 1863, the first major military action since the truce of March 1861. Had Governor Grey's repudiation of the Waitara deal been published by the end of April, it is likely that on May 4 his troops would not have come under renewed attack by Maori. By the time the Waitara announcement was made on May 11, it was too late: the country was plunged into a new and even more vicious round of warfare.

As an example of how far relations had sunk, what began as ripples from a single stone thrown into the Waitara river all those years ago had escalated into tidal waves of hatred on both sides. Where missionaries had worked so hard and so successfully to educate Maori in Judeo-Christian principles – resulting in the almost total abandonment of cannibalism within one generation and creating great leaders with a better sense of ethics than many Pakeha politicians today – out of the new hatred sprang Hauhauism, a firebrand mix of Maori tohunga beliefs and old Testament Judaism, manifesting itself in terror attacks, spells, ripping out the hearts of victims, and the return to cannibalism.[280]

---

280 The Hauhaus believed they also enjoyed supernatural protection from bullets. It wasn't one of their most successful policies: "The soldiers who were all hidden behind their high parapet, did not open fire on us until we were within close range. Then the bullets came thickly among us, and close as the fingers on my hand. The soldiers had their rifles pointed through the loopholes in the parapet and between the spaces on top (between bags filled with sand and earth), and thus could deliver a terrible fire upon us with perfect safety to themselves. There were two tiers of rifles blazing at us. We continued our advance, shooting and shouting our war-cries. Now we cried out the 'Hapa' ('Pass over') incantation which Hepanaia had taught us, to cause the bullets to fly harmlessly over us: 'Hapa, hapa, hapa! Hau, hau, hau! Pai-marire, rire,

In one Hauhau attack, a group of soldiers resting without their weapons were ambushed. Seven men, including their commander, Captain Lloyd, were killed, stripped naked and then beheaded. Their heads were then used in a recruiting drive to illustrate the power of the new spiritual movement. In response, Government troops on Grey's orders were carrying out systematic torching of villages and pas to prevent ongoing guerrilla attacks, in a "scorched earth" policy that even Grey's military commander, General Duncan Cameron, felt was over the top.[281]

The Waitara affair, then, was shaking everything that Maori had believed in to the very core. The old ways were coming back, the fires of Maori nationalism were being stoked, and New Zealand would never be the same.

While the Waitangi Tribunal quoted a comment from the time, "We seem to be fast approaching a settlement of the point, whether Her Fair Majesty or His Dark Majesty shall reign in New Zealand,"[282] referring to Victoria vs the Maori King, many Christians, Maori and Pakeha both, would have seen that comment in an entirely different light as they watched what the Kohimarama conference had described as "this evil" spread across the map like freshly spilt ink. Godzone was anything but.

---

rire – hau!' As we did so we held our right hands uplifted, palms frontward, on a level with our heads – the sign of the ringa-tu. This, we believed, would ward off the enemy's bullets; it was the faith with which we all had been inspired by Te Ua and his apostles. The bullets came ripping through our ranks. 'Hapa, hapa!' our men shouted after delivering a shot, but down they fell. 'Hapa!' a warrior would cry, with his right hand raised to avert the enemy's bullets, and with a gasp – like that – he would fall dead. The tuakana (elder brother) in a family would fall with 'Hapa!' on his lips, then the teina (younger brother) would fall; then the old father would fall dead beside them." – Te Kahu Pukoro, quoted by James Cowan, *The New Zealand Wars: A History of the Maori Campaigns and the Pioneering Period: Volume II: The Hauhau Wars, 1864–72*, published 1956. See http://www.nzetc.org/tm/scholarly/tei-Cow02NewZ-c2.html

281   Cameron resigned his post in early 1865.

282   Waitangi Tribunal, Taranaki Report, chapter 3

CHAPTER THIRTEEN

Of Church And State

This book is not intended to be the definitive complete New Zealand history, there simply is not space available to concentrate on everything to the level of detail we've managed so far on the key periods and issues. Most New Zealand history books have not indulged in anywhere near the depth offered on those selected issues here. Better perhaps to understand the major milestones well, at the risk of jettisoning some of the more minor events.

It is acknowledged that the breakdown in Maori-Pakeha relations during the land wars and the decades that followed resulted in major breaches of the Treaty, justifying investigation and settlement. Vast areas of Maori land, for example, were confiscated by the Government as punishment after the land wars, without the Government declaring the Treaty to be void. As a result, those confiscations breach Article 2 of the Treaty as they relate to undisturbed possession of the land.[283]

There is no easy way around that.

The question of "why" things got so bad is perhaps the real issue.

Despite promising Maori equality under the law and all the rights of British citizens, the reality of language and cultural barriers hit home in the first two decades after the Treaty. It wasn't helped by a Governor who believed in leaving Maori to do their own thing; tino rangatiratanga by default.

"In one all-important direction," wrote historian James Cowan, "Gover-

---

283   For the sake of balance, Maori lawyer and cabinet minister Sir Apirana Ngata disagreed, saying the ceding of sovereignty gave the Crown the right to make laws, and when they passed a law allowing confiscation as a punishment for armed rebellion, this was within their powers under Article 1 of the Treaty.

nor Grey's strength was weakness. Sir William Fox, in his criticism of the native policy of the day, says that Grey in his first administration [1845-53] whilst personally ingratiating himself with the Maoris, utterly failed in attaching them to British laws and institutions. 'Under him they continued a separate people, almost as much as when Tasman or Cook saw the first canoe. But this personal link was one which necessarily snapped when he left the colony. No permanent or stable bond of union had been established between the native race and British authority. He sacrificed our national position to his personal position; and when he departed (in 1853) he left the natives without helm or pilot'."[284]

Sir George Grey

In Grey's defence, William Pember-Reeves argues he had acted decisively with strong military action to clean up the wars in Wellington and Kororareka that had been left to fester by FitzRoy.

"Peace quickly came. It is true that at the end of the year 1846 there came a small outbreak which caused a tiny hamlet, now the town of Wanganui, to be attacked and plundered. But the natives, who retired into the bush, were quietly brought to submission by having their trade stopped, and in particular their supply of tobacco cut off."[285]

Continuing to think laterally, when a Maori chief refused permission for a road to be punched through his territory, "Grey said nothing, but sent the chief's sister a present of a wheeled carriage. Before long the road was permitted."

"But it was in the use he made of the restored tranquillity that he showed his true capacity. He employed the natives as labourers in making roads, useful both for war and peace. They found wages better than warfare. As navvies, they were paid half a crown a day, and were reported to do

---

284   Fox, quoted in James Cowan's biography, *Sir Donald Mclean*, Chapter 17, Reed Publishing, 1940, see http://www.nzetc.org/tm/scholarly/tei-CowDona-t1-body-d0-d17.html
285   *The Long White Cloud*, page 171-172

more work as spade-men than an equal number of soldiers would. At no time did the Maori seem to make such material progress as during the twelve peaceful years beginning with 1848.

"With his Brown subjects, Grey, after once beating them, trod the paths of pleasantness and peace. The chiefs recognized his imperturbable courage and self-control, and were charmed by his unfailing courtesy and winning manners. – He found time to learn their language. The study of their character, their myths, customs, and art was to him a labour of love and bore practical fruit in the knowledge it gave him of the race... Few men have ever understood the natives better. He could humour their childishness and respect their intelligence.

"On the all-important question of the validity of the land clause in the treaty of Waitangi, the Governor gave the Maori the fullest assurance. Striving always to keep liquor and fire-arms from them, he encouraged them to farm, helped to found schools for them, and interested himself in the all-important question of their physical health, on which he consulted and corresponded with Florence Nightingale."

The image left, however, was of a father figure rather than a man with a plan for integrating the races.

For twenty years, although the Government had appointed Maori "assessors" or Magistrates, European justice only stepped in when Europeans were involved as a rule. So by 1860, little wonder that Maori chiefs at Kohimarama were begging to be included within the European justice umbrella, and seeing Crown titles for their land.

"The Governor came, bringing with him the laws. The Maories who are now dead and gone received them gladly. I will now tell you where I find fault with the pakeha. This is where the pakeha was wrong: he did not fully explain and tell us that this meant so and so, and that meant so and so. When they gave us the laws, they allowed us to have only a part and withheld a part. Now listen, and I will tell you where I find fault with the Maori: after selling land to the pakeha he attempts to keep it back," exclaimed Wiremu te Wheoro, a Waikato chief attending the conference.

Prior to the full outbreak of the land wars, Tamihana Te Rauparaha had been an advocate of the King movement as a means of advancing Maori in parallel with Pakeha. After the wars broke out, he cut his ties to Kingitanga, and favoured a greater integration: "What you say, Hetaraka, about educating the Maories in the schools – that the boys and girls may learn Pakeha customs – is correct...Schools are good. It is right that the children should be instructed in what is good. It was the law of Christianity that put an end to our cannibal practices. It is right that when murder is committed by a Maori or a Pakeha he should be tried by the English law and hanged for his crime; and that minor offences should be treated with a summons."

Modern New Zealanders, Pakeha and Maori alike, probably have little awareness of just how much they owe the Christianisation of the Maori for their current lives in New Zealand. Regardless of whether one personally believes or not, the Maori did, and the spiritual impact of washing away past sins in the baptism of Christ played a massive part in helping Maori to wipe their slates clean with each other in tribal disputes that once would have provoked war and cannibalism. If we can be forgiven, then we can also forgive, became the rule many lived by. Likewise, the social justice message of Christianity played a huge role in allowing an openly Christian British administration to take sovereignty over New Zealand. In the same way that the US declares, "one Nation under God", so too did Maori believe that if the British followed biblical principles then their own interests would be protected.

An example of how deeply this penetrated the Maori psyche is furnished by the original Te Rauparaha, Tamihana's warrior father. Arrested by Governor Grey in 1846 and imprisoned during a native uprising (he was subsequently released)[286], the elder Te Rauparaha told his son from behind bars: "'Oh son! Both you and Matene [Te Whiwhi], go to your people! and say: repay only with goodness on my account; do not incur ill-will with the Europeans on my account – for only by Goodwill is the salvation

---

286 The story behind Te Rauparaha's arrest is told by William Pember-Reeves. Maori insurgents had been waging guerrilla war against Pakeha settlers near Wellington, and Governor Grey sent in troops to the bush to flush out the guerrillas: "And there was one story of heroism. An outpost of the fifty-eighth regiment had been surprised at dawn. The bugler, a lad named Allen, was raising his bugle to sound the alarm, when a blow from a tomahawk half severed his arm. Snatching the bugle with the other hand, he managed to blow a warning note before a second tomahawk stroke stretched him dead. Grey adopted the Fabian plan of driving the insurgents back into the mountain forests and slowly starving them out there. In New Zealand, thanks to the scarcity of wild food plants and animals, even Maori suffer cruel hardships if cut off long from their plantations.

Rauparaha, now a very old man, was nominally not concerned in these troubles. He lived quietly in a sea-coast village by the Straits, enjoying the reputation earned by nearly fifty years of fighting, massacring and plotting. The Governor, however, satisfied himself that the old chief was secretly instigating the insurgents. By a cleverly managed surprise he captured Rauparaha in his village, whence he was carried kicking and biting on board a man-of-war. The move proved successful. The mana of the Maori Ulysses was fatally injured in the eyes of his race by the humiliation. The chief, who had killed Arthur Wakefield and laughed under Fitzroy's nose, had met at length a craftier than himself. Detained at Auckland, or carried about in Grey's train, he was treated with a studied politeness which prevented him from being honoured as a martyr. His influence was at an end." See *The Long White Cloud*, page 170, http://www.nzetc.org/tm/scholarly/tei-ReeLong-t1-body-d1-d12.html

251

Te Rauparaha

of Man, Woman and Child'."[287]

When academics claim Maori had "no concept" of sovereignty in 1840, they overlook the deep impact of the Bible's accounts of Kings, Pharaohs, judges, commandments and laws, and the teachings of Jesus Christ and the Apostle Paul in the New Testament as to the power of Caesar.[288]

Compare Te Rauparaha and the Ngatitoa tribe's dignity following his arrest, in 1846, with the massacre of the *Boyd* only a little over 30 years earlier, resulting in the deaths of 70 passengers and crew on the ship, and feasting. You can see, then, how far New Zealand had come in just 40 years. It didn't happen through the efforts of a secular bureaucracy.

It's worth returning to the letter of Charles Darwin and Robert FitzRoy – the Captain of the *Beagle* who later became Governor of New Zealand briefly – because their letter from 1835 foreshadowed precisely some of these points.

Darwin was particularly interested in the social evolution of Pacific societies, and he noted that in his travels only one thing had radically transformed cultures for the better: Christianity.

"For refreshments and supplies, only those islands can, with safety, be now frequented, on which either European or native missionaries have established themselves. When a merchant ship approaches a remote island in the Pacific, her first object is to ascertain whether it has ever been visited by a missionary. If it has, she knows she may approach with confidence; if it has not, she keeps under sail in the offing, and if she does communicate with the shore, it is with the utmost caution, and with much reluctance."[289]

---

287 Biography of Tamihana Te Rauparaha, by Steven Oliver, *Encyclopedia of New Zealand*, http://www.teara.govt.nz/en/biographies/1t75/1
288 For evidence of the Bible's influence on their understanding of sovereign actions, look no further than Wiremu Tarapipipi's warning to the Ngaruawahia Kingites to be careful of supporting an unjust war: "They (the Europeans) have forsaken the right way, they have become deranged like the King of Babylon who was turned into the forest. But let us not take up arms in an unrighteous cause...I do not forget some of the kings of Judah who engaged in unrighteous war, how they perished in their sin..."
289 Darwin & FitzRoy's letter, 28 June 1836, reprinted in *South African Christian Recorder*, 2, 1836

Why is it, Darwin then asks, that non-Christians are so dismissive of what the missionaries achieved?

"But even while profiting by the influence of the missionaries, and even assisted by them in intercourse with the natives, many persons have not hesitated to ridicule the means by which the missionary has gained that very influence by which they are profiting; and, in direct opposition to his entreaties, or well-known wishes, encourage the natives in immorality, and in the use of spirits?"

Darwin described such people as "secular embarrassments", undoing the very work that made New Zealand and other islands safer to visit and settle. Moreover, wrote Darwin and FitzRoy, such people try to deflect from their own moral shortcomings by attacking the missionaries:

"They abuse, and seek for faults in a system, and in the conduct of individuals, which has a tendency to check, or expose, the impropriety of their own hitherto unrestrained morality."

It was, said Darwin and FitzRoy, Christians who tamed and stamped out cannibalism, not secular justice. It was missionaries who brokered an end to wars and slavery, not secular justice.

First came the cannibals. Then came the Christians as lion-tamers. Once Christians had made the place comparatively safe, every godless man and their dog thought they had a right to come in and pontificate on how the laws should be, wrote Darwin, having done none of the hard work and in fact done much to undermine it.

Which is a similar state of affairs to today. Seven generations later, there is no real appreciation of why Maori signed the Treaty and how much hard work went into it. The missionaries enabled New Zealand to be settled on Christian principles. The Maori only agreed to the Treaty out of respect for Christian principles. The waves of settlers and politicians who followed didn't share the same values, didn't appreciate the ground work that had gone in, and the result was unmitigated disaster.

Darwin noted the resentment springing up already, in 1835, towards the fact that the Church missions owned the 'best' land. Were ordinary settlers present in New Zealand in 1814, he posed, placing their families "among hostile and cannibal savages", or was it the missionaries doing the hard yards?

"If a missionary, and a recent settler, are each in treaty for a particular piece of ground, and the former obtains it upon easier terms than the latter, in consequence of the goodwill of the natives, is it not a natural and legiti- mate advantage earned in the fairest and the most honourable manner?"

Ngatitoa's Matene te Whiwhi summed it up nicely at Kohimarama:

"Mr. McLean, there is nothing else to be said. Light has been thrown upon the subject by you, by the Europeans. My word to-day is, The Europeans are parents to us. In the first instance, when the Europeans began to flock hither, Mr. Marsden came: afterwards came Governor Hobson, then the Europeans began; to find a footing in the country, and they began to find (work for) hands. You brought the system hither.

"First you brought baptism, and we were baptised in the name of Christ. That was completed. There has now become only one Christ, and one Governor: we have become one in (our allegiance to) the Queen. For this reason…these races should become united under the Queen. Let there be but one Sovereign for us, even the Queen. We have been invited hither by the Governor to express our opinion. It is well, therefore, that there should be but one system. Leave it not for the hidden voice, or unknown tongue, to disapprove, or cause to misunderstand. Yours is a hidden, or unknown tongue; as ours is also. Even though it be so, let the Queen unite us."

Chief Ihakara Tokonui likewise expressed relief that the old ways were gone: "In former times the evil that prevailed in this Island was War: now the Gospel has been received. Under the old system, Peace was established, and on the morrow another war was commenced.

"When Christianity came, then for the first time were made manifest the good things of the Pakeha and the evil things of the Maori. The people of this island are committing two thefts. One is the "Maori King," for they are robbing the Pakeha of his name. You alone, the Pakeha. possess what is good: we, the Maories, have nothing good. When I first saw you I was ashamed of myself. And here is the other. You know what the bee is. Some bees work, some bees are lazy. You are like the working bee. You fill your hive, whether it be a box or an empty tree. But the Maori is like the other bee – the lazy one. And the Maori takes advantage of your work."

It sounds inflammatory today and was probably an example of what today would be called "cultural cringe" but nonetheless it's sometimes a good thing to compare yourself against another to work out where you could be doing it better. A similar comment was made at Ngaruawahia by another chief:

"Look at his (the Pakeha's) work in other lands," lamented Chief Karaka Tomo te Whakapo, at the great meeting of May 1860, "never too late, never behind time." The centre of discussion in this case was a still uncompleted pa site.[290]

---

290 From Buddle's transcript of the Ngaruawahia great meeting, Appendix to Journals of the House, 1861, Session I, E-01, page 41

For Rotorua's Eruera Kahawai, "It was the introduction of the Gospel that put an end to our evil ways. Yes, my friends, it was Christianity alone that did it. It put an end to thieving and many other sins. I have already entered the Queen's party. We have now a new parent, the Queen. We have now the protection of the Queen. We have abandoned our old ways. The rule now is kindness to the orphan (charity), peace, and agricultural pursuits. I shall not turn to the Maori side I have now come under the wings (protection) of the Queen. The father on that side is the Governor."

In response to complaints from delegates that the Queen's law had not yet penetrated deeply enough into Maori society, a set of suggested punishment guidelines for minor offences was delivered to the chiefs, written by former Chief Justice Sir William Martin. McLean told the chiefs when it came to equality under the law Maori people needed to partake gradually:

"These rules have been put forth by the Governor for the guidance of those tribes who have not yet been accustomed to the administration of English law. They have been carefully prepared by your friend Dr. Martin, with a view to assist the native tribes in outlying districts in administering justice amongst themselves. They are not applicable to those districts where English law is regularly administered, as, for instance, the Bay of Islands and Port Nicholson.

"Some of the chiefs have expressed a wish that there should be but one law. This is much to be desired by all but is not so easily attained. A child does not grow to man's estate in a day. It took the English many generations before they brought their system of law to its present state. While such a difference exists in the usages and customs of the two races in this country. it is necessary that some of you should be gradually initiated into the elementary principles of law before you can appreciate it.

"With this object, and with a view of superseding some of the objectionable customs to which mamy of your old people still cling, your friend Dr. Martin has taken much pains to prepare these rules. They are simple and easy of comprehension by all. They are not put forth as law, but merely as a set of plain rules to guide your assessors in dealing with cases referred to them where access cannot be had to an English court. Where it is possible to refer to an English magistrate, it will always be proper to do so," assured McLean.

The culture and tikanga of Maori who signed the Treaty in 1840 had rapidly given way, by 1860, to an appreciation of the different things the Pakeha system had to offer, if only they were allowed to share in it. Donald McLean noted these changes in his support for iwi seeking Crown title to their lands:

"As I remarked on a former occasion, the old men among you are passing away – Paikea, Te Amohau, and a few others, are all that remain. Those who are versed in Maori laws and usages are disappearing; their children must take their places. The ancient land marks and boundaries will not be known to the children. This will give rise to endless confusion, unless some new system be adopted. Let some new law be recognised, so that, when your relatives die, there will be no difficulty afterwards in disposing of their land and other property."

Kohimarama was the first time the chiefs had been gathered since Waitangi, and it was a perfect opportunity to address problems and come up with long term solutions. After hearing the pleas from chiefs like Tuhaere for Crown title, Governor Gore Brown instructed Native Secretary Donald McLean to read out the Governor's response to the chiefs:

> "In his opening speech the Governor assured the Chiefs assembled at Kohimarama, that the Treaty of Waitangi will be maintained inviolate by Her Majesty's Government. He now invites them to consider the difficulties and complications attending the ownership of land, and trusts they will be, able to devise some plan for removing or simplifying them.
>
> "It is well known that nearly all the feuds and wars between different tribes in New Zealand, have originated in the uncertain tenure by which land is now held. Very many disagreements would in future be avoided if the possession of land from any fixed date – say, 20 years, – were recognised as giving the possessor a good title.[291]
>
> "Such a limitation would be in accordance with the law which prevails in England.
>
> "It is very desirable that some general principles regulating the boundaries of land belonging to different tribes should be generally received and adopted; for, until the rights of property are clearly defined, progress in civilisation must be both slow and uncertain. When disputes arise between different tribes in reference to land, they might be referred to a committee of disinterested and influential chiefs, selected at a conference similar to the one now held at Kohimarama.

---

291 This would convert aboriginal title to a defined legal title, provided you had occupied or administered the said land for the next twenty years.

"There is also a simpler plan universally adopted in Hindostan, which appears well suited to the circumstances of New Zealand, viz., when men cannot agree as to their respective rights, each party chooses two persons – and these four choose a chief of another tribe having no interest in the matter disputed. Then the five sit in judgment, and decide who is right and who is wrong; but before they pronounce judgment, both the contending parties solemnly engage to abide by it.

"The Governor earnestly desires to see the chiefs and people of New Zealand in secure, possession of land, which they can transmit to their children, and about which there could be no dispute. Some land might be held in common for tribal purposes; but he would like to see every chief and every member of his tribe in possession of a Crown Grant, for as much land as they could possibly desire or use. When a dispute arises about a Crown Grant, the proprietor need neither go to War nor appeal to the Government: he can go at once to the proper Court, and, if he is right, the Judge will give him possession, and the Law will protect him in it.

"Tribal jealousies and disputes, however, interfere to prevent individuals from obtaining Crown Grants; and they will continue to do so, and cause quarrels and bloodshed, until men grow wiser, and learn that the rights of an individual should be as carefully guarded as those of a community.

"It is essential to the peace and prosperity of the Maori people that some plan for settling disputes about land should be adopted; the Governor therefore hopes that the Chiefs will consider the subject carefully and dispassionately, and assures them that he will gladly co-operate with them in carrying into effect any system that they can recommend, provided it will really attain the desired end.

"Government House, July 18, 1860."

It is clear from the statement above that disputes over land were far more complex than we imagine today, and not simply confined to Pakeha ripping off Maori. Maori, under the old ways guaranteed to them in the Treaty, were continuing to dispute amongst themselves.

As the official Maori newspaper, *Te Karere*, reported it, Native Secretary Donald McLean then gave his analysis:

"The Chiefs present were all aware that land was the main source of many of their difficulties; occasioning loss of life, and affecting the property of both races. No fixed law on the subject could be said to exist, except the 'Law of Might'. It was true, various customs relating to Native tenure existed; but these were not in any way permanent; and the endless complications of such customs were eventually resolved into the law of might.

"Paora, one of the Ngatiwhatua Chiefs present, had stated that one law did not exist with the Europeans and Natives about land. This was true, inasmuch as the Native has no fixed law to regulate the rights of property. How, therefore, could it be expected that one law should prevail? The European has a law to guide him on this subject; the Native has no well-defined law.

"The Governor had long thought of this subject, and he availed himself of the present Conference of Chiefs to place his own views before them, in the hope that they would co-operate with him to devise such a measure as would simplify Native tenure, and enable them to leave the land they inherit in the quiet and undisturbed possession of their children.

"Scarcely a year passed without our hearing of war about land in some part of New Zealand. At Tauranga the Natives had been fighting very lately. Also at Whakatane, Tunapahore, Upper Wanganui, Hawkes' Bay, Ngapuhi, Te Ihutaroa, and now at Taranaki. It was asserted by some, that these wars had been occasioned by Government land purchasers. This was untrue. The Government used every endeavour to prevent quarrels in conducting the purchase of land; and at those districts throughout New Zealand where no land had been purchased, such as Te Ihutaroa, and other places with which the Government did not interfere, bloody feuds were carried on between the different tribes from time to time.

"Powerful tribes took possession of land by driving off or exterminating the original inhabitants. Those in their turn drove off other less powerful tribes. The conqueror enjoyed the property while he had the power of keeping it. None were certain how long they could occupy the land in peace. It was true that Christianity introduced a different state of things. By its influences the conquered were permitted to re-establish themselves on the lands of their ancestors. In process of time, however, the conquered encroached too far on the formerly recognised rights of the conqueror, occasioning up to the present day, much bitterness of feeling between these two classes of claimants.

"Tribes vary in their customs about land, but after all, their various customs are liable to be superseded by the Law of Might. He would not detain them longer, but wished them to consider this message well before they expressed an opinion on it. If any felt anxious to express their opinion at once, he invited them to do so," reported *Te Karere* of McLean's comments.

Interestingly, the response from the chiefs was incredibly positive. Most saw the benefits of Crown title: by identifying genuine "commons" to be reserved for the whole tribe, and then subdividing off the land occupied by individual tribal members with titles they could pass to their children or sell for profit, chiefs realised their people could share the benefits of the new system.

Some chiefs, in fact, had already twigged to the fact that tribes with large European settlements nearby were becoming rich through trade and employment opportunities, and went so far as to offer large tracts of land to the Crown during the Kohimarama conference:

Tamati Hapimana Wharehinaki, (Tapuika,) Maketu: "We are waiting to hear it said, 'You (the Pakeha) want to get possession of the whole of the Island'. I now, for the first time, say that I will enter on your side; for on this day it has been said that Maketu is your soil. That is the place which has cherished me from childhood even untii now. Do you ask me to give my parent (referring to the soil) to you? Be it according to your will. Let me have one hundred thousand pakehas on my land, that it may be filled.

Paora Tuhaere, (Ngatiwhatua.) Orakei: "I belong to another tribe, but I rise to speak because I observe that the speeches of the Ngatiwhakaue and Ngaiterangi chiefs are one. I have been listening to the correctness of their words. Formerly they were at enmity; now they co-operate for the cession of their land. I say, let all lands hereafter be treated in this way."

Maihi, Ngatihoko, Tauranga: "Now there are two Lords, the Queen and a king. One of these Lords has become jealous about his servant being taken by the other, and if he is taken by the one then the other will be angry. Hence I can see that there is death in this the Maori King project."

Tukihaumene, (Ngatiwhakaue,) Maketu: "Let the Queen's Sovereignty spread and extend to every place. From the Reinga (in the north) to where the sun rises, and on to Port Nicholson. The acknowledgment of the Queen has been agreed to by us all."

Te Makarini (Ngatiawa, Bay of Plenty): "I came here suffering pain (or concern) on account of three things, namely, – first, death (mate); secondly, power (mana); thirdly, the king. I do not mean ordinary death, I mean death by the hand of man (murder). Listen, all of you to these words. Had the Queen's tikanga become generally acknowledged by us, these evils would have been averted, and the tikanga would have prospered. I mean by this to blame you."

Raniera Te Iho: "I first came to understand in the time of Governor Grey – under him and Mr. McLean. They came and planted the tikanga at Wairarapa. As yet I know only the name of the Pakeha. Justice rules in New Zealand. I offer my land, in the proper manner, to the Governor. True the land passes across to the Governor, but then I get my price for it. Should I afterwards stretch forth my hand after my land, that would be wrong. I prove my allegiance to the Queen by parting with my lands…I give up my land to Queen Victoria, and to the Kings and Queens, her successors. As to that talk at Waikato I know nothing about it. Had our forefathers handed down that name (the Maori King) then it would be right. My choice is with the Pakeha who first brought that name here. I have no other subject to speak on, inasmuch as my land is parted with. Two objects have my adherence, God and the Queen."

Ngapomate, (Ngatiwhakaue,) Rotorua: "Listen you of the Conference, the new comers, and you others! I will hold up to you my grievance that the Conference may consider it. The grievance is between Rotorua and Taupo. Now observe: this is Tutukau, and there is Rotokakahi. Henare Te Pukuatua is a party concerned in this grievance. There was a piece of land which Henare considered to belong to his mother, and he went to survey it (to mark boundaries). This resulted in the death of forty persons. By placing ourselves under the Queen's protection we shall get this grievance redressed. If the Queen administers a remedy it will be effectual. That disease extended to Rotomahana involving Rangihinea; then we of the Arawa suffered and one hundred men perished. …This sort of thing is constantly going on. There was a healer at Rotorua who should have restored me, but I was not made whole. I therefore bring my grievance here in order that the Queen may find a remedy."

Keep those comments in mind when you read the Waitangi Tribunal reports accusing the Crown of forcing land reform on Maori without their consent: "The purchase of individual interests began as soon as individual interests were created. The practice continued even when the extent of Maori landlessness was plain, so that little Maori land now remains."[292]

As has been shown, they consented. Maori were begging for land reform.

That, then, is how Maori viewed the Treaty of Waitangi and its implications. To sum up, let's quickly recap the main points emerging from Kohimarama's ratification of the Treaty:

292   Waitangi Tribunal: The Taranaki Report, Chapter 1, http://www.waitangi-tribunal.govt.nz/scripts/reports/reports/143/78820F29-BB30-4C59-B1FC-89AFE53AD8F3.pdf

SOVEREIGNTY: Despite the Maori (signed and official) version of the Treaty using the word 'kawanatanga' for 'sovereignty', there is no credible basis to keep arguing that "governorship" meant something less than sovereignty to those who signed the Treaty, and those who followed afterward. Guided by Bible accounts, most Maori leaders had a good understanding of sovereigns and laws. In the stories of the tribes of Israel, much resonated with their own circumstances.

TINO RANGATIRATANGA: Article Two of the Treaty guaranteed Maori tino rangatiratanga over their lands and treasures, so long as they wished to retain ownership of them. Modern academia argues tino rangatiratanga meant "absolute sovereignty" and therefore meant sovereignty had not passed to the Crown as suggested. You have seen that Maori – in their own words and almost without exception – "abandoned" many of their old customs and laws in favour of "the Queen's Law", making tino rangatiratanga somewhat of an empty concept if it really meant sovereignty. Whatever the clause meant in 1840, it was absolutely defined by the 1860 Kohimarama runanga, and they did not understand it to mean what the modern Treaty industry says it is.

LAND: One of the big bones of contention arising from the Treaty at the time was its promise to let Maori own and control their tribal lands by way of their existing tikanga, a real life example of tino rangatiratanga in action. Unfortunately, tribes found aboriginal title vastly inferior to Crown title and wanted to know why they'd been left with a 'pup'. The problem was a logical consequence, however, of tino rangatiratanga. Maori land had traditionally been tribally owned rather than individually owned. That meant tribes could not easily sell their land or convert it to individual wealth units. It was all very well owning vast tracts of land as far as the eye could see, but if you couldn't put it to use the way your pakeha neighbours were, you slowly slipped behind. At the same time, one must acknowledge that Maori had genuine and valid fears that too much of their land was slipping away for low prices.

So the question at the start of this chapter remains: what went wrong? In short, the Crown had built up a huge amount of political and social capital in the eyes of probably the majority of Maori, and they squandered nearly all of it.

While many Maori saw the error of Wiremu Kingi's Waitara claim, and the Waikato King movement's support of it, the "scorched earth" military response made reasonable Maori both weary and wary. Where hope, faith and love had guided them in 1860, a dark cynicism was growing by the end of the decade.

More than a million acres of Maori land – some from tribes loyal to the Crown – had been confiscated by the Government in the wake of the land wars, and the King movement's Maori nationalism which had been soundly rejected at the Kohimarama conference was rapidly gaining followers, disillusioned with the betrayals of a supposedly Christian government.

On the other hand, some former rebels had become loyalists, like Gate Pa defender Enoka te Whanake:

"It is true that I fought against the Queen at the Gate Pa; but I have repented of this evil and am now living under the shadow of her laws. As for this Tawhiao, who styles himself the 'King of the Maoris,' let him be brought hither as a footstool for the son of our Queen, whom we welcome among us this day," he declared in an 1870 speech welcoming Queen Victoria's second son, Prince Alfred, to Tauranga.[293]

Support for the Crown's land confiscations from rebel tribes came from a surprising quarter down the track – Cabinet Minister and lawyer Sir Apirana Ngata:[294]

"Some have said that these confiscations were wrong and they contravened the articles of the Treaty of Waitangi, but the chiefs placed in the hands of the Queen of England, the Sovereignty and authority to make laws. Some sections of the Maori people violated that authority, war arose and blood was spilled. The law came into operation and land was taken in payment. This in itself is Maori custom – revenge – plunder to avenge a wrong. It was their chiefs who ceded that right to the Queen. The confiscations cannot therefore be objected to in the light of the Treaty".

Despite Ngata's well reasoned argument and its appeal to Maori customary tikanga, it seems to fall at a fundamental hurdle. The Crown never declared the Treaty void over alleged Maori breaches, and yet then passed laws thinking it had the right to seize Maori land despite the Treaty provision.

While people can, and have, made arguments that the rebellion was a breach of the Treaty that justified punitive action, New Zealand operated under the rule of law. The Government failed to dot the I's and cross the t's. By not ripping up the Treaty, it continued to be bound by it no matter how aggrieved it felt.

Perhaps that's why Ngata added there were grounds for compensation,

293 Letter from Governor Bowen to the Earl of Kimberley, 26 December 1870, regarding Royal visit. See http://www.nzetc.org/tm/scholarly/tei-TurEpit-t1-g1-t1-g1-t2-g1-t102.html
294 *The Treaty of Waitangi: An Explanation*, by Sir Apirana Ngata, 1922, see http://www.nzetc.org/tm/scholarly/tei-NgaTrea-t1-g1-t1.html

not by the fact of confiscation but by the scale:

"The objections should be made in the light of the suffering of some of the tribes by reason of the confiscation of their lands. The wrongs were done by others while lands belonging to others were confiscated. Consequently many tribes suffered through having no lands. Some tribes were too severely punished. It was from these objections that earnest supplications were made to Ministers or by way of petitions to Parliament. While the Government could not defend itself under the provisions of the Treaty, Governments have used the Treaty as a shield against these supplications and claims."

Sir Apirana Ngata

Those were some of the big clouds, but Maori faith in Pakeha integrity was also being worn down by a death of a thousand cuts. Take the plight of Auckland's Ngatiwhatua. Before the Treaty was signed, Ngatiwhatua had already invited European settlers to live on its land with a view to buying it down the track. A Deed of Sale was eventually drafted which did not properly identify the lands being purchased, and ended up inadvertently scooping up Taurarua Bay (modern Parnell).

By the time Ngatiwhatua realised their lands at Parnell had gone awol on them it was too late, settlers and "fine people" were already building houses on it. Chief Paora Tuhaere's pleas for compensation were batted from Governors to bureaucrats and back again, from the early 1840s onward.

In a petition to Parliament in 1871 for compensation, the very patient Tuhaere explained:[295]

"That Sir George Grey returned to the Colony as Governor in place of the said Thomas Gore Browne, and your petitioner knowing that it was in the time of the said Sir George Grey that your petitioner's land had been taken away, waited upon the said Sir George Grey, accompanied

---

295 Petition of Paora Tuhaere to the General Assembly, 1871, see http://www.nzetc.org/tm/scholarly/tei-BIM767Paor-t1-g1-t2.html

by Te Keene Tangaroa. The said Sir George Grey asked your petitioner what he had to say. Your petitioner replied, 'I have come to converse about Taurarua, the land you heard of at the time of your first arrival in the Colony as Governor'."

Sir George Grey replied, "That is correct, Paul; but what is to be done in the matter?"

"I want payment for that piece of land."

"Paul," said Grey, "don't demand too heavy a payment. How much do you require?"

"Four thousand pounds."

"That, is far too much," objected the Governor. "You had better compromise it."

Tuhaere looked at him for a moment. "Now, according to your idea, how much should it be?"

Sir George Grey answered, "One thousand pounds."

Tuhaere sighed. "The reason I ask four thousand pounds is that my land was taken away for no reason, and without my consent."

"Agree to take the one thousand pounds," repeated Grey.

"Will the one thousand pounds be paid at once?"

According to Tuhaere, Sir George Grey said he would speak to his Council, and he asked the chiefs to return on the following day. When they did, they found the Governor kicking for touch, saying he was sending the land dispute to "arbitration". Tuhaere, naturally, felt disillusioned.

His arbitration panel, Symonds and Heaphy, couldn't reach a decision because of the vague wording of the Deed of Sale and so, years later, Ngatiwhatua was still without payment.

A thousand pounds spent in Parnell today would barely buy you a flat white coffee, let alone the entire suburb from Judge's Bay across to the central city.[296]

Tuhaere reminded Parliament of the words of Governor Gore Browne at Kohimarama all those years earlier:

"At the conference of the Native chiefs held at Kohimaramara, near the said city of Auckland, on the 10th day of July, 1860, His Excellency Thomas Gore Browne, who succeeded the said Sir George Grey as Governor of the said Colony, stated in the eleventh paragraph of his address to the chiefs there assembled: – 'Your lands have remained in your pos-

---

296 Bernard Hickey's website, interest.co.nz, noted some key real estate sales for 2010 in ancestral Taurarua: "$3,100,000 St Stephens Ave (The PM's Street); $3,490,000 Awatea Road; $3,600,000 Taurarua Tce; $3,700,000 Takutai Street; $4,900,000 St Stephens Ave".

session or have been bought by the Government at your desire.' And in the twelfth paragraph of the said address: 'It is your adoption by Her Majesty as her subjects which makes it impossible that the Maori people should be unjustly dispossessed of their lands or property…Every Maori is a member of the British nation; he is protected by the same law as his English fellow-subject'."

Apparently not, muttered Tuhaere – a man almost single-handedly responsible for allowing the creation of the metropolis of modern Auckland.

"Your petitioner does not wish your honorable Assembly to restore Taurarua aforesaid to him, as Europeans are now inhabiting the land, and Crown grants have been issued for portions of the same, but he wishes to obtain compensation for the loss of his said land.

"Your petitioner would most respectfully remind your honorable Assembly that in the early times of this Colony the Government obtained lands for little or no payment, and the Maoris were glad to receive the Europeans among them, and the Europeans were allowed to acquire large tracts of valuable land for a few blankets and articles of clothing. Even the missionaries pursued this plan of acquiring land, giving in exchange a few axes, iron pots, or fish-hooks; telling the Maoris to believe in God, engaging their attention heavenwards, and whilst they were in that position, ere the eye had turned to the earth, bought the land and none remained. When the Maoris were wiser, the missionaries ceased to buy land," Tuhaere noted with wry humour.

"Your petitioner would most respectfully remind your honorable Assembly that he has never allowed his claim to rest."

These were the things, then, that chipped away at Maori/Pakeha relations, chipped away at trust. After steering two peoples almost onto a common purpose, the winds of revolution and stupidity in the sixties blew them off course for more than a century. Where Maori had sought Pakeha men with spirits in the image of God, they found instead ordinary, fallible men with feet of clay. If the Pakeha bureaucracy had acted on a more principled basis, history might have turned out differently.

The rules of balance require consideration of a different perspective on this. There is utterly no doubt that the Kohimarama Conference was a total ratification of the English version of the Treaty of Waitangi. It meant that the English concept of sovereignty had been discussed, understood and accepted by the combined chiefs of New Zealand. Whatever arguments might exist around the exact meaning of tino rangatiratanga, Kohimarama trumped them.

However, for those who've been jumping up and down in the aisles thinking, 'yay, my side won', consider this.

The Kohimarama Conference is also clear evidence that the Colonial Government, post Waitangi, recognised a limited duality of justice and administration. The mere fact that a Maori Parliament had been convened and passed binding resolutions at the government's request is proof of that. So too is the content of speeches by Governor Gore Brown and Colonial Secretary Donald McLean.

Tino rangatiratanga was not an entirely vacuous concept; the practicalities of Maori self-administration underneath an overlaid Government infrastructure were recognised and encouraged as Treaty benefits, two decades after the treaty was signed. One can hardly turn around now, a century and a half after Kohimarama, and say that wasn't part of the deal. Clearly it was.

The question now is whether some devolution of local authority back to tribal iwi bodies is legitimate in a 21st century framework where most Maori are either urban or living in Australia, or whether the relationship has now evolved to the extent that such efforts would be redundant.

CHAPTER FOURTEEN

Fast Forward

At the time of writing, the latest round of Treaty settlements (there have been several rounds of 'settlements' over the past century and a half) had reached more than a billion dollars, and expected to trigger 'top-up' provisions for some of the early settlements.

It would take another book to lay out in full detail the intricacies of the latest settlements, and compare them to the previous payments received by some of those tribes.

Alternatively, some might argue that a billion, or even two or three billion, is a small price to pay to clear away 170 years of baggage and move the country forward – especially when you consider investors in South Canterbury Finance received a bigger bailout from taxpayers ($1.5 billion) than Maori have.

The compensation for "forests and fisheries" is to a large extent a side issue. The real danger in the Treaty settlements is not really the money, it is the precedent being set and the willingness of the government to accept the mystical 'legal' arguments as valid. There is a very real risk that myths and fabrications about the Treaty of Waitangi will be written into law for all time.

The Great Divide has, hopefully, illustrated the real context behind why Maori signed the Treaty of Waitangi. The actual 1840 Treaty is almost totally legally irrelevant in a real sense, because it was superseded by a much wider and more informed discussion of its merits at the 1860 Kohimarama runanga.

In every respect, Kohimarama is the new Treaty, the real Treaty, between Maori and Pakeha. Where there was any hint of ambiguity in 1840, that had vanished with the extensive debate and resolutions passed at Kohimarama.

It has been argued before that New Zealand's parliamentary system is unconstitutional, and extensive legal argument and confirmation of that has been published.[297] Doubts about the validity of our constitution behind the scenes are one of the reasons Parliament is now holding a major constitutional review.

However, here's the rub: that review is most likely going to enshrine the modern interpretation of the 1840 Treaty of Waitangi as the foundation for our new constitution. After what you've read here, do you think your friends and neighbours are well enough informed about the Treaty and what it really promised, to have any sensible input into our new constitution when the time comes? Or will your friends and neighbours be bullied into submission because they don't have any facts at their fingertips to argue with?[298]

This is a debate and a constitutional review that will affect the lives of every single living New Zealander, their children and generations to come. Ignorance of the facts, on this issue, is not bliss.

Do you want to be ruled by two sovereigns, the Crown and some kind of Pan-Maori organisation, or is it time for the constitution to make the people – all the people, *he iwi tahi tatou* – sovereign instead, placing the will of the people above the Crown and any Maori entity as described?

If sovereignty is vested in all New Zealanders, of whatever race, and then delegated down to the Crown and or its Treaty-partner mechanism with appropriate checks and balances so the public can veto bad law, isn't that a better safeguard for all of us than allowing a cosy clique of vested political interests to deliver up a fait accompli that will keep them in power and feeding at the public trough forever?

The question that arises from this book is a very simple one. The Treaty was a response to changing circumstances. Circumstances have continued to change over the seventeen decades since it was signed. At the time of the Treaty, the Crown was an absolute sovereign, with people as subjects, not citizens. Likewise in Maori society chiefs performed a similar role, to the extent of the limits of the "might is right" doctrine.

297 See the final two chapters of *Absolute Power: The Helen Clark Years*, by Ian Wishart, Howling At The Moon Publishing, 2008
298 Author, official Waitangi researcher and advisor to the Ministry of Maori Affairs, Dr John Robinson, has recently published a book alleging the New Zealand Government required him to lie in official reports about our history, in order to make "facts" fit the modern Treaty interpretation. His devastating allegations show the Government and its agencies cannot be trusted to give the public the full story. His book is *The Corruption of New Zealand Democracy* by John Robinson, Tross Publishing, an extract of which is published in the Oct/Nov 2011 *Investigate* magazine, see http://www.investigatemagazine.co.nz/Investigate/?p=2717

Therefore, it is easy to see why two large bureaucracies with free and unfettered access to taxpayer funding, the Crown and tribal iwi organisations, might like to see that power sharing arrangement continue with the two 'treaty partners' as apex predators over their 'subjects' underneath.

Can New Zealand afford to tie its future to a document essentially drafted on the back of a napkin in 1840, or is it time to give the document its due respect, but construct a new future path, together, where the people control the politicians and bureaucracy, not the other way aroud?

This is the question *The Great Divide* asks you, and hopefully the book provides you with enough information to make an informed choice when the time comes.

Our story is one of passion, of ordinary humans and pioneers on both sides who tried to make a go of things during incredibly difficult times. Sometimes they made grave mistakes. Sometimes they enjoyed great successes. But without their efforts together, and without the Treaty, none of us would be here debating it today. It is time to stop beating ourselves up over the past, and instead build a brighter future.

Treaty Of Waitangi

English version based on drafts from 3 February 1840

The following version of the Treaty is taken from the first schedule to the Treaty of Waitangi Act 1975.

Preamble

HER MAJESTY VICTORIA Queen of the United Kingdom of Great Britain and Ireland regarding with Her Royal favour the Native Chiefs and Tribes of New Zealand and anxious to protect their just Rights and Property and to secure to them the enjoyment of Peace and Good Order has deemed it necessary in consequence of the great number of Her Majesty's Subjects who have already settled in New Zealand and the rapid extension of Emigration both from Europe and Australia which is still in progress to constitute and appoint a functionary properly authorised to treat with the Aborigines of New Zealand for the recognition of Her Majesty's Sovereign authority over the whole or any part of those islands – Her Majesty therefore being desirous to establish a settled form of Civil Government with a view to avert the evil consequences which must result from the absence of the necessary Laws and Institutions alike to the native population and to Her subjects has been graciously pleased to empower and to authorise me William Hobson a Captain in Her Majesty's Royal Navy Consul and Lieutenant Governor of such parts of New Zealand as may be or hereafter shall be ceded to her Majesty to invite the confederated and independent Chiefs of New Zealand to concur in the following Articles and Conditions.

Article the First

The Chiefs of the Confederation of the United Tribes of New Zealand and the separate and independent Chiefs who have not become members of the Confederation cede to Her Majesty the Queen of England absolutely and without reservation all the rights and powers of Sovereignty which the said Confederation or Individual Chiefs respectively exercise or possess, or may be supposed to exercise or to possess over their respective Territories as the sole Sovereigns thereof.

Article the Second

Her Majesty the Queen of England confirms and guarantees to the Chiefs and Tribes of New Zealand and to the respective families and individuals thereof the full exclusive and undisturbed possession of their Lands and Estates Forests Fisheries and other properties which they may collectively or individually possess so long as it is their wish and desire to retain the same in their possession; but the Chiefs of the United Tribes and the individual Chiefs yield to Her Majesty the exclusive right of Preemption over such lands as the proprietors thereof may be disposed to alienate at such prices as may be agreed upon between the respective Proprietors and persons appointed by Her Majesty to treat with them in that behalf.

Article the Third

In consideration thereof Her Majesty the Queen of England extends to the Natives of New Zealand Her royal protection and imparts to them all the Rights and Privileges of British Subjects.

W HOBSON Lieutenant Governor.

Now therefore We the Chiefs of the Confederation of the United Tribes of New Zealand being assembled in Congress at Victoria in Waitangi and We the Separate and Independent Chiefs of New Zealand claiming authority over the Tribes and Territories which are specified after our respective names, having been made fully to understand the Provisions of the foregoing Treaty, accept and enter into the same in the full spirit and meaning thereof: in witness of which we have attached our signatures or marks at the places and the dates respectively specified.

Done at Waitangi this Sixth day of February in the year of Our Lord One thousand eight hundred and forty.

Māori Version of the Treaty of Waitangi

The following version of the Treaty is taken from the first schedule to the Treaty of Waitangi Act 1975.

Preamble

KO WIKITORIA, te Kuini o Ingarani, i tana mahara atawai ki nga Rangatira me nga Hapu o Nu Tirani i tana hiahia hoki kia tohungia ki a ratou o ratou rangatiratanga, me to ratou wenua, a kia mau tonu hoki te Rongo ki a ratou me te Atanoho hoki kua wakaaro ia he mea tika kia tukua mai tetahi Rangatira hei kai wakarite ki nga Tangata maori o Nu Tirani-kia wakaaetia e nga Rangatira maori te Kawanatanga o te Kuini ki nga wahikatoa o te Wenua nei me nga Motu-na te mea hoki he tokomaha ke nga tangata o tona Iwi Kua noho ki tenei wenua, a e haere mai nei. Na ko te Kuini e hiahia ana kia wakaritea te Kawanatanga kia kaua ai nga kino e puta mai ki te tangata Maori ki te Pakeha e noho ture kore ana. Na, kua pai te Kuini kia tukua a hau a Wiremu Hopihona he Kapitana i te Roiara Nawi hei Kawana mo nga wahi katoa o Nu Tirani e tukua aianei, amua atu ki te Kuini e mea atu ana ia ki nga Rangatira o te wakaminenga o nga hapu o Nu Tirani me era Rangatira atu enei ture ka korerotia nei.

Ko te Tuatahi

Ko nga Rangatira o te Wakaminenga me nga Rangatira katoa hoki ki hai i uru ki taua wakaminenga ka tuku rawa atu ki te Kuini o Ingarani ake tonu atu-te Kawanatanga katoa o o ratou wenua.

Ko te Tuarua

Ko te Kuini o Ingarani ka wakarite ka wakaae ki nga Rangitira ki nga hapu-ki nga tangata katoa o Nu Tirani te tino rangtiratanga o o ratou wenua o ratou kainga me o ratou taonga katoa. Otiia ko nga Rangatira o te Wakaminenga me nga Rangatira katoa atu ka tuku ki te Kuini te hokonga o era wahi wenua e pai ai te tangata nona te Wenua-ki te ritenga o te utu e wakaritea ai e ratou ko te kai hoko e meatia nei e te Kuini hei kai hoko mona.

Ko te Tuatoru

Hei wakaritenga mai hoki tenei mo te wakaaetanga ki te Kawanatanga o te Kuini-Ka tiakina e te Kuini o Ingarani nga tangata maori katoa o Nu Tirani ka tukua ki a ratou nga tikanga katoa rite tahi ki ana mea ki nga tangata o Ingarani.

(Signed) WILLIAM HOBSON,
Consul and Lieutenant-Governor.

Na ko matou ko nga Rangatira o te Wakaminenga o nga hapu o Nu Tirani ka huihui nei ki Waitangi ko matou hoki ko nga Rangatira o Nu Tirani ka kite nei i te ritenga o enei kupu, ka tangohia ka wakaaetia katoatia e matou, koia ka tohungia ai o matou ingoa o matou tohu. Ka meatia tenei ki Waiangi i te ono o nga ra o Pepueri i te tau kotahi mano, e waru rau e wa te kau o to tatou Ariki.

Ko nga Rangatira o te wakaminenga.

Kawharu Translation

The following translation of the Māori text of the Treaty was done by former Tribunal member Professor Sir Hugh Kawharu.

Preamble

VICTORIA, THE QUEEN OF ENGLAND, in her concern to protect the chiefs and the subtribes of New Zealand and in her desire to preserve their chieftainship[1] and their lands to them and to maintain peace[2] and good order considers it just to appoint an administrator[3] one who will negotiate with the people of New Zealand to the end that their chiefs will agree to the Queen's Government being established over all parts of this land and (adjoining) islands[4] and also because there are many of her subjects already living on this land and others yet to come. So the Queen desires to establish a government so that no evil will come to Māori and European living in a state of lawlessness. So the Queen has appointed 'me, William Hobson a Captain' in the Royal Navy to be Governor for all parts of New Zealand (both those) shortly to be received by the Queen and (those) to be received hereafter and presents[5] to the chiefs of the Confederation chiefs of the subtribes of New Zealand and other chiefs these laws set out here.

The first

The Chiefs of the Confederation and all the Chiefs who have not joined that Confederation give absolutely to the Queen of England for ever the complete government[6] over their land.

The second

The Queen of England agrees to protect the chiefs, the subtribes and all the people of New Zealand in the unqualified exercise[7] of their chieftainship over their lands, villages and all their treasures.[8] But on the other hand the Chiefs of the Confederation and all the Chiefs will sell[9] land to the Queen at a price agreed to by the person owning it and by the person buying it (the latter being) appointed by the Queen as her purchase agent.

The third

For this agreed arrangement therefore concerning the Government of the Queen, the Queen of England will protect all the ordinary people of New Zealand and will give them the same rights and duties[10] of citizenship as the people of England.[11]

[signed] William Hobson Consul & Lieut Governor

So we, the Chiefs of the Confederation of the subtribes of New Zealand meeting here at Waitangi having seen the shape of these words which we accept and agree to record our names and our marks thus.

Was done at Waitangi on the sixth of February in the year of our Lord 1840.

Footnotes by Professor Kawharu

1. 'Chieftainship': this concept has to be understood in the context of Māori social and political organisation as at 1840. The accepted approximation today is 'trusteeship'.

2. 'Peace': Māori 'Rongo', seemingly a missionary usage (rongo – to hear: ie, hear the 'Word' – the 'message' of peace and goodwill, etc).

3. Literally 'Chief' ('Rangatira') here is of course ambiguous. Clearly, a European could not be a Māori, but the word could well have implied a trustee-like role rather than that of a mere 'functionary'. Māori speeches at Waitangi in 1840 refer to Hobson being or becoming a 'father' for the Māori people. Certainly this attitude has been held towards the person of the Crown down to the present day – hence the continued expectations and commitments entailed in the Treaty.

4. 'Islands': ie, coastal, not of the Pacific.

5. Literally 'making': ie, 'offering' or 'saying' – but not 'inviting to concur'.

6. 'Government': 'kawanatanga'. There could be no possibility of the Māori signatories having any understanding of government in the sense of 'sovereignty': ie, any understanding on the basis of experience or cultural precedent.

7. 'Unqualified exercise' of the chieftainship – would emphasise to a chief the Queen's intention to give them complete control according to their customs. 'Tino' has the connotation of 'quintessential'.

8. 'Treasures': 'taonga'. As submissions to the Waitangi Tribunal concerning the Māori language have made clear, 'taonga' refers to all dimensions of a tribal group's estate, material and non-material – heirlooms and

wahi tapu (sacred places), ancestral lore and whakapapa (genealogies), etc.

9. Māori 'hokonga', literally 'sale and purchase'. 'Hoko' means to buy or sell.

10. 'Rights and duties': Māori at Waitangi in 1840 refer to Hobson being or becoming a 'father' for the Māori people. Certainly, this attitude has been held towards the person of the Crown down to the present day – hence the continued expectations and commitments entailed in the Treaty.

11. There is, however, a more profound problem about 'tikanga'. There is a real sense here of the Queen 'protecting' (ie, allowing the preservation of) the Māori people's tikanga (ie, customs) since no Māori could have had any understanding whatever of British tikanga (ie, rights and duties of British subjects). This, then, reinforces the guarantees in article 2.

The Littlewood Treaty Version

4th of February 1840

Preamble

Her Majesty Victoria, Queen of England in Her gracious consideration for the chiefs and people of New Zealand, and her desire to preserve to them their land and to maintain peace and order amongst them, has been pleased to appoint an officer to treat with them for the cession of the Sovereignty of their country and of the islands adjacent to the Queen. Seeing that many of Her Majesty's subjects have already settled in the country and are constantly arriving; And that it is desirable for their protection as well as the protection of the natives to establish a government amongst them.

Her Majesty has accordingly been pleased to appoint me William Hobson a captain in the Royal Navy to be Governor of such parts of New Zealand as may now or hereafter be ceded to her Majesty and proposes to the chiefs of the Confederation of the United Tribes of New Zealand and the other chiefs to agree to the following articles.-

Article first

The chiefs of the Confederation of the United Tribes and the other chiefs who have not joined the confederation, cede to the Queen of England for ever the entire Sovereignty of their country.

Article second

The Queen of England confirms and guarantees to the chiefs & tribes and to all the people of New Zealand the possession of their lands, dwellings and all their property. But the chiefs of the Confederation and the other chiefs grant to the chiefs Queen, the exclusive right of purchasing such land as the proprietors thereof may be disposed to sell at such prices as shall be agreed upon between them and the persons appointed by the Queen to purchase from them.

Article Third

In return for the cession of the Sovereignty to the Queen, the people of New Zealand shall be protected by the Queen of England and the rights and privileges of British subjects will be granted to them.-
Signed,
William Hobson
Consul & Lieut. Governor.

Now we the chiefs of the Confederation of the United tribes of New Zealand being assembled at Waitangi, and we the other chiefs of New Zealand having understood the meaning of these articles, accept of them and agree to them all. In witness whereof our names or marks are affixed. Done at Waitangi on the 4th Feb. 1840

Appendix

THE CRITICS ON *BREAKING SILENCE*:

"*Breaking Silence* is not on my recommended read list. I firmly believe it is *compulsory* reading for anyone over 18." – Andrew Stone, *Albany Buzz* business magazine

"The book has real value" – Larry Williams, Newstalk ZB

"I found it an incredibly surprising book, and a very relevant book, and a very important book". – Anna Smart, Newstalk ZB

"I had no particular views on the case before this book came out but I have to say it's a powerful read. An influential read, one might say... All those people who poured out their invective when it became known the book was about to hit the book shops really should just read it for themselves. It may not be quite what they think." – Helen Hill, *The Marlborough Express*

"*Breaking Silence* is a chilling narrative and the most important I have read. Adults may need to read the story to gain any understanding. Younger people should read in it a warning: that it is the way we make decisions early on that may determine the course of our life and the lives of those entrusted to our care." – Pat Veltkamp Smith, *Southland Times*

"The book so many maligned before it came out reveals a mother we haven't met. When I last wrote about Macsyna King, I said I didn't think I'd like her. I've changed my mind. I certainly think she outclasses the Wellington radio announcer who posted on Facebook that after receiving her advance copy of *Breaking Silence*, she had "spat on it, wiped my ass on it, and ripped it up". – Tapu Misa, *NZ Herald*

"Actually, the rumours of Wishart's death as an investigative journalist turn out to be greatly exaggerated. *Breaking Silence* will likely enhance his reputation considerably. As we said at the outset – we are very, very glad to have read the book." – John Tertullian, *Contra Celsum*

BREAKING
SILENCE

THE KAHUI CASE

MACSYNA KING AND
THE REAL STORY OF THE
MURDER OF HER TWINS

IAN WISHART
#1 bestselling author

THE CRITICS ON *THE INSIDE STORY*:

"Undeniably...when Wishart hits he hits big. *Arthur Allan Thomas: The Inside Story* is a book two generations of New Zealanders have waited for... Wishart...offers an explosive new theory about who pulled the trigger of the gun that killed the Crewes in their Pukekawa farmhouse and theorises about the mystery woman who fed their infant daughter, Rochelle, for days after the murders.

"...With his thorough analysis of the evidence and his generous use of first-person accounts it's a stellar piece of journalism..." – *Southland Times*

"Wishart has a brand new prime suspect and he lays out his case in this fascinating and highly readable book. Wishart is painstaking in his investigation, and his interviews with the man at the centre of the case, Arthur Thomas, offer a remarkable insight into one of New Zealand's most memorable characters. " – Kerre Woodham, Newstalk ZB

"Wishart's report of Detective Sergeant Len Johnston's brazen arrogance collecting items for later use as evidence from Thomas's farm – pieces of wire, .22 shells and axle stubs - exposes a dark and scary side to our guardians.

"Through the book Wishart lays the ground for his claim that Johnston was actually the murderer and by his position on the inquiry team and proximity to Hutton, was able to influence an outcome which saw Thomas convicted twice of a double murder. Wishart's conclusions are disturbingly possible in my view.

"The question of to what extent Hutton had the wool pulled over his eyes by Johnston is moot. Based on Wishart's debunking of transcripts and evidence previously recorded, I think Hutton could well have been fooled by his best mate. Which means so too were the rest of the team deluded." – former Det. Insp. Ross Meurant, *NZ Herald*

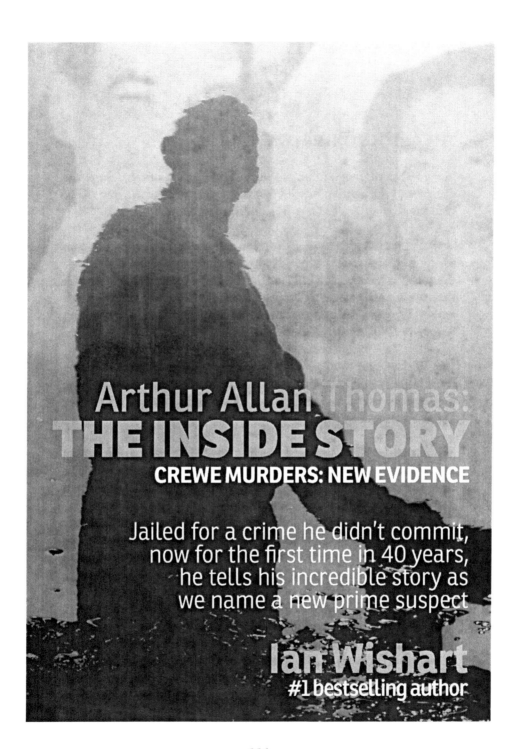

Arthur Allan Thomas:
THE INSIDE STORY
CREWE MURDERS: NEW EVIDENCE

Jailed for a crime he didn't commit,
now for the first time in 40 years,
he tells his incredible story as
we name a new prime suspect

Ian Wishart
#1 bestselling author

THE CRITICS ON *AIR CON*:

"*Air Con* is a thorough summary of the current state of the debate, the science and the politics; it will be an important reference in any AGW skeptic's arsenal." – Vox Day, *WorldNetDaily*

"I started reading this book with an intensely critical eye, expecting that a mere journalist could not possibly cope with the complexities of climate science...[But] The book is brilliant. The best I have seen which deals with the news item side of it as well as the science. He has done a very thorough job and I have no hesitation in unreserved commendation." – Dr Vincent Gray, *UN IPCC expert reviewer*

"Ian Wishart's *Air Con* is another masterpiece of scientific reason, letting the thinking world know that so-called man-made global warming is the greatest scam ever aimed at humanity. Please read this book." – Professor David Bellamy, England

"This book by New Zealand journalist Ian Wishart – a #1 bestselling author four times – surprised me by the completeness with which he reviewed and presents alternatives to the plethora of IPCC inspired spin and publicity which floods our media today.

"His sixteen chapters examining aspects of the debate are meticulously footnoted and thus are a valuable reference resource for those wishing to dig deeper or keep up to speed with the unfolding global warming / carbon reduction political drama in years to come." – Dr Warwick Hughes, climate scientist

"Ian Wishart carefully and painstakingly looks at the topic, examining the evidence and weighing up the pros and cons. He not only finds the science to be unconvincing, but believes that following the proposed remedies will well-nigh bankrupt the West and in fact compound problems. An eye-opening treatment of a controversial issue. – *Quadrant* magazine, Australia

AIR CON

seriously

THE INCONVENIENT TRUTH
ABOUT GLOBAL WARMING

IAN WISHART   #1 BESTSELLING AUTHOR

THE CRITICS ON *LAWYERS, GUNS & MONEY*:

"Wishart has grown as an author" – *Otago Daily Times*

"He's onto another winner. Wishart is...exceptionally thorough. He skilfully blends official documents with his own observations and material from his own inquiries, giving a more informative picture than could ever have been possible in the daily media." – *Manawatu Evening Standard*

"If you like to mix business with pleasure, take *Lawyers, Guns & Money* to your beachside accomodation with you" – *North & South*

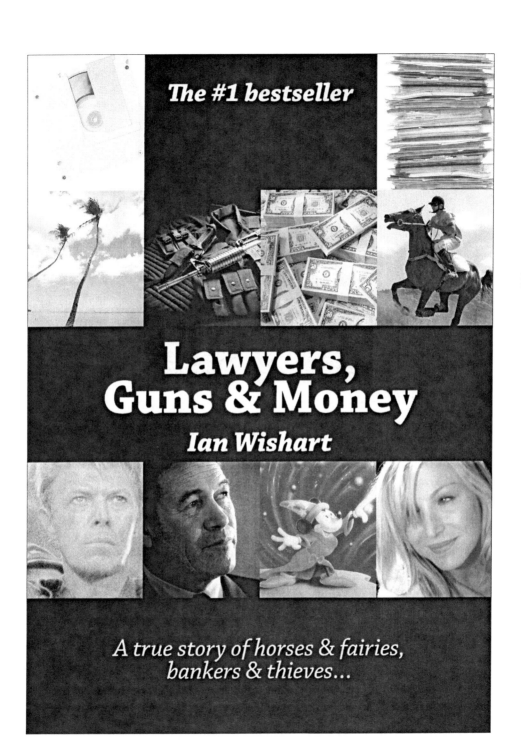

The #1 bestseller

Lawyers,
Guns & Money

Ian Wishart

*A true story of horses & fairies,
bankers & thieves...*

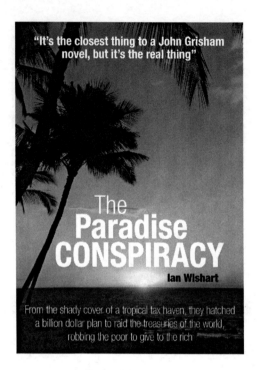

"It's the closest thing to a John Grisham novel, but it's the real thing"

The **Paradise CONSPIRACY**

Ian Wishart

From the shady cover of a tropical tax haven, they hatched a billion dollar plan to raid the treasuries of the world, robbing the poor to give to the rich

THE CRITICS ON *THE PARADISE CONSPIRACY*:

"*The Paradise Conspiracy* is required reading...pacey, penetrating scrutiny" – *New Zealand Herald*

"It is the closest thing to a John Grisham novel, but it is the real thing... among the best investigative stories about New Zealand business for many years" – *Waikato Times*

"...a compelling book...a Watergate-type tale" – *NZ Listener*

"Sensational stuff and hard to fault. Wishart is a professional...it is the most controversial New Zealand book that I can remember" – Bruce Jesson, *The Republican*

"Wishart presents facts he can totally substantiate, and leaves readers to draw some obvious conclusions...compelling, revealing and worrying reading" – *BOP Times*